The Lost Pho
A Kilvert Family Story

We smile as we remember the old family groups, some of them stiff and inappropriate, some of them a bit faded and dim with the years, but close to every smile lurks a tear, for 'the touch of a vanished hand and the sound of a voice that is still' comes vividly before us with the memory.

Jessie Robinson Bisbee, Photography – Then and Now, 1917

The Lost Photo Album

A Kilvert Family Story

by
John Toman

Revd F. Kilvert

PUBLISHED BY THE KILVERT SOCIETY

First published in Great Britain in 2013 by The Kilvert Society.
Copies obtainable from the hon Publications Manager of The Kilvert Society
(contact details available through the Society's website, www.thekilvertsociety.org.uk)

Edited, typeset in Adobe Caslon and designed in InDesign at
Gwasg Boase, Vauxhall House, Monmouth NP25 3AX

ISBN 978-0-9576266-0-7

Printed and bound by CPI Group (UK) Ltd, Croydon, CR0 4YY

Contents

Album people

Acknowledgements

Special thanks are due to Margaret McGregor without whose help and guidance this book would not have been written. She put at my disposal her thirty years' experience at Bristol Record Office in piecing together the lives of the Kilvert Album characters by pursuing them in a wide range of sources, many of which were unknown to me. This extended my knowledge far beyond the basic census and town directory data which I had examined. Margaret was fired by the Album as an intriguing historical source and by the challenge of unlocking it. She produced many details which helped to make the characters come alive.

I was also very fortunate to find that in Bristol there was an expert on nineteenth-century albums: Dr. Samantha Matthews, Senior Lecturer in Victorian Literature, University of Bristol. She was interested to have the Kilvert Album brought to her attention. I have benefited enormously from discussions with her about the carte de visite phenomenon and about the meanings and purposes lying behind the compilation of family photograph albums. She commented on parts of the book. She also recommended relevant books and loaned me some from her personal collection. The interest and confidence I could bring to my researches were strengthened by her involvement.

I have been greatly supported in writing this book by the enthusiasm of Alan Brimson, Secretary of the Kilvert Society. The Preface is testimony to his determination that the Album should come into the Society's possession so that its membership could have first call on the knowledge and insights contained in it. From the outset, he could see its potential for adding to our understanding of the Kilvert family and of their social milieu.

Colin Johnston of the Record Office at Bath has patiently answered many queries out of his wide knowledge of all things to do with that city. I am very grateful to Leanne McCredden and Philip Kent of the University of Melbourne, Victoria, Australia, who undertook the copying of the biography of Henry Hewitt held in the University's Baillieu Library.

Ann Smith of Reading Local Studies Library kindly copied parts of Wendy Koe's The Jackdaws for me.

I have learned much from Ron Cosen's website 'Photographers of Great Britain and Ireland 1840-1940'. He also answered a number of my queries. Another online source on the history of photography which I have found useful is 'Victorian and Edwardian Photographs – Roger Vaughan Personal Collection'. Help has been forthcoming too from the Royal Photographic Society, Bath, and from Geoff Blackwell of the Society's Historical Group.

I should also like to thank Julian Reid, Archivist of Merton College, Oxford; Philippa Mole, Assistant Archivist, Royal College of Surgeons; Dorian Levecque of the British Library's Asia and Africa Reference Service; staff of the Wiltshire and Swindon History Centre and of Bristol City Library; Andrew Lee-Hart, Local History Librarian, Sefton Metropolitan Borough Council; Paul Collett, Assistant Curator, Chippenham Museum.

Biographical note on Francis Kilvert

FRANCIS KILVERT was born on 3 December 1840 at Hardenhuish near Chippenham, Wiltshire. His parents were the Rev. Robert Kilvert and Thermuthis Kilvert. After schooling at home, Kilvert attended the private school run by his uncle Francis in Bath. He was at Wadham College, Oxford, from 1859 to 1862. In spring 1865, he became curate to the Rev. Richard Venables in the village of Clyro near Hay-on-Wye. He became vicar of Bredwardine, Herefordshire, in 1877. He married Elizabeth Rowland on 20 August 1879 but died five weeks later from peritonitis. He was thirty-eight years old.

He began writing his diary in January 1870, working steadily at it, redrafting many passages until he was satisfied with them. It is a highly imaginative piece of work, which often reads like a novel. Frederick Grice wrote of it: 'As a social document its value ... is beyond question', but also one which 'communicates the feelings and moods of his time ... a chronicle not only of the events of the time but of its inner life'. The original notebooks containing the diary were passed by Kilvert's widow to their nephew Percival Smith, son of the diarist's sister Thersie. He sent them in 1937 to the publisher Jonathan Cape, whose reader William Plomer was greatly impressed by them. The first volume was published in 1938, followed by two others in 1939 and 1940. They became bestsellers. Plomer's typescript of the entire diary was destroyed, making further study of it impossible. The National Library of Wales brought out two unabridged diary editions for April-June and June-July 1870 in 1982 and 1989.

Jonathan Cape's three-volume edition of Kilvert's Diary was reissued in 2006 by O'Donoghue Books, Hay-on-Wye, Powys HR3 5WZ. Copies may be obtained from Mr. C.B. Dixon, Archivist, The Kilvert Society, Tregothnan, Pentrosfa Crescent, Llandrindod Wells, Powys LD1 5NW.

Preface

EARLY in February 2012, the committee of the Kilvert Society were alerted that a Kilvert Family Photograph Album was coming to auction at Chippenham. The Society's Archivist, Treasurer and Secretary met at the auction room to inspect the album, to validate its authenticity, and genuine it most certainly was! The auction house was unable to consider a private sale so the album would go to auction on 24 February.

The committee of the Society then met in full to discuss and approve a bid for the album, and set a maximum price it was prepared to pay.

Then came the fateful day: the Secretary of the Society along with several committee members gathered at the auction room to make our bid. We waited some 90 minutes before Lot 169 came up. You can just imagine the tension; here was the most exciting primary source of insight into the life of Francis Kilvert since the Diarist's notebooks first appeared on the desk of William Plomer, at the publishers Jonathan Cape, in 1937.

Our only competitor appeared online. The bids opened at £500 and within seconds went to £600, £700, £800, £900 and finally reached £1,000 but hallelujah! The winning bid was ours and so was the album! It has not been possible to learn the identity of the person who put the album up for sale. It is understood that it originated in Scotland.

The Album's auction had created a great interest in the local media and our successful bid was reported that evening on the local television news. Immediately on my telephone came an excited John Toman, the Society's foremost researcher on all things Kilvertian. He had seen the local television news and was eager to hear all the details of the photograph album.

With his usual infectious enthusiasm, he set to work to research each individual image of those who appear in the album. After many months of painstaking work he has produced this fine volume that has a wonderful story to tell; along with the reproduction of each photograph, it greatly expands our knowledge of Francis Kilvert, his family and its connection with the City of Bath.

This most important and original piece of research is essential reading for all interested in the Rev. Francis Kilvert, his life and his *Diary*.

Alan Brimson
Hon. Secretary, the Kilvert Society, January 2013

Introduction

THE Kilvert Album is an historical document not only because it tells us about the family at a certain period in its development but also because it marks a stage in the history of photography. Experiments to fix photographic images had continued throughout the 1830s and 1840s with considerable success. In the 1850s effort was directed to discover processes enabling prints to be made from negatives. The successes achieved made possible pictorial coverage of such world events as the Crimean War (1854-6) and suddenly photography's potential for widening people's horizons had been realised. But the personal and family uses of the new medium also made a massive appeal to the Victorian public. Photography made it possible to record what ordinary people were experiencing every day within a familiar, intimate world. The family album emerged in the 1860s as part of a movement which popularised photography on a scale never seen before. The Kilvert Album belongs to this phase.

Kilvert's *Diary*, written between 1870 and 1879, included evidence that photography and collecting photos in albums were of considerable interest to him, as they were to many of his contemporaries, including Anna Maria Kilvert, the Album's compiler. Anna Maria (1827-1902) was the diarist's cousin. Victorian compilers of albums were usually women and the following exploration of the Kilvert Album is also an exploration of the lives of women, of the activities they pursued – or were allowed to pursue. Middle-class ladies were not employed and were surrounded by servants who did the bulk of domestic chores. My discussion takes account of such domestic matters as the number of servants employed in Album households in order to give some idea of the extent to which ladies in them were free to engage in other activities. The best that they could hope for was marriage, which enabled them to escape from their family homes and from ageing parents, to run their own homes, to create their own circle of friends, and of course to have children. Kilvert's sister Emily showed a clear understanding of this situation when she referred to the family of her uncle Francis and his wife. They had three children, she wrote, 'all daughters'. The eldest, Anna Sophia, 'a remarkably lady-like girl, never married'. She ended up, as did many unmarried women, in a religious community: 'an Associate of St. John the Divine, Kennington'. The next sister, Elizabeth Frances, was unusual in having employment: she became Matron of Derby Infirmary (*and* married). The youngest, Adelaide, possessed what Emily recognised as the greatest possible advantage for securing a husband: 'being very good looking, she married at the age of 22 ...'[1]

The Album concerns the Kilvert family which originally settled in Bath in 1780 in the person of the diarist's grandfather, who set up as a coachbuilder, determined to win his share of the money being spent there by the spa town's élite. The account that follows deals with the next generation, which had to make its way in the ruthless society of the early nineteenth century. Although Bath was the home of most of the subjects portrayed in the Album, some lived in, or had connections with, Cheltenham, as well as with Gloucester and Chippenham. The Album story is therefore a regional one.

However, the story also takes us much further afield, particularly to India. India was of momentous significance for Victorians. It provided vast revenues for Britain and much of the capital that fuelled its industries. It provided thousands of jobs for its menfolk. The many wars fought in India claimed many British lives, as did its climate. Thousands of British families went out to live there and their experiences formed a substantial component of national consciousness, of the content of newspapers, of everyday conversation, and of family histories. The fact that more than a third of Album characters (14 out of 35) spent part of their lives there is one measure of its importance.[2] Their memories of the heat and dust of the plains, of the cool havens of hill-stations, of Indian servants, of Indian wildlife, of parties and balls, of endless boredom in settlement bungalows,[3] of disease and death, haunt the Album's portraits. India drew the Album's subjects as it drew generations of others because it was a place to make a fresh start, get married and get on in life. However, if one came home rich, one was lucky; indeed, one was lucky if one came home at all. And always there was the strong likelihood that one would be changed by India in ways that were disturbing and destructive of one's better self.

Two statements in J.M. Bourne's *Patronage and Society in Nineteenth-Century England* explain much about the society which these Album characters represent. The first is this: 'The great domestic problem for middle-class parents was how to get their daughters "off" and their sons "on".' Dr. John Kilvert had three sons (one died young) and six daughters;

photographs of most of them and their marriage partners figure in the Album, mostly near the beginning. Getting his sons 'on' in some suitable profession was a major problem for Kilvert's coachbuilder grandfather, Francis, and his grandmother Anna (née Parsons), who had no less than seven sons, among whom were Dr. John and Robert, father of the diarist. When grandfather Francis died in 1817, leaving the family virtually penniless, the problem became acute.

Dr. John Kilvert (born 1797) had to face the problem when he was little more than a child. Robert Kilvert in his 'Memoirs' told how John (the fourth son of their father) 'obtained the rank of midshipman onboard Admiral Duckworth's flagship, the *Antelope*'. Sir John Duckworth (1747-1817) distinguished himself in naval engagements against the French after war broke out in 1793. He himself began as a midshipman at the age of eleven. Robert Kilvert also recorded that his brother John was 'for several years on the Newfoundland station'. Duckworth was Governor of Newfoundland from March 1810 so we know that John Kilvert arrived there then – aged thirteen – and returned to Portsmouth in the *Antelope* in November 1812. His post as midshipman had, it is important to stress, come through patronage; he obtained it, Robert Kilvert wrote, 'through some interest that my uncle at Worcester possessed' (i.e. Richard Kilvert, Prebendary of Worcester Cathedral). Robert referred again to patronage as the means by which the Kilvert sons were to 'get on'. His eldest brother, Francis, obtained pupils for him to teach, which 'put [Robert] in the way of forming useful connections ... among these were Sir William Hotham's family'.[4] Patronage had to be sought by poor but genteel families such as the Kilverts in early nineteenth-century England. To obtain positions in the Church, the law and medicine needed an expensive university education. It was afforded somehow by Dr. John Kilvert who, after his years as a midshipman, studied to become a surgeon and qualified M.R.C.S. in 1820. These were the beginnings of the man whose family and friends are pictured in the Album.

Bourne's second pertinent statement is this: '[India was] truly the paradise of the middle classes'. India offered to poor but genteel middle-class families opportunities for work, advancement and escape from poverty. 'Out in the East lay security, status, opportunity and the promise of wealth'. Insecurity was the paramount fear of this class: 'Employment, health and money were precarious in the extreme'. To escape these dangers, they had to seek patronage or, increasingly, advancement by means of the 'rational "middle-class" values of merit, efficiency and competence'.[5]

Although the CDV album is no longer with us, the keeping of albums of family photographs is. The album as physical object has given way to a degree to the showing of photographs on TV and computer screens and mobile phones, but the function is the same: recording the history of a family, representing its members and their friends, including those who have died, highlighting its significant locations, its activities, its interests, its claim to social importance. Martha Langford emphasises another element common to the keeping of a family album in Victorian times and in the present: people's usual experience of an album includes a person who acts as its interpreter. Thus, in order to understand an album's meaning, it is necessary to attempt to tell its story the way its original compiler would tell it. The importance of speech in this process leads Langford to assert that since an album is an 'oral-photographic performance ... something like the compiler's performance must take place if the album is to be unlocked'. An album is 'an instrument of collective show and tell ... and functions as a pictorial *aide-memoire* to recitation, the telling of stories'. One source of help for the compiler's memory is the order of photographs in an album, their adjacency suggesting links and relationships. An effort has been made in what follows to interpret the order of the photos in the Kilvert Album in relation to its stories.

Behind a family album is a voice, a conversation; understanding it depends on reanimating that voice, hearing what it has to say. Each compiler of an album had purposes, intentions in its compilation, something unique to communicate. We have to discover what that was in Anna Maria's case. To her, as to all compilers of family albums, the chosen photographs were emblems of the stories of lives, 'giving voice to the intensity of human experience'.[6] Her album was her version of events. In the chapters that follow, the stories of individual characters have been pieced together and fitted into what it is hoped is a coherent narrative of events, interesting in itself, but one which evokes the intensity of one family's experience, illustrating the ways in which the drawing-room album offers a very personal and intimate insight into the values of a Victorian family.[7]

A note on costume

MUCH can be understood about the world of the Album from the clothes which its subjects, especially the women, are wearing in their portraits. The points that follow are a guide. The clothes would have been chosen with some care since they were a major element in the image which their CDVs presented to the society in which they moved. The purpose of dress was to show how wealthy, how fashionable, how well-educated, how successful its wearers were; in other words, clothes signified status. Hobsbawm emphasises that the mid-Victorian period was one in which the middle class reached its highest point in terms of power and confidence, a state manifested in 'the appearance of the clothes its members wore, [and] the interiors which surrounded them'. The drive to move up the social scale 'could actually place numerous people into the historically novel situation of playing new (and superior) social roles and having to wear the appropriate costume'. Hobsbawm also underlines the way that the over-filled, over-decorated and sumptuous interiors of middle-class homes were expressly designed to assert 'status and achievement [and] personality'. The studios of some Album photographers sought to capture, in a rudimentary way, the feel of wealthy domestic interiors, as we shall see.

The Victorian middle class was well able to express its status through material goods in this period because it was one of booming industries and increasing prosperity. With prosperity came a desire for both domestic comfort and luxury. An article entitled 'Luxury', published in the Cornhill Magazine in July 1860, argued that the society of the time could fairly be described as 'luxurious' in the sense that excessive importance was attached to material possessions. The fashions of the time reflected the demand for consumer goods: 'Women's clothes were more opulent, making use of a wide range of materials and rich colours'. The rich colours were made possible by means of synthetic dyes, which were introduced in the 1860s following experiments by Sir William Perkin, who produced an aniline dye in 1856. Mass production techniques were also making clothes cheaper. The photographer, John Mayall, advised ladies about the most suitable clothes to wear when having their photographs taken: 'Dark silks and satins are best for dress; shot silk, checked, striped or figured material provided they be not too light, and colours to be avoided are white, pale blue and pink'.

Crinolines appeared in the 1850s and were still widely worn during the next decade. Made of rich fabrics, which had become lighter in weight by this latter period, they often had lace or silk trimmings. Many layers of under-petticoats, a fashion introduced in the 1840s, were replaced from 1856 by the crinoline frame of flexible steel, but by the late 1860s crinolines were out of fashion. The wide skirts of the 1860s-1870s period had 'their width exaggerated by tiered flounces and crinoline petticoats'. By the 1870s the fashionable large skirts were projected backwards by the bustle. (It is visible in the photo of 'E.F. Kilvert' – i.e. Eliza Kilvert; she stands sideways as though to display her fashionable shape.) The bustle was one of the styles focused on by Hobsbawm in his examination of 'the powerful sexual element' of middle-class costume, 'an extraordinary combination of temptation and prohibition'. Heather Toomer notes the important role played by lace: 'lace designs were at their most opulent. Deep flounces, mantles and square shawls, six feet wide, were all made in hand-made lace or machine fabrics'. Hand-made lace was always expensive but machine lace, usually black, worked into a net, made large objects such as shawls affordable for the less well-off. A wide range of lace was available in this period but 'the lace shawl was a major accessory for both day and evening wear'. It is very much in evidence in the Album.

Poke bonnets (i.e. close-fitting bonnets with projecting brims), which had appeared when Queen Victoria came to the throne in 1837, were still fashionable in the mid-1850s and beyond. Worn on the back of the head, they were made of ribbons and lace and sometimes surmounted with artificial flowers, usually roses. Bonnets had diminished in size by the 1860s, allowing hair to be visible. Two of the (older) Album women are wearing bonnets in their photographs. One of them also wears the side-curls, also known as ringlets, popular in the early 1840s and still popular in the mid-1850s. Several of the Album women have the centre partings and large buns that were favoured in the 1860s and 1870s. Chignons were also fashionable at this time.

CHAPTER ONE
Albums and daughters

A good deal of the challenge and the fascination of the Kilvert Album lies in identifying its subjects. Very often old family albums contain no verbal information at all, so that even the subjects are unknown and there is nothing to indicate when the photographs were taken or what links them. We are fortunate that the Kilvert Album features not only captions identifying subjects but a few photographs are dated and, in the case of some of the children, their ages at the time are given. Most importantly, the inscription 'A.M. Kilvert 1861' inside the front cover suggests that the Album's compiler was Anna Maria Kilvert, eldest surviving daughter of Dr. John, and that she began her collection in 1861. Since one photograph is dated 1883, we have some idea of the period in which collection went on.[1]

1861 is a significant date with regard to the kind of photographs in the Album: they are all of the cartes de visite (CDV) type, which became very popular in the summer of 1860 when the well-known society photographer, J.E. Mayall, published a collection of photos of the Royal Family, which had great appeal for the public of the day. James Ryan noted that many family albums began with portraits of the Royal Family, as though it were an ideal to which ordinary families could aspire.[2] The CDV had been patented in 1854 in France by André Disdéri and quickly began to replace the calling-card presented at the time of a social visit. Families would often provide decorative baskets or trays for such cards. Although it took some time for the CDV to gain acceptance, by 1860 the public had embraced the idea of photographic calling-cards. A photograph, approximately 2.25 inches wide by 3.5 inches tall, was pasted onto a standard-sized mount measuring 2.5 inches by 4 inches.

The images were taken in multiples of eight or fewer, and since they could be taken on a single plate, they were cheap to produce. A slit in the bottom of the mount enables photos to be easily inserted and removed. Furthermore, photographers regularly advertised that extra copies could be produced in the future when subjects needed more (several of the Album photos bear this message on their backs). This provided a lucrative source of income for photographers.

'The introduction of the CDV meant that photographic portraits were now within the grasp of almost everyone in society, regardless of their social status'.[3] Prior to that time, it was only the very rich who could afford to have full-length portraits painted of themselves. Photography itself owed much to this tradition of portraiture. As a profession it grew enormously from 1850, concentrating largely on portraits. In the 1841 census it was not even listed as a profession but by 1851 the census recorded 51 photographers, and by 1861 the figure was 2,879.[4] People were keen to collect cartes both of family members and of what today we would call 'celebrities': 'For the first time ordinary people could see, and possess, photographic images of their heroes and heroines, be they royalty or religious persons, actors or actresses, writers, politicians, military figures or simply people who had achieved notoriety'.[5] The fashionable new habit of collecting cartes became known as 'cartomania' or 'cardomania'. The American writer, Oliver Wendell Holmes, was writing in *The Atlantic Monthly* in 1862: 'Card portraits have become the social currency, the "green backs" of civilisation'. The craze had spread not only to the USA; it was an international phenomenon by the time Anna Maria began her album in 1861.

At this point CDVs were being produced primarily to be collected in albums and not as visiting cards. The Kilvert Album is typical of those specially produced for card collections and of those from 'the early 1860s ... with pages cut out to accommodate two cartes back to back in cardboard sleeves'. It is typical too in its appearance, 'designed to reflect the external features of Bibles and prayer books, most notably the heavy leather bindings and metal clasps. Such measures suggested to the public that the photograph albums were worthy of the same awe and respect afforded to religious texts'.[6]

One element in the cartomania phenomenon was the thrill, in those early days of photography, of seeing one's 'likeness' reproduced. Helen Vafeas, descendant and biographer of Henry Hewitt, one of the Kilvert Album characters, noted his keenness to have CDVs made of himself when he was living in Bath in 1860. She quoted the diary he kept at the time: 'September 5 1860. J.W.W. came to see me, gave me his likeness' and 'Col. Cotgrave and I had our carte likenesses taken' and 'went with Gilbert to have his likenesses taken at Perkins'. Perkins of Bath took the photos of several of the Album characters, including Hewitt himself and Kilvert's sister Emily. Vafeas commented: '"Having one's likeness taken" was popular. Exchanging "likenesses" was a mark of special friendship and affection'.[7] When Henry Hewitt went to live in France for eight months in 1862, he gave his 'likenesses' to close friends and family and also when he left for Australia at the end of 1864. He also took with him to Australia a large album of likenesses given to him. An aspect of the desire to have likenesses made was explained by Tagg: 'To "have one's portrait done" was one of the symbolic acts by which individuals from the rising social classes made their ascent visible to themselves and others'.[8]

The comments Henry Hewitt made about having CDVs done for himself and accompanying friends to have theirs done show that there was an attendant excitement about it. CDVs were not only fashionable but were a form of conspicuous consumption. Since they were relatively expensive, those who had them done were advertising their wealth, just as the CDVs themselves were designed to assert status, proof of having got on. The poses and clothes of Album subjects have therefore been described in this chapter and in later ones in some detail because they reveal something of the images of themselves which the subjects wished to project.

Kilvert had arranged with his photographer to be posed in profile, looking serious and dignified against a plain backdrop, seated on a straight chair next to a low table, on which rests his right arm. His hands hold what is perhaps meant to be a religious book. Down the side of the chair hangs the tail coat of a dark suit, relieved only by a watch chain. His sideways pose does full justice to his large black beard. He took pride in his watch and chain and was concerned for the latter's safety on a visit to London on 11 May 1875:

I forgot to bring my watch key with me to London, having left it on the gold chain for which I substitute a steel one when I come to London, fearing that the gold chain may be stolen.

Kilvert's photograph has on its back the words 'E. Thomas, Causeway, Chippenham' and the date 1872 in the diarist's own handwriting. The photographer who helped to construct the image by which Kilvert has become known worldwide has particular relevance to the Album story. There were two photographers in Chippenham in the 1870s by the name of Thomas and with a first name beginning with 'E'. One was Edward but he was unlikely to have taken Kilvert's picture because he was only twenty-three in 1872, unusually young to have been able to set up such a business. He also gave his occupation as deputy minister of the Causeway Primitive Methodist Church at the time of the 1871 census. He had no home of his own then and was lodging with that Church's minister.

Edwin Thomas, on the other hand, was proud to declare in Spinke's Chippenham Almanac for 1877 that he had been 'established for upwards of thirteen years'. In 1881, he was advertising 'A Varied Assortment of Views of Chippenham' and 'Views of Bowood House, Terraces, Waterfall etc.' Bowood House, the mansion of Lord Lansdowne, was a short distance from the village of Derry Hill, where Edwin was then living. The lives of Edwin and that of his wife Elizabeth make an interesting case-study in terms of the struggle to get on and get off in mid-Victorian times. Both can be seen in census records making their way in the world from humble to more exalted stations. They also did their best to provide homes for a variety of nieces.

Edwin's father James was born in 1809 in Kington Langley, the village near to Chippenham where Kilvert's mother was born in 1808. She probably knew of James's family. Edwin's mother was Esther, born in 1813, in Cold Ashton, twenty miles from Chippenham. Edwin himself was born in Devizes, the eldest of six children. The fact that he was living in 1851 on the Derry Hill farm of his grandparents, John and Ann, may mean that he was employed there, along with the farm's two labourers and fourteen horses. By 1861, John had died and Edwin continued to live there but now his occupation was that of teacher. A log book exists for Derry Hill School from 1863 onwards but his name does not appear in it. Nor can it be found in schools of adjacent parishes, so it is not known how long he taught. He was clearly seeking to better himself by becoming a teacher, though it was a low-status, ungentlemanly occupation at that time. He was still living with his grandmother in 1871, by which time he had become a photographer, his 1877 claim to have been established thirteen years making 1864 the date when he abandoned teaching. His grandmother had died by 1881 and he was living with his parents and a sister at the Derry Hill farm. He was still working as a photographer.

The woman Edwin married in September 1885 was Elizabeth Sarah Tanner, born in 1844 in the hamlet of Easton, two miles out of Chippenham. She was the fourth of the six children of James Tanner, a mason, and of Lucy, née Reynolds. Both James and Lucy were born in Chippenham. Elizabeth was working in 1861 as a house servant to a married couple there. The 1871 census shows her as housekeeper to William Newman, landlord of the Five Alls pub in The Causeway, Chippenham. She lived there with her seven-year-old niece Emily. At the end of 1871, Elizabeth married Newman: he was fifty-nine and she was twenty-seven. When he died in September 1884, she had the satisfaction of knowing that she had both married her employer and inherited his property. Edwin Thomas may have been a regular at the Five Alls pub because his photography business was in The Causeway, though he didn't live there then. However, after his marriage he set up home there: the 1891 census shows him with Elizabeth and his two nieces Agnes (13) and Helen (7). Photography was behind him at this point; his occupation is given as rate collector. That was his occupation too in 1901, when Helen, now a dressmaker, was living with him, plus Elizabeth's niece Emily Tanner. House numbers had been introduced by then and Edwin's was 47 The Causeway. He died there in June 1911; Elizabeth died in March 1929.

Some who sat for the CDV portraits taken by photographers like Edwin Thomas sought to aggrandise their actual social position, a pretence in which most photographers colluded by posing subjects against backdrops suggestive of wealthy drawing-rooms. 'For the customer, such backgrounds allowed them the pretence of moving beyond their normal social constraints, appearing instead with the trappings of wealth, educa-

tion and status often completely at odds with the reality of their position'. Album characters were, by and large, used to comfortable drawing-
rooms but they too would have enjoyed the opportunity to present their
best self. The challenge facing photographers was to show subjects' best
features. The pose was 'the major indicator of character' and needed to
match 'the sitter's age, stature and manner', and 'the pose of women was
required to reflect their natural poise and grace'. Maintaining poses was
eased by giving subjects chairs and tables, balustrades and pillars to lean
on. 'Clearly placed props could be used to draw attention to certain at-
tributes – for example a book placed under the hand of the sitter implied
literacy, highly valued in the days before compulsory education'.[9] Elizabeth Siegel made similar points about CDV portraits:

> The goal of these images was to obtain the proper combination of an ac-
> curate likeness and an elevated expression, in keeping with the belief that
> outer features were clues to inner character ... most viewers understood
> the signs of gentility through his or her clothing or setting as readily as
> they discerned character through his or her countenance.[10]

These aspects of the photographer's art can be seen in the Album
pictures examined in the following pages.

The taking of 'likenesses' and the use of the word (although 'photo' was also used) were still current in the 1870s, as Kilvert's *Diary*
shows. On being shown a photograph of Wordsworth on 1 April
1871, the diarist commented: 'This photograph is by far the best and
most pleasing likeness I have seen of the poet'. On 5 October 1874,
he wrote about a girl in his class at Clyro school: 'Gipsy Lizzie never
looked more beautiful than this morning. I wish I could get a likeness of the child'. These *Diary* entries are reflections of his general
interest in photography and collecting photographs. His mother too
was a compiler of albums as the *Diary* entry for 12 May 1874 records:
'Dora and I went to Bath and bought a handsome square album for
her [birthday] as a joint present from the family'. On his birthday on
3 December 1871, he recorded: 'Emily sent me two beautiful photographs for my scrapbook'. The involvement of daughters of middle-
class families in album-keeping is illustrated in the following entry:
'Alice Dew has been pasting my photographic scraps into my scrapbook and illuminating their titles under them'.[11] When in London

on 12 January 1871, Kilvert 'went into a photograph shop [in the Burlington Arcade] to get some scraps ...'

Was Kilvert referring to photographic calling cards in the *Diary* entry for 16 May 1870: 'Some of the Awdrys from Monkton called during dinner but went away leaving cards'? It appears that CDVs were still being used as calling-cards in 1871 from Kilvert's *Diary* entry for 6 November which stated that he bought a CDV stand made of walnut from his friend Fanny Bevan when he visited the Bevan home. Fanny (Frances) was then eighteen, a daughter of the Rev. William Bevan of Hay-on-Wye. The fact that she had carved the stand herself is another indication of the genteel activities undertaken by daughters of middle-class families in this period. (More will be said of these activities later.) The collecting of photos by women in family albums, which seems to have been the particular responsibility of Dr. John's daughter Anna Maria, appears in Kilvert's record of visiting his distant relatives, the Miss Mascalls, on 15 February 1875. He wrote of comparing pedigrees with Miss Mascall and of looking 'at the family pictures'. Assertion of pride in one's family appears to be a factor here. Kilvert noted, on an earlier visit – 8 October 1872 – to these 'gentlewomen', that he was 'entertained with genealogical talk' and was shown 'old family pictures'. On 1 August 1870, he spent the afternoon 'looking through the photograph albums' of his friend Mrs. Hockin. The Mascall entries support the Wichards' observation that 'the photograph album would take over the formal record of family history normally found on the front page of the family Bible'. This was one of the functions of the CDV album: 'it recorded the genealogy of the family (and established its respectability)'. Another function, visible when Kilvert visited the Miss Mascalls on 8 October 1872, was that it 'provided a rich source of entertainment and stimuli for conversation'.[12] A Victorian commentator summed up what cartomania meant in 1866:

> [it] created a new passion ... a system of portrait exchange and portrait collection was initiated... Albums for the reception of these pictures were provided, and these once obtained must be filled, first with family and friends, and then with popular favourites, and the photographic album containing the domestic portrait gallery, soon became a necessary adjunct of every drawing-room table.[13]

Album making was a key feature of the lives of middle-class and aristocratic women in the nineteenth century. Elizabeth Siegel shows that a variety of meanings and functions was expressed through the broad range of albums popular among women: 'presentation albums of artistically accomplished ladies, the more common albums of verses and sketches that displayed contributions from acquaintances, and albums filled with portraits of family members and friends'. For women who had artistic aspirations and talent, 'albums were a place of creative exploration' and albums comprising collections of drawings 'demonstrated the "accomplishment" of the artist'.[14] Siegel's book, *Playing with Pictures,* deals chiefly with aristocratic women's experiments with photocollage, in which CDVs were often blended with drawings and paintings.

Before considering Anna Maria Kilvert as compiler of the Kilvert Album, account will be taken of what the *Diary* tells us of the domestic activities in which its middle-class women were routinely engaged. One entry which touches on photographic albums is that for 3 December 1874 (again it was Kilvert's birthday): 'Fanny and Dora had each had a picture framed and glazed for me. Katie had made a very pretty picture frame of paper'. Fanny and Dora were two of his sisters (their photos do not appear in the Album) and Katie was his niece, daughter of his sister Emily. In general, the *Diary* pictures women doing artistic things such as singing and playing the piano. Sometimes they are doing sewing and embroidery, which is presumably what Mrs. Kilvert was busy with when her son noted that she 'sat on the wall and *worked* and read' (my italics) while he and others, including women, played croquet (croquet and archery were popular female activities). Often women did drawing and painting, as in the following examples. In the home of his Clyro friends, the Bridges, Kilvert found Miss Child: 'She showed me her clever drawings of horses ...' His friend Mrs. Webb spent much of her time drawing and painting, as on 29 August 1870 when he referred to 'a series of water colour sketches of Alpine scenery ... beautifully executed by Mrs. Webb'. On 4 October 1870 he wrote: 'A fair-haired pretty German girl ... showed us some beautiful drawings and illuminated texts'. She pressed him into buying 'a six shilling set, of which she has ordered 1000 copies to be printed'.

Collage seems to have played some part in the German girl's work as it did in the additions Alice Dew made to Kilvert's photograph album referred to earlier. She had 'illuminated' the titles of the photographs just as the drawings of the German girl were blended with 'illuminated texts'. Perhaps these 'illuminations' were drawings and paintings of the whimsical and fantastical kind that appeared in photocollage albums. Kilvert showed marked interest in the work of Gertrude Headley, daughter of the Vicar of Hardenhuish, near Chippenham. On 27 January 1875, he wrote:

> She showed me some scrap books which she had made and some matchcases she was making of millboard covered with black glazed paper dotted with little coloured pictures taken from crackers and valentines and glazed with copal gum.

It is evident Gertrude also liked to play with pictures. Kilvert approved of her experiments: 'Very pretty handiwork', he commented.

Just as it was expected that ladies would be engaged in producing beautiful objects with which homes could be enhanced, so it was expected that gentlemen would admire them. Something of an exception was Mrs. Crichton, a Clyro lady much admired by Kilvert for being spirited and intelligent, who had, he discovered, 'painted herself, the door panels, wainscot, etc' of her boudoir. 'The wainscot she was obliged to do lying on the floor' (my italics). However, she also did more artistic painting: 'The walls were hung with paintings of her own in oil and water colours'. Perhaps, on the whole, Kilvert was more impressed by her painting the woodwork of her boudoir because that challenged the contemporary image of the perfect lady, which made her unusual.

Further investigation of Kilvert's attitude concerning women's role shows however that he accepted that their place was in the home. On 16 November 1870 he stated that a recent article in the *Saturday Review* 'described Mrs. Crichton to the life'. He was referring to the piece called 'Great Girls' by Mrs. Lynn Linton, which appeared in that journal on 12 November, one of a series on the 'Woman Question' in the period 1868-1870. (Kilvert, who read the *Saturday Review* regularly, must have seen them all.)[15] By the 1860s, amid increasing agitation over women's rights and increasing sexual assertiveness among middle-class girls, Mrs. Linton was becoming anxious about what she had called 'The Girl of the Period'. Her article insisted that the 'Great Girl' had 'a receptive brain', was 'quick to learn ... intellectually as well as emotionally alive ... interested in the current questions of history and society'. However, she also retained the qualities of the perfect lady: her past was 'innocent', she had no 'moral uncertainties' and the path of her duty was 'plain'; she didn't wish to rival her husband or 'to desire an individualised existence'. She was intolerant only of those who seek to disturb the existing state of things', and this included 'the shrieking sisterhood', i.e. those women who spoke up for enlarged rights for themselves. In essence, she accepted her current subordinate, domestic role because she believed a woman's life to be bound up with her home.

In her article 'The Girl of the Period' (*Saturday Review*, 4 March 1868), Mrs. Linton waxes nostalgic for an earlier English ideal of womanhood, which meant a woman of 'innate purity and dignity – neither bold in bearing nor masculine in mind; a girl who, when married, would be her husband's friend but never his rival'. She would make his house a real home. The girl of the period, however, got married in order to secure freedom from the 'boredom and bondage' of her life: 'She has to sell herself to purchase her freedom'. It was only the 'old-fashioned' girl, 'not Girls of the Period, who marry for love'.

Mrs. Linton was doing her best to resist forces in society that were seeking to give a woman a role beyond that of wife and mother. The middle-class daughter was inevitably going to chafe at the narrowness of that role, at its 'boredom and bondage'. Martha Vicinus has emphasised the excessively narrow nature of the Victorian ideal of the lady. The predominant ideology ruled that she was devoid of sexual feeling. However, she was capable of family affection and desire for motherhood because they were innate. Once married, she did not work; she had servants for domestic work and nannies and governesses looked after her children. Such social and intellectual growth as she enjoyed came from schooling and her social circle. Her primary function was to marry. If she didn't marry, her position was lamentable. Since society prepared women for the sole function of marriage, and encouraged a marriage 'market', then failure to capture a husband was regarded the same way as a business failure.[16] Gorham echoed this view of the unmarried woman's predicament: 'Marriage was the only acceptable adult role for a middle-class woman'; the position of the girl who didn't marry was 'bleak indeed'. As a dependant in her home or that of a relative, she would find herself in the position of an unpaid servant. Becoming a governess was the only alternative because it required gentility.[17] 'Throughout the nineteenth century unmarried women were generally regarded as social failures, and treated with alternating pity and contempt. Most of all they were re-garded as anomalies'.[18]

In two remarkable *Diary* entries (2 and 11 October 1870), Kilvert showed that he was acutely aware of the painful predicament of the unmarried daughter. When the news came of the death of Kilvert's aunt Mary, sister of Dr. John, Kilvert reflected that she was the last of that generation. He was particularly concerned for her daughter Elizabeth: 'Poor Elizabeth, what will she do now?' A few days later, he had his answer. In order to recuperate after the strain of Mary's illness and death, Elizabeth and her brother Edward were first going on holiday to the seaside. Then they were to 'settle together in Lon-don, he is going into a lawyer's office. She keeps house for him after a fashion. He is certainly very good to her'. There was no possibility of her marrying: 'I hear she is a deplorable object to look at, no teeth left, but improved mentally and morally by her mother's illness and death'. Three years later, Kilvert had further news of 'Poor Elizabeth' from Edward, who was at aunt Marianne's when Kilvert visited: 'He told me what I was surprised to hear and could hardly understand, that his sister Elizabeth is now staying at the Angel at Chippenham without our knowing anything about it'. It seems that the loneliness and stress of a spinster's life and the duty of keeping house for her unmarried brother had taken its toll of her for 'it was of no use to ask her to Langley for she would not go near any of her relations or old friends'. Inevitably, large numbers of women were in the position of 'Poor Elizabeth' at this time.[19] In 1851 there were half a million more women than men in Britain. 'From the 1860s onwards, many 'surplus women' chose to live in institutions (including religious orders) as a positive alternative to living as low-status appendages in the house-hold of a brother'.[20] This pattern is apparent in cases of relatives of some Album characters (see later).

The picture that has been outlined of the middle-class lady supplies the context in which to consider Anna Maria as compiler of the Kilvert Album. Daughters were valued because 'they could offer the family a particular sort of tenderness and spirituality. The image of the ideal middle-class daughter was that of the sheltered flower'.[21] Anna Maria had been such a 'sheltered flower' until she eventually secured a husband in 1870 at the age of forty-three. After her marriage, she went to live in Liverpool with her husband and his family so the period of the Album's compilation extended from 1861, when she was living at home in Bathwick,[22] to 1870 and beyond. No children were born of her marriage and her husband's children were largely grown up; she had the leisure to attend to album compilation. 'To understand the social functions of album-keeping, we need to consider it as part of a feminine culture ... constructed by and through the image of the "lady"'. The practice of compiling albums was seen as a predominantly feminine one, with genteel, even aristocratic connections, part of a lady's femininity.[23]

It has already been noted that the family album functioned as a record of a family's history. More can be said of its purposes. Patrizia Di Bello places the practice in the history of photography: 'Women's albums were an important aspect of the visual culture of the time, crucial sites ... in the meaning of photography, as a new modern medium'. She also drew attention to album compilation as 'a thoroughly modern collecting practice which played an important role in the construction of the genteel identity of women and their families'.[24] Langford quoted Susan Sontag's view of the purpose of a family album: 'each family constructs a portrait-chronicle of itself − a portable kit of images that bears witness to its connectedness'. Sontag envisaged photography's role in mid-Victorian times helping to 'memorialise ... the vanishing extendedness of family life', with photographs providing 'the token presence of the dispersed relatives. A family's photograph album is generally about the extended family − and often is all that remains of it'.[25] This view of an album's purpose seems to fit Anna Maria's role particularly closely because her compilation embraced relatives dispersed by distance or death and, because so many of its characters were friends of her relatives, she was in effect chronicling an extended family composed of both. As the modern world of railways, steamships and geographical exploration tended to disperse them, the album could reunite them.[26] Many of Anna Maria's relatives and friends had been halfway round the world, most to India, and had in the main returned. Some lived, or had lived, in different parts of Britain. Some had been born abroad or had died abroad.

Di Bello's exploration of how Victorian women learned to use and to 'read' photography, especially when it was so new, helps us to understand Anna Maria's approach to her album. Di Bello considers such questions as: what did the pictures in family albums do, what uses did they have, why were they kept? One of her answers was that they were about 'family ties and resemblance, longing and memory'. Another concerned the particular way in which photos encouraged a close and intimate form of looking, unlike paintings,[27] which seems to have been the atmosphere characterising the afternoons during which Kilvert examined the family albums of Mrs. Hockin and the Miss Mascalls. The following extract from Elizabeth Barrett Browning's letter of December 1843, in photography's very early days, illustrates this intimate approach to photographs. She referred to that

> ... wonderful invention of the day, called the Daguerrotype... I am longing to have such a memorial of every Being dear to me in the world. It is not merely the likeness which is precious ... but the association, and the sense of nearness in the thing ... the fact of the very shadow of the person lying there fixed for ever.[28]

It was the almost supernatural dimension in this account of photography's fascination that led Di Bello to refer to its 'magic' – its power of summoning up a person – and to emphasise its tactile quality, the sense that (particularly) women had, as compilers of albums, of touching photographs possessing this mysterious power. In modern times, we have lost that sense of excitement and wonder because we have lived so long in a world of pictures and actually touch photographs less and less.

In Langford's view, the compiler, in the act of telling a story through an album, is reanimating the past and blending it with the present in a nostalgic desire to summon up absent individuals. Furthermore, since compilers intend their images and the story they constitute to be 'read' by those who came later, 'All compilers appeal in some way to the future'. An album's story necessarily depended on the individuals who appeared in it and the shape and pattern they collectively gave to it. Some albums were sold containing introductory verses stressing albums' role. For example:

> I wish my album to contain
>   The old familiar faces
> Of all my true and valued friends,
>   They'll here find welcome places.
> And hope you'll not intrusive deem
>   The request that now I make,
> A portrait true of each dear friend
>   I ask for friendship's sake.

Anna Maria must have requested portraits from those individuals who figure in her album. One intriguing aspect of it concerns her 'audience', those who heard her story. Who was meant to see the album, who actually saw it, how widely was it shared? Did Kilvert and his family ever see it? His carte de visite is dated 1872, which was possibly the date he gave it to Anna Maria, though it could have been later. Did he ever see it in its album setting as part of the total album story? Did his sisters Thersia and Emily see their cartes de visite in that story setting? Did some members of the family or some friends contribute their images to it but were never allowed to see the collection and their place in it? Were they deliberately barred from seeing it because they would become aware of omissions from it which they would find hurtful? It is the case, for example, that though Kilvert and two of his sisters appear in it, two other sisters, a brother and their parents do not.

Langford underlines how much depends on the compiler: 'A family album is not by a family, but about it and its reasons for continuance. The album synthesises those reasons; a member of the family synthesises the album'. Anna Maria's reasons were no doubt ones shared by compilers of other albums: to commemorate her (extended) family, to record its existence, to assert its activities and their value, to express pride in it. Looking at her album now, we are bound to ask 'who is this family, who is the presenter of it and why did she take on that role?' The role would tend to set its performer apart, as Langford pointed out, because 'Photography was, and continues to be, an isolating hobby'. And yet, the compiler has emotional attachments to her album's subjects; she may be 'the daughter to one woman and the sister to another' and therefore 'her voice could never be objective or omniscient'.[29] The images she chooses are linked by kinship and association but while those links are based in part on objective facts (e.g. that this person was married to that person), the compiler's interpretation of links is also subjective (e.g. that these persons shared the same outlook).

An album's subjectivity resides in other factors. The compiler's decision to include some photographs and to exclude others is based on personal predilections and attitudes. Thus the story that an album tells is one whose pattern and emphases can be changed. CDV albums would accompany their compilers on social visits to relatives and friends and would be available to have additions made. The fact that some photographs come first or early in an album carries emotional meanings. The compiler was always free to change the order and arrangement of photographs to show relationships, friendship groups and so on, and changes to these over time. In addition, the compiler's own stance towards subjects could change over time, resulting in the reordering of some pictures or even the complete exclusion of others. The captions below (almost all) the photos in the Kilvert Album, while they enable individuals to be identified, pose problems. If, over a period of time, photos were added to or removed from it, new captions would be needed and old ones would need to be changed. However, there is no sign that captions have been erased or overwritten. Furthermore, the captions, all in the same handwriting and therefore written by the same person, seem also to have been written at the same time. There are several reasons for this conclusion. Firstly, there are no variations in the colour of the ink used; variations in colour would be visible if written at different periods. Secondly, an individual's handwriting varies over time but no variations are evident in the captions – which relate to photos collected over twenty years. Thirdly, no captions have faded noticeably more than others. These points tend towards the conclusion that the captions were added at a late stage in the compilation of the Album when it was no longer fluid, when Anna Maria rationalised or reordered it and wanted to ensure, before she died, that future viewers of it would know who its subjects were.

Caution needs to be exercised over attaching excessive importance to the individuals who finally found a place in the Album and to those who might have been expected to and did not. Langford warned: 'While [gaps] can never be resolved with unquestionable finality, they are no different from any other ambiguous element in a work of art, neither mistakes nor secrets'. They are just 'silences'.[30] Furthermore, the people who appear in the Kilvert Album may simply be those who were keen to have CDVs made, who were happy to board the cartomania bandwagon. Dr. John, Anna Maria's father, does not appear, nor is there a space or a caption for a photo of him (both exist for her mother but the photo is missing). Dr. John died in 1861, when the Album was apparently begun, and may have been too ill to bother with CDVs or indifferent to carto-mania. It is easy to believe that the devout Mr. and Mrs. Kilvert, parents of the diarist, chose not to have CDVs made because they regarded them and cartomania as worldly vanities. However, the knowledge that there was a degree of distance between the diarist's family and that of Dr. John disposes one to see other significance in it.

One commentator, cited by Langford, saw the family album as an attempt to idealise the family as an institution by presenting only its positive aspects and ignoring or failing to represent 'images of divorce, antisocial behaviour, illegitimacy, disability, and violence'. Bearing this in mind, Langford herself advises that, when seeking to learn the meaning of a family album by re-presenting it orally, we should be careful about what questions we ask: 'Is it polite to pry?' She concludes her study of albums with this statement: 'the main thing is to develop an empathetic relationship with the compiler of the album' and to achieve an 'imagina-tive reconstruction' of it.[31] The chapters that follow aim to draw close to the mind and character of Anna Maria Kilvert, without whose care and devotion to her extended family the Kilvert Album would not have existed, and to reconstruct its story by tracing out what it has been pos-sible to gather about the lives of its subjects and the ways those lives interconnected.

CHAPTER TWO

Doctor John and his family in Bath

Getting on in Bath in the first two decades of the nineteenth century was particularly hard. It was a city of fierce competition and of booms and busts. 'There could have been few other places in England where the contrast between the life styles of the rich and poor was as sharply drawn as Bath'.[1] The coachbuilding business of Francis, Kilvert's grandfather, had failed in 1793 in the depression caused by the declaration of war against France and he became bankrupt in 1794. The family re-established itself in 1799 in Widcombe outside Bath proper, a relatively poor area populated mainly by artisans, tradesmen, and workers in Bath's woollen industry. Robert Kilvert noted that when their father died in 1817 'it became needful that all of us who were of an age to do so should set to work'. William, the next in age above Robert, was to go into commerce but he died in 1819. (Another brother, Thomas, had died in 1816.) Richard sought his fortune in Canada. Francis, Edward and Robert went into the Church. The son who eventually became Dr. John had escaped, as we have seen, from the anxiety, overcrowding, and relative poverty of Caroline Buildings, the terrace in Widcombe incorporating the Kilverts and their Falkner relatives, to become a midshipman. John's exciting naval exploits made him a hero in the eyes of Robert: 'He had plenty of chances to see some stirring work and meet with some hard knocks'.[2] We don't know where John obtained the education which enabled him to train as a doctor. Robert himself, but not John, attended King Edward VI School, Bath, where his eldest brother Francis had managed to obtain the position of assistant master even before going to Oxford. When Robert became a pupil there in 1811, annual fees for a day boy (which he was) were £8.8s., equivalent to £400 today. Perhaps he received a discount because his brother was a master; certainly school fees could not have been afforded for any other brothers. Studying to become a doctor must have been a severe financial struggle for John. Nor was he to enjoy, as did his three brothers who went into the Church, the prestige and honour of attending Oxford University.[3]

When one reads the memoirs of Kilvert's father Robert and Kilvert's sister Emily, one becomes aware of an interest in and a respect for doctors. Robert Kilvert recalled from his time at King Edward's Grammar School in Bath a boy called Bally who 'was many years afterwards an M.D. in Bath'. When Robert was taking his first professional step in 1827 by obtaining a curacy in Keevil, Wilts., he was succeeding a Rev. Griffiths. He made a point of noting that Griffiths's father was 'an M.D. of Bristol'. Emily Kilvert was interested in all kinds of doctors. She was fond of 'dear old Doctor Colborne', who was their family doctor when they lived in Hardenhuish, Wiltshire. He was a family friend, often having tea in the Kilvert drawing-room and playing chess with 'Papa' afterwards.[4] After he retired, he was replaced as the Kilverts' family doctor by his elder son William who, Emily emphasised, 'had taken his M.D. degrees'. The family liked William less than Colborne senior, 'but I believe he was really a cleverer man than his father, though with nothing like his experience'. Emily recalled too 'our other medical attendant', Francis Spencer from Chippenham. One of her childhood memories that stayed with her until she was seventy was her 'first sight of a frog's leg under a magnifying glass', shown her by Dr. Charles Bailey of Chippenham. Her respect for doctors possessing the degree of M.D. is apparent in her account of her first meeting with her future husband: he was, she noted, 'Samuel Wyndowe, M.D.'

Emily's awareness of different categories of doctors, with holders of M.D. degrees at the top of the ladder, was no doubt more acute because she had an uncle in the profession. Heads of middle-class families aspired to live like gentlemen and becoming a member of a profession was both a means to this end and some guarantee of security. Emily's family had been blighted by her grandfather's loss of fortune and bankruptcy, a fate common in the middle class. Entering the medical profession was, however, not easy because a good education was necessary and competition was severe. Training for professional examinations was worth paying for 'in a world each year more full of young gentlemen than of good remuneration and respectable jobs for them to go into'.[5]

Peter Gay has outlined the basis of the medical hierarchy, of which Emily Kilvert showed some knowledge. At the start of the nineteenth century, the nation's health was in the hands of three groups: physicians, surgeons, and apothecaries. The Royal College of Physicians controlled the first, and to become a member required a university degree plus a doctorate in medicine (M.D.). In 1850, only 1,700 of Britain's 14,700 medical men were recognised as physicians. Surgeons, which was what Emily's uncle John was, were 'lesser mortals' (Gay's phrase) than physicians. Emily, however, referred to John as 'a consulting physician'. Surgeons did the nasty cutting work which physicians declined to do. For a long period, 'surgeons were tainted by their association with the barber's trade, they sliced like butchers and stitched like cobblers'.[7] Membership of the Royal College of Surgeons of England (RCSE, founded 1800) was open to all surgeons from 1843. Those who had hospital experience had higher status than those who had none. Apothecaries, who from the middle ages had been dispensers of medicines, also improved their professional status in the nineteenth century through courses of study and examinations.[8] Apothecaries had the lowest status in the hierarchy: 'Apothecaries were shopkeepers akin to grocers'.[9] Dr. John conducted an apothecary's shop at his Widcombe surgery.

The Apothecaries Act of 1815 set out a course of study which had to be followed before candidates could take an examination, thus guaranteeing a certain standard of education. The RCSE adopted a similar approach in order to raise the status of its members. Until the nineteenth century, surgeons were seen as inferior to physicians and apothecaries, as men of little education. Prior to this, surgeons followed no compulsory course of study. After some time spent in one of London's medical schools or hospitals, they took one examination in anatomy and surgery at the end of a seven-year apprenticeship. The examination was not a demanding one and there were few failures.

By the time that Dr. John was training, the RCSE had instituted a five-year (minimum) apprenticeship requiring attendance at two courses of lectures in anatomy and physiology and two courses in the theory and practice of medicine, plus six months' practice in a hospital (St. George's

Hospital, London, in John's case). He became a member of RCSE on 4 February 1820, first appearing in its list of members in 1821. It was in 1821 too that he became a Licentiate of the Society of Apothecaries. He continued to appear in the RCSE list of members until 1860. That year he failed to register himself under the Medical Act, which was requesting that information in November 1860.[10] Illness may have prevented him from registering since he died early in the next year.

The expansion of medical knowledge in the nineteenth century encouraged professionalisation: doctors grouped themselves into different bodies according to their different education and specialisms. All the professions struggled in this period to gain government backing through the establishment of rules under which they could conduct their business in return for the right to police themselves within their own professional organisations. 'In the Victorian age, a profession was a guild of gentlemanly practitioners bound together by shared interests and institutions'. In what follows, Dr. John can be seen playing an active part in a professional association bent on asserting and raising the status of its members. In particular, he can be seen defending his apothecary role against the charge that it degraded the profession through its association with 'trade'.

After qualifying as a doctor in 1820, John returned to Bath, to Claverton Street, Widcombe, where he had set up a surgery. The plaque commemorating him in St. Mary's Church, Bathwick, states that he lived there from 1824.[12] Bathwick was a relatively new part of Bath, separated from it by the River Avon and swampy meadows. No factories were ever built there and by the end of the eighteenth century it was home to some of Bath's most well-to-do families, living in a few scattered houses. The area had become part of the Pulteney Estate in 1727 and was linked to Bath in 1773 by the Pulteney Bridge. It might be said that the wealthy Pulteney family created Bathwick as a new town, which would become a suburb of Bath. St. Mary's churchyard opened in 1809 but the new church, built by John Pinch the elder for the growing population, didn't open until 1820.[13] Houses began to be built up Bathwick Hill by 1810. By 1835, Bathwick had become part of Bath and five thousand people were living there in 1840.

This was the place where Dr. John chose to settle – a burgeoning location which was appropriate for one making a new beginning. It was also to be home to several Album people. It is barely half a mile from Dr. John's family home in Widcombe, another Bath suburb known to several Album characters. St. Mary's Church, Bathwick, apart from commemorating Dr. John's death, had considerable significance for him and his family. It lies just across the road from his home at 12 Darlington Street. He was married in the Church in 1826 and was a worshipper there; a single headstone marks both his own grave and those of two of his children – his infant son John and his twenty-two year old daughter Antoinette – in its nearby graveyard. His oldest brother Francis preached at the Church,[14] and was, for a while, his neighbour at 7 Darlington Street, where he tutored private pupils.

Another of Dr. John's brothers was the Rev. Robert Kilvert (1804-1882), father of Francis the famous diarist, named after his learned uncle Francis. The diarist's sister Emily noted in her memoirs that there was always some distance between her family and that of Dr. John: 'I don't know why we never went to stay at 12 Darlington Street, but we never did', adding 'I don't think [Mama] cared much for Aunt Marianne' (the wife of Dr. John).[15] The few references Kilvert made in his *Diary* to Marianne seem generally favourable. He sympathised with her over the death of her son William and was pleased at an improvement in her health when visiting her at her daughter's house in London. He slept at her home during the 1873 Bath Church Congress. He conducted the marriage ceremony for two of her children.

Neither of Kilvert's parents, Robert and Thermuthis, appears in the Album, confirmation perhaps of the distance between their family and that of Dr. John. Anna Maria's awareness that Mrs. Kilvert did not 'care much' for her mother was possibly a reason for omitting photos of her and her husband from the Album. An important clue to the basis of Mrs. Kilvert's antipathy appears to lie in the observation Emily made immediately before stating that her mother didn't like Marianne: 'though [Mama] was very fond of Uncle John [she] had a great horror of what she called "Bathy" people'. Emily offered no explanation of her mother's 'Bathy' expression. What it meant can be deduced from her family background. She came from Quaker merchant stock and had attended a Moravian school whose motto was 'Busyness'.[16] In addition, she was devoted to Evangelical philanthropy, enterprise, and missionary work in Africa. Her husband Robert was a very fervent Evangelical clergyman. These influences meant that she believed passionately in the value of work and effort; to be idle was sinful. In the early nineteenth century, when Evangelicalism was at its strongest, the idleness of the rich, particularly in fashionable centres, came in for much criticism. Emma, wife of the Evangelical Wiltshire clergyman, the Rev. William Money, was censorious of Cheltenham gentry on a visit there in 1824: 'Their dress, manners, and idle habits, to us sober people are really disgusting and ... what is of much greater consequence, sinful in the sight of God'.[17]

Bath in its heyday had been labelled a city of 'Loungers' by the Rev. Anstey in his *The New Bath Guide* (1776). That reputation had endured until the 1820s when Mrs. Kilvert (born 1808) was a young woman. Lewis Weston Dillwyn (1778-1855), Swansea landowner and industrialist, had engaged Robert Kilvert's Evangelical friend the Rev. Henry Moule as tutor for his sons in 1823, on the recommendation of Robert's eldest brother Francis. When visiting Bath on 15 December 1828, Dillwyn referred in his journal to 'lounging about this idle busy place all day'. He could see the town was 'busy' but only with pleasure and frivolity, not productive work. By 1829, one of his sons had become a boarder at uncle Francis Kilvert's Bath school and Dillwyn, when visiting his son on 14 May, wrote: 'Did nothing but lounge about in Bath'. The ethos of such spa towns, whose ethos was idleness, offended him. Visiting Cheltenham on 12 September 1843, he was again irritated: 'Dawdled away my time Cheltenham fashion'.[18]

Kilvert had been brought up to recognise, like his mother, that towns like Bath bred idleness in people not driven by more elevated notions of the purpose of human life. In the very revealing *Diary* entry for 23 October 1872 he wrote: '[Bristol] is a grand city. How much greater than Bath. I breathe freely here. Here is life, movement and work instead of the foolish drawl and the idle *lounge*' (my italics). Dillwyn would have applauded Kilvert's assertion because his town of Swansea was Bristol's equivalent. He himself was engaged not only in managing his ceramics factory there but also in all kinds of municipal and intellectual endeavours. He served on committees concerned with paving, lighting, harbour and hospital improvements. In addition to being an F.R.S., he took an interest in natural history, mineralogy, geology, scientific and technological inventions. He brought his children up to follow the same interests. When he entrusted his son to uncle Francis, he was acknowledging that they both belonged to the up-and-coming, progressive middle class. It will be shown later that the Album people belonged to this class. Another crucial thing that Dillwyn and Francis had in common was their religious outlook, in which productive work had a central role: both men were Evangelicals, both had Quaker connections.[19]

The hostility of Emily Kilvert's Quaker mother to 'Bathy' people stemmed from a background she shared with Dillwyn. The juxtaposition of Emily's remark with her observation that her family was distant from that of her uncle may seem to suggest that Mrs. Kilvert saw the latter as belonging to Bath's idle, fashionable circle. Emily was clearly uncertain as to the basis of the coolness between the families of the two brothers. Mrs. Kilvert's antipathy to Aunt Marianne was, it seems, a chief factor, though Emily couldn't, or wouldn't, explain it. In the account that follows of the lives of those given a place in the Album by Anna Maria, it is very obvious that they in no way were part of a sector of Bath society dedicated to pleasure and idleness. They were rather a middle- and upper-middle-class, professional group representing medicine, education, the Church, the law, and the army. Evidence suggests too that they were religious people, 'sober' people in Emma Money's sense of the term. Some were adventurous and prepared to risk their lives in unhealthy climates. Some pioneered scientific discoveries, some wrote learned books, some were involved in commerce. They were all busy, all worked when they could. They either were from Bath or had links to Bath; they were decidedly not 'Bathy' people according to Mrs. Kilvert's definition.

Kilvert's *Diary* provides us with an entry which both reveals something of Anna Maria, the compiler of the Album, and illustrates this 'busy' ethos. She was forty-five years of age when she took much pleasure in showing the diarist round Liverpool in June 1872. She enthused about its commerce and wealth and took him to meet her husband, Mr. Gwatkin, a merchant dealing in wine and ship's stores. Later they gave Kilvert a tour of the docks, which put him in 'dancing spirits'. Kilvert appears not to have had much previous contact with the Gwatkins for he wrote 'I like the Gwatkins exceedingly... I think we are fast friends now'.

They were his kind of people. His remark about being 'fast friends *now*' (my italics) suggests again the distance between his family and Anna Maria's referred to by Emily Kilvert.

A *Diary* entry three months later (25 September) suggests further cementing of Kilvert's friendship with Anna Maria and her husband. Noticeably, he was inducting them into the history of his own family by showing them Langley Burrell Church and, more importantly, Langley House, home of the wealthy and influential Ashe family. Walter Coleman, father of Kilvert's mother, had married on 15 April 1807 Thermuthis Ashe, the daughter of Robert and Thermuthis Ashe. Robert was the squire of Langley Burrell. He was the patron of its Church and founder of its school. For a time he was High Sheriff of Wiltshire. His wife was a haughty, autocratic woman, used to being obeyed. Their daughter's marriage to Walter was deeply resented by her parents because he was a Quaker, causing a long-standing rift between them and the Kilverts. Quakers' refusal to acknowledge rank and clergymen might be expected to antagonise the Ashes, a gentry family proud of its social status, several of whose menfolk had been in the Church.

Kilvert took Anna Maria and her husband, Theophilus Gwatkin, into Langley House 'to see the family pictures' in the dining room. These pictures were not photographs, such as those which recorded some of the history of Anna Maria's family in her album, but painted portraits of the Ashe forebears of Kilvert's mother, and as such possessed higher prestige than photographs in a family album. Kilvert was recalling the rift between his family and the Ashes when he wrote in his account of the visit to Langley House: 'Of my great-grandmother's picture I have a peculiar hatred'. It was she who had been particularly bitter at her daughter's marriage to a Quaker. There was an element of pride in Kilvert's view of this marriage, which it would have been hard for him to suppress as he presented the Ashe family pictures to the Gwatkins. He admired Quakers in general and particularly admired his grandfather Walter Coleman, who was known for being honest, straightforward and unassuming. It might be said that Walter had married well by marrying into a wealthy family who lived in a mansion, but his own people had a fine house and wealth derived from their merchant business. Kilvert strongly resented the Ashe prejudice against his grandfather on the grounds that he was a Quaker.

Kilvert had been brought up with a lively awareness of what it meant to marry well. Around his parents' marriage lingered the idea that Robert Kilvert had moved up socially by marrying Walter Coleman's daughter Thermuthis, as Robert himself noted:

> The common people, according to the wisdom given to them, said he had 'done well for himself' because he had married the daughter of one whom they thought one of the great ones of the earth – a landed proprietor of old family, with county connections.[20]

Thus, there was no prejudice against Quakers in Robert's stance towards Walter Coleman. The *Diary* entry for 16 September 1874 is one of several showing Kilvert's awareness of 'doing well' for oneself in the marital stakes. Miss Bynon, a former Clyro parishioner of his, told him that 'she understood that Mr. Pope had "married into a noble family".' Andrew Pope, from a Bristol trade background, was a clergyman friend of the diarist. He married into the Money Kyrle family, Herefordshire landowners.

The Ashe / Kilvert rift paralleled in some ways that between the diarist's branch of the Kilvert family and that of Anna Maria, and he must have been aware of it as he acted as oral presenter of the family portraits in the dining room of Langley House. Anna Maria's marriage to a tradesman thirteen years her senior with a grown-up family, while not as controversial as marrying a Quaker, would have provoked some criticism.[21] It is quite possible that behind Kilvert's invitation to the Gwatkins to tour Langley Burrell Church and Langley House lay a desire to reconcile his family with theirs by sharing common ground. He no doubt knew of Anna Maria's interest in family history (he would have known of her album, to which he had contributed his CDV). The idea that he was actively seeking reconciliation with her is further strengthened by the *Diary* entry for 22 January 1874. On that occasion, he took Gwatkin and 'Annie' (the familiar form of Anna Maria's name shows how much their friendship had deepened)[22] to another location which was of central importance to both their families – Widcombe. Kilvert was actually staying with the Gwatkins from Thursday to Saturday at their Upland Villa home up Bathwick Hill, and on Thursday afternoon they walked together to Prior Park. Their route would have taken them past Caroline Buildings, the terrace of modest houses in Widcombe into which the Kilvert family moved after the collapse of the coachbuilding business of Kilvert's paternal grandfather. During the Langley House visit with the Gwatkins, the focus was on the maternal side of Kilvert's family; during the Widcombe visit, he and Anna Maria could share the knowledge they had of their respective fathers' years of poverty there. Robert Kilvert was born there in 1804 and John, Anna Maria's father, was raised there from 1799 when he was two.

There are good grounds for supposing that Theophilus Gwatkin would have found much to admire in Walter Coleman, the upright, honest Quaker businessman. Not only was Gwatkin a businessman himself, but he was critical of the shady practices of many of the Liverpool businessmen with whom he regularly dealt:

> Mr. Gwatkin did not seem to have a high opinion of the solvency or honesty of Liverpool merchants. Pointing to the great crowd buzzing and surging below he said, 'I don't believe there are ten men there who could pay 15/- in the pound'. He pointed out to me however three honest men.

Kilvert clearly warmed to Gwatkin's sentiments, adding wryly, 'one felt uncomfortably like being in Sodom and ten righteous men nowhere to be found'.

Quakers were known for business ethics that were the polar opposite of those which drew Gwatkin's criticism. They were strong believers in thrift and in having the capital to back their business enterprises. Hardworking and honest, their word was their bond. They believed in the fair price and liked to set the 'single price', in other words the price at which their goods would be sold, maintaining this practice in periods when bargaining was the norm.[23] Their reputation for fair-dealing and integrity attracted customers and was the basis of their success.[24]

There is no doubt that Kilvert worked to establish a friendship with Anna Maria, the compiler of the Album which is the subject of this study. There is no doubt also that he gave her his CDV for inclusion in it. The CDV is dated 1872 – the year when he stayed with her in Liverpool and when he declared: 'I think we are fast friends now'. (The CDV would, of course, have been *made* in 1872 and given to her later.) The deepened friendship between him and her and the shared exploration of their family backgrounds did not result in the inclusion of the photographs of Mr. and Mrs. Kilvert in the Album. The reason for this may have been Marianne's antipathy to them, which Anna Maria continued to respect. Could the germ of that antipathy have been prejudice against Quakers, which Mrs. Kilvert's family were? A later chapter suggests that Marianne was capable of fierce religious prejudices.

Anna Maria had been happy to marry someone in trade. Any idea that her mother Marianne might have felt herself superior to trade is perhaps dispelled by the fact that her father was in trade (unless that was the very reason for the feeling) as we can see from an indenture, dated 4 August 1789, which bound Andrew Berkeley Becks, son of John Becks of Duke Street, Westminster, Gentleman, deceased, to Henry Holland Stationer of London 'to learn his Art'. The terms of the apprenticeship were severe. It was to last seven years. Apart from keeping his master's secrets and commandments, doing no damage to him and wasting none of his goods, the apprentice was not to 'commit Fornication, nor contract Matrimony'. 'He shall not play at Cards, Dice, ... he shall not haunt Taverns, or Play-houses'. His master agreed to teach Andrew the 'Art and Mystery' of his trade and to provide his 'Meat, Drink, Apparel and Lodging'.

Andrew Becks had been out of his apprenticeship two years when he married Elizabeth Martha Cole at St. George's, Hanover Square, London, in 1798. Three daughters were born of the marriage: Marianne[25] (born 2 September 1800), Martha (born 1805), and Eliza (born 1811). Although it is possible that Dr. John met Marianne in London during his medical training, the fact that a 'Mr. Becks' was living at Sydney Parade, Bathwick, in 1826 suggests that the bride of Dr. John was local. They married on 24 October 1826 at St. Mary's, Bathwick; she was twenty-six, he was twenty-nine. In 1841 Andrew (aged sixty-five and described as 'of independent means') and Elizabeth (aged sixty) were living at 14 Pierrepoint Street, overlooking the Avon, in St. James's parish.[26] With them were their daughters Martha (aged thirty-five) and Eliza (aged thirty); both of the latter were unmarried and worked as governesses. Andrew died in December 1843 and by 1851 his widow and daughters had moved to 35 Henrietta Street, an elegant street in Bathwick half a mile from Dr. John's, a better-class address than Pierrepoint Street. Elizabeth Becks made ends meet by taking in boarders, one of whom in 1851 was a forty-eight year old woman living on an annuity, the other a young bank clerk. At no.36 lived an accountant and his wife and Augustus Price, an army captain in the service of the East India Company. His father, a 'landed proprietor', lived next door at no.37. Elizabeth Becks was still occupied, at the age of eighty-three (1861 census), as a 'boarding-house keeper'. After she died, her daughters Martha and Eliza became boarding-house keepers. In 1871, their boarders were a colonel's widow and a retired banker and his wife, among others. Marianne's mother and spinster sisters had managed to be genteel, independent and respectable, while living at a respectable address, during long years in Bath. It seems unlikely that Mrs. Kilvert, from a Quaker merchant background herself, would have resented Marianne's background, so the reason for the former's dislike of the latter was not an objection to trade.

The marriage certificate of Marianne and Dr. John throws no more light on this matter. The wedding service was conducted by John's brother Francis. The witnesses were Andrew Becks, Martha Becks (sister of the bride), and John's sister Mary. The fact that Robert Kilvert was not a witness cannot be taken as further confirmation of distance between his family and John's; it is likely that he was present.[27] However, it is perhaps significant that he was not a witness at the marriage on 3 January 1837 of John's sister Mary to the Rev. John Matthews when Robert's three other brothers were witnesses. It is odd that this wedding did not take place at St. Mary's, Bathwick, nor at Lacock, where the bridegroom was vicar, but at Langley Burrell Church; Robert *later* became Rector at Langley Burrell but in 1837 he was Vicar of Hardenhuish. Anna Maria's interest in Langley Burrell Church would have been increased during her visit there in September 1872 by the knowledge that it was the location of her aunt's marriage.

By the time of the 1841 census, John was settled at 12 Darlington Street with his growing family: the record shows six children, ranging in age from thirteen to one, plus a surgeon's apprentice aged fifteen. In 1851, John's household included a cook, a housemaid and a footman. In the year in which he died (1861), his next door neighbour was another surgeon, Dr. Lloyd, with whom he had been in partnership in an earlier period. The 1846 *Bath Directory* lists him as partner to Dr. Evans, with their surgery located at 12 Darlington Street. Evans, like John, was a member of the Provincial Medical and Surgical Association (PMSA).

Dr. John showed he was a forward-looking individual when he became one of the fifty founder members of the PMSA, inaugurated in July 1832 at Worcester Infirmary.[28] Its secretary stated its aim as the promotion of cooperation among doctors in provincial towns in order to develop and share knowledge. Such men, he wrote, 'do not hold the rank in the community to which they may attain'. He referred to the hostility which some London doctors were fomenting among different branches of medicine. The PMSA clearly intended to enhance the social and professional status of its members and in part this meant resisting the influence of metropolitan doctors. In 1853, the PMSA extended its membership to London doctors and became the British Medical Association in 1856.

Something of John's character can also be gathered from two letters which he submitted to the editors of the PMSA *Journal*. In the first (dated 24 July 1850) he was responding to a letter that appeared in the *Journal* on 10 July from James Tunstall, who was an M.D. One of Dr. John's friends had brought to his attention 'objectionable passages' in the letter and John had hoped that they would have been focused on at his PMSA branch meeting but they had not. Nor had any correspondent to the *Journal* taken them up so John felt 'constrained' to comment, though 'in no unkind spirit'. (He had to tread carefully because Tunstall worked in Bath as he did.) The issue Tunstall had raised was the practice carried on by some doctors of preparing and supplying medicines for patients. John himself had a surgery and apothecary's shop at 33 Claverton St., Widcombe in partnership (in 1837) with Dr. Lloyd. Tunstall had argued that the practice of providing medicine caused the medical profession to 'sink into a *trade*' and that 'No person who "sends out his own physic" should be allowed to become a Fellow of the Royal College of Surgeons' (the italics were Tunstall's). To give up this 'trade' would, he insisted, 'elevate the character of the professional man'. It was one of the means by which the profession could reform itself.

John declared himself entirely opposed to Tunstall's proposal. 'Pharmacy,' he wrote, 'having taken its place amongst the legitimate studies of the medical profession, its practice ought not, in fairness, to be called "the trade in physic".'Traditionally, GPs across the country had charged fees which covered both the patient visit and the medicine prescribed. In his view, every doctor should possess 'a competent knowledge of drugs' and therefore it was impossible to 'detach and discard pharmacy as an unworthy and degraded branch' of the medical profession. Dr. John could glimpse in Tunstall's proposal a desire to make the medical profession more exclusive and less democratic. He also resented its snobbish hostility to 'trade' and to those whose living came from it. He was also sensitive to the fact that the hostility came from an M.D.

Another letter to the *Journal* from John dated 12 August 1850 confirmed his outlook. At the last meeting of the Bath / Bristol branch of the PMSA it had been decided to elect members of its council by ballot and John was urging that this 'new feature of management' be adopted by the Parent Society whose 'present mode of selection', as in all its branches, had too much partaken of the character of a close corporation' because councillors were 'self-selected'. Behind John's last phrase lay his awareness of the Municipal Reform Act of 1835 which swept away town councils whose members preserved their own seats through nepotism and cronyism, replacing them with councils elected by ratepayers. He was giving voice to the 'notorious thirst for independence' typified by towns like Bath.[29] For a man so keen on democratic ballots, it is odd that in the Bath parliamentary election of January 1835 John chose not to vote. He also declined to vote in the election of July 1837. He did vote in 1847 but not in 1852. His brother Francis voted in all these elections.[30]

One might have expected John to have been a member of the Bath Literary and Philosophical Association (BLPA) founded in 1825, whose aim was to circulate information about literature and science. Francis, John's brother, was the driving force behind this body, serving regularly on its committee and becoming chairman in 1859. The membership always included businessmen, clergymen, army and navy men, and especially doctors. In 1859 its treasurer was a M.R.C.S. as John was. Members could attend programmes of lectures on all kinds of literary and scientific topics. The period in which Lit and Phil societies like the BLPA flourished – 1770s to 1820s – was one in which science became extremely popular. The significance of Lit and Phils was that they represented the interests and aspirations, and shaped the identity of, the expanding middle classes of provincial towns. For some reason, the BLPA didn't appeal to John, in spite of (it could have been because of) the fact that his brother was its leading light.[31] John's brother Edward was a member in the 1836 season. Among topics regularly featured in BLPA programmes was geology. John was such an enthusiastic palaeontologist that on 27 October 1859 he was writing to the pioneering photographer Henry Fox Talbot of Lacock Abbey (Wilts.) enclosing plates and photographs of fossils found in Forrest Marble clay, which is composed of crushed shells of ancient sea-creatures. The fossils had been found in cuttings for the Wilts.-Somerset railway near Lacock. In another letter the same day, John requested Talbot to apply a new photographic process of his to the fossils to bring out their 'intricate forms'.[32]

This chapter has given a glimpse of the beginnings in Bath of Dr. John Kilvert's family. It had a humble and difficult start but to qualify as a doctor as John did was a creditable step in the struggle to gain security and respectability. Emily Kilvert's admiration for those who had achieved this step was no doubt shared by John's daughter Anna Maria. A respect for determination and energy in the struggle to get on is one element in the latter's motivation to memorialise her family and its circle of friends. The photos of Emily Kilvert, one of her sisters and her diarist brother found places in the Album; other members of her branch of the Kilvert family do not. Later chapters will explore the question – a problematic one – of who of the Kilvert family is in the Album and who is not.

The period of the Album's compilation was one in which the cult of attaining respectability and independence gained ground on a massive scale. Lord Palmerston gave powerful expression to it in a speech he delivered in April 1865 at the prize-giving of the South London Industrial Exhibition. The speech was reported in the *Illustrated London News*, a newspaper much favoured by Kilvert's family and the social group represented in the Album. Palmerston emphasised that the British constitution 'opens to every man having talents, energy, perseverance, and good conduct any honours and distinctions which his turn of mind and attainments may qualify him to aspire to'. He urged his audience to 'look at your Army, your Navy, your Law, your Church, your statesmen. You will find in every one of those careers men who have risen to the highest points, who have ... started from the smallest beginnings'. He added: 'You may not all become Generals or Admirals; you may not all become Lord Chancellors or Archbishops; ... but you will, by systematic industry, raise yourselves in the social system of your country – you will acquire honour and respect for yourselves and for your families'.[33]

This cult underpins the Kilvert Album: its male subjects, labouring in their chosen professions of the army, the law, medicine, education, the Church, and business (which in this period was aspiring to become a profession), can be seen as the kind of success stories with which Palmerston sought to inspire his audience. Anna Maria sought to represent in her Album the success stories of members of her extended family, people who had made their way by *merit* – a key value in its ethos.

CHAPTER THREE
Getting on and getting off

To the British public of the nineteenth century, the annals of India always had a romantic character. The subject of India always produced strong reactions in Kilvert. One insight into the whole complex of issues represented by it for him is the extraordinary *Diary* entry initially sparked off by an east wind on 8 October 1870. He hated east winds, usually referring to them as 'poisonous'[1]. The entry reads: 'In the night the wind had gone round from the cursed East into the blessed West. All evil things have always come from the East, the plague, cholera, and man'. His reference to Man as one of the evil things to have originated in the East is explicable in terms of his belief in the doctrine of Original Sin, a very strong belief for Evangelicals.[2] The Middle-East is the location of Man's origin in *Genesis*. The East for the diarist was a place of threats and dangers, it did things, usually bad things, to people; those who went there often didn't come back, or became ill, or were otherwise *changed*. Examples abound in the *Diary*. In February 1872, the sister of Lechmere Thomas of a family that lived near Clyro told Kilvert that she feared that Lechmere would soon be returning to Ceylon where he was a coffee-planter; 'it was dreadful,' she said, 'and for so many years'. Lechmere went out on 12 July and Kilvert saw him off. On 3 September 1878, the dreaded news arrived by telegram that he had died of cholera. Stories Kilvert heard compounded his view of the East as the home of savagery. James Gough, who had served as a soldier in India, told him that 'the Mussulmans [i.e. Muslims] were savage and murderous and would kill English soldiers if they found them alone or even in small parties'. He also said that cholera 'played havoc' with his regiment.

Kilvert was shocked by a terrible incident in the East, which he reported on 14 February 1872: 'horrible news from India that the Governor-General Lord Mayo had been stabbed in the back by a fanatic convict in the Andaman Islands'. The shock waves throughout the nation at this event were particularly strong because Lord Mayo (1822-1872) was an energetic and caring Governor-General, who had actually introduced reforms in the Andaman Islands penal colony which reduced mortality from malaria by 90%. His murderer was a convict there.

Kilvert was content to record the murder as the deed simply of a 'fanatic convict' and leave it at that. The background to it has been explored by Helen James and is relevant to the Album story. Mayo's killer, Shere Ali, had been convicted of the murder of an old enemy in a blood feud, his death sentence commuted to life imprisonment by a judge sympathetic to the cultural circumstances of the crime. Ali felt his crime was justified and resented his imprisonment; he determined to kill some high-ranking European in revenge. He was a Pathan and a Muslim from north-west India and had served in the Punjab mounted police. The area he came from was known for its resistance to British rule. Lord Mayo had declared shortly before leaving Calcutta for the Andaman Islands visit, that he intended to destroy Muslim elements in north-west India who had announced holy war against Britain. The authorities at the penal colony were aware of threats to Mayo's safety during his tour of inspection. The colony was a hotbed of resentment towards British rule. Rebels from the Indian Mutiny had been sent there in 1858 when it was in the charge of 'Dr. Walker, a ferocious superintendent inclined to use execution as punishment for the slightest infringement of the penal colony's rules'. Among prisoners there were several Muslim leaders who had preached holy war before the 1857 uprising. Sentenced to death initially, they were later condemned to life imprisonment. Although James acknowledged that 'it is possible that [Shere Ali] was not motivated by politico-cultural causes, but by a sense of injustice at being punished by those whom he had served so well', she indicated that his background and the current political atmosphere were very likely to have been factors. She characterised his killing of Lord Mayo as a 'political assassination' and drew attention to others in previous months, such as that of Judge Norman, Acting Chief Justice of Calcutta on 20 September 1871.[3] 'Fanatic' Shere Ali may have been but he was a believer in his own religion, which the British had rejected. In 1856, Lord Dalhousie had incurred deep resentment among both Hindus and Muslims by annexing the Kingdom of Oudh, the last independent Muslim kingdom in India. When asked by the authorities why he had killed Mayo, Shere Ali's answer was 'God made me do it'; then they hanged him.

Against this background, the case of Kilvert's cousin, William Kilvert, oldest surviving son of Dr. John, comes sharply into focus. His is the first photo in the Album, as though Anna Maria had taken special care to remember her dead brother. He poses self-consciously debonair and handsome in the fashionable clothes of the early 1860s: white trousers, three-quarter length black coat buttoned at the very top, coloured cravat, white gloves in one hand and very shiny black top hat in the other. Of all the Album men, he cuts the most impressively stylish figure. Briggs noted that when the artist Whistler settled in England in the late 1850s, he was 'conspicuous for wearing white duck trousers' ('duck' was strong untwilled linen or cotton). Other Album men have light-coloured trousers but none as bright as William's. He had also chosen to pose with a 'topper', characterised by Briggs as 'the indispensable symbol of good form'.[4] Behind William (chosen specially for its soldier subject?) is mountain scenery suggestive of far horizons and a life of manly activity, and he leans casually on a plinth, one leg crossed over the other, its weight resting on the toes. He has dark curly hair and the facial hair – sideburns and a dashing moustache – popular in the period (and said to have been copied from Sikh soldiers in India). The photo's sense of joy and promise is belied by its caption: 'William Kilvert, late 92nd Highlanders'. Very shortly after the picture was taken he was dead.

The 3 January 1873 entry in *Kilvert's Diary* informs us that his death was surrounded by controversy and bitterness:

> Aunt Marianne has at length heard certain news of the death of my cousin William Kilvert. He died at Calcutta of diarrhoea after a very short illness 7 years ago. Captain Harold Child knew of his death all the while but concealed it from his family through a mistaken idea of kindness. He heard of William's death by a letter from Mrs. Morgan who had dined with William in Calcutta a few days before his death. The family have thus been kept in cruel suspense about his fate for 7 years.

The 'diarrhoea' that killed him was probably dysentery – or cholera.

Uncertainty over William's fate may have made Anna Maria unwilling to include him in her album until she was sure.[5]

In his effort to 'get on', William had gone out to the East as an adventurer and it had cost him his life, as it had Lechmere Thomas. William, born 13 August 1837, had emulated his father by entering military service at an early age. He was only seventeen when he became an ensign (the lowest rank of commissioned officer) on 30 April 1855, becoming a lieutenant on 4 October 1855.[6] His regiment, the 92nd Regiment of Foot, was created in 1794.[7] It went to the Crimea in September 1855 just after the fall of Sebastopol and remained there till May 1856. Presumably William served there. It went to India on 6 March 1858 to help quell the Mutiny and was involved in many small fights and pursuits. His Album photo could have been taken in the 1861-2 period.[8] *Allen's Indian Mail* [9] reported his arrival back in India on 16 August 1862.

While on leave in spring 1861, William was acting in a play at Bath's Theatre. The *Bath Chronicle* for 2 May reported his appearance in Tom Taylor's comedy (in three short acts), *Still Waters Run Deep*, one of several pieces in the Theatre's night of 'Amateur Theatrical Performances'. The male members of the cast were mainly soldiers like William. He played the part of Dunbilk, the accomplice of the villain, Captain Hawksley, who persuades a wealthy elderly gentleman to buy fraudulent shares in his 'Galvanic Navigation Company'. William was required to maintain a broad Irish accent because Dunbilk is a stage Irishman whose speech is full of rich oaths and folksy Irish allusions. He refers, for example, to the villainous Hawksley as 'as sharp as Corney Rooney's pig'.

Tom Taylor (1817-1880) wrote many popular plays. His *Still Waters Run Deep* was first performed in 1855 and was still appealing in 1916 when a silent film was made of it. After graduating at Cambridge in 1840, Taylor worked as a journalist for several newspapers including *Punch*, of which he became editor in 1874. His play *Our American Cousins* (1858) became famous because Abraham Lincoln was watching a performance of it when he was assassinated. It featured a character called Lord Dundreary, a brainless English aristocrat. The actor who made the part famous grew very long side whiskers for it, worn without a beard, which thereafter became known as 'Dundrearies'. Most of the Album men had adopted them (those of Col. Cholmeley, William Macrone and Arundel Rogers are particularly impressive).

That William Kilvert was to be found performing comic parts in amateur theatricals suggests that he was confident, reasonably talented, lively, and ready for fun. The *Bath Chronicle*'s reviewer of *Still Waters* wrote of William's performance: 'Dunbilk is a rattling rollicking Irishman, not over refined but sharp enough. [It] is a role in which there is little to do but that little must be well done, and on this occasion it was most efficiently performed'. The unfortunate thing about William's participation in *Still Waters* is that the day afterwards his father died, an event announced in the same issue of the *Bath Chronicle* that recorded William's theatrical success. Furthermore, his father had witnessed that success, as the *Chronicle* noted in its 2 May report 'Sudden Death of a Citizen': 'On Saturday evening he attended the Theatre, his son Mr. W. Kilvert being one of the amateur performers on that occasion'. The report also paid this tribute to Dr. John:

> We record with much sorrow the sudden death of an old and esteemed citizen, J. Kilvert Esq., surgeon, of Darlington Street. Mr. Kilvert retired to his chamber on Saturday night last, in his usual health, but was seized with cramp in the stomach, and died before morning. He was a man highly respected in the city for many excellent qualities, and his unexpected decease will be generally regretted.

In Dr. John's death certificate, the coroner gave the cause of his death as 'Disease of heart'. William was to die two years after his father.

Kilvert's reference to William's death '7 years ago' shows that uncertainty still surrounded it because it had actually occurred ten years before – in 1863. The National Probate Calendar for 1880 records his death date as May 1863, in Calcutta, and his personal estate as £800 (£30,000 today). Probate was granted to Anna Maria as the oldest of his siblings. Kilvert referred to William's 'very short illness' but his regiment left India for England without him on 24 and 28 January 1863 and he didn't die until May. He was perhaps already too ill to travel in January, and was dead when it arrived in Gosport on 20 May 1863.

We don't know what Kilvert knew or remembered of his cousin but it can't have been much. To Emily, Kilvert's sister, William was 'a boy I never liked. He used to tease us children on our infrequent visits to his father's house'.[10] The photo that follows William's (making it the second in the Album) is that of 'Grandmamma', born Anna Parsons in 1764. She looks straight at the camera, in a 'serious' pose, one hand in her lap, the other resting on a large book, suggestive of a devotional work. Her clothes are black in the main; a dress with fitted bodice and a skirt made all the fuller by two or more petticoats. On top of her dress is a black lace shawl. The black ensemble is relieved by a 'best' cap, white with frills (such caps were fashionable in the late 1850s), and a white collar – both imparting a Puritan or Quaker look to her. She sits very upright in a high-backed chair. Her family, the Parsons of Shropshire, the county that had also bred the Kilverts, were yeoman farmers several of whose sons became army and navy officers. In 1791 Anna had married Francis Kilvert, the coachbuilder grandfather of the diarist. Emily Kilvert re-called being taken when she was very young (she was born in 1842) to Lacock Vicarage where Anna was lying ill. It was the home of Emily's aunt Mary, sister of her father and of her uncle Dr. John Kilvert. Anna was to die there. We learn something of her from Robert Kilvert: 'devotedly affectionate, untiringly active, utterly self-forgetful, ever contriving for our happiness and welfare'.[11] Robert also observed that his grandmother disapproved of the marriage of her son Francis to Anna because she disliked the Parsons family. No reason for this antipathy is given.

It is necessary here to say something of the East India Company (EIC), an organisation of considerable significance to the story of the Album. It was founded in 1600 by wealthy merchants and aristocrats in order to gain access to the cotton, indigo and tea trade of the Far East. The history of British India is that of the EIC. The Company occupied large parts of India, especially from the eighteenth century onwards. It built trading posts, had its own armies and administered its territories on which it levied taxes. Anna Parsons's older brother William (born 1755) was one of those eighteenth-century young men who 'got on' by becoming a 'writer' in the EIC. 'Writer' meant clerk and William worked in this role at Fort St. George, Ingeram, Madras, an EIC 'factory' or trading post. His family jocularly referred to him as a 'nabob', a corruption of the Indian word 'nawab' meaning prince. People in England used 'nabob' to refer to EIC servants who amassed illegal fortunes in the East. Their reputation for corruption stemmed from the fact that their salaries were low and to augment them they engaged in India's internal trade alongside their official work – the Company's trade.[12] EIC servants, as a social group, came usually from mercantile families, although not all were the 'eager and ambitious neophytes' described by Lawson.[13] William Parsons does not seem to have been notably rich or greedy and certainly believed that young men should devote themselves to business and hard work.

Richard Gott's book *Britain's Empire* is groundbreaking because it views the subject from the position of the Empire's subject peoples. One theme of the book is that those peoples always resisted their British invaders, so that 'In almost every colony they had to fight their way ashore', and the Empire 'was established, and maintained for more than two centuries, through bloodshed, violence, brutality, conquest and war'. The career experiences of several of the Album characters bear witness to the truth of this statement. Gott is keen to explode the myth, the product largely of past histories of the Empire (and of some recent ones), which paint a cosy picture of rulers and ruled living in harmony. Gott, however, insists that a true record shows that 'the British were for the most part loathed and despised by those they colonised'. That there was always resistance is clear from the numerous revolts of the latter. India could only be controlled by two strategies. One was the making of alliances with willing Indian princes, who were bribed, bullied and exploited. The other was through armies of 'sepoys', Indian soldiers paid to make war on their countrymen. Sepoy armies were used all over the Empire to enforce conquest and defeat resistance. 'Sepoys who served the British did so because they were paid to do so, and because they were too terrified to withdraw their labour'.[14]

They were used, for example, to subjugate Ceylon in 1818 when the people rebelled. British settlers began to arrive in the 1820s to grow coffee. In 1848, when rebellion reared its head again, there were several causes. New taxes had been imposed, plus a new law requiring all able-bodied men aged sixteen to sixty to work on roads, the main value of which was to facilitate transport to and from coffee plantations. Viscount Torrington, Ceylon's Governor, commented: 'Our coffee estates are a source of deadly hatred to the Kandians' (i.e. inhabitants of Ceylon). European and Malay troops were used to suppress the revolt of

1848. Hundreds of Kandians were killed, 'the troops went among the people, and shot them like birds before sportsmen' one British eye-witness observed.[15]

A recent *Kilvert Society Journal* article has shown that the Thomas family mansion of Llanthomas near Clyro depended throughout much of the latter half of the nineteenth century on income derived from both coffee and tea plantations in Ceylon owned by Lechmere Thomas and his brother Walter, in partnership with their cousin Edward. Edward, who also worked as a solicitor, 'had earned his wealth mainly through investments in Ceylonese tea companies and rubber companies in the Federated Malay States'.[16] In 1949, Ifor Thomas of the family was still seeking, like his father Walter before him, to make his living out of the Empire: he emigrated to Southern Rhodesia where land and black servants were cheap, and where it was still possible, barely a year after India had at last gained its independence, for Europeans to pretend that nothing had changed.

The history of the EIC is one of wealth and corruption to the extent that it became a scandal in the eighteenth century when William Parsons was one of its humble servants. Lord Clive, part-hero and part-villain, was the founder of the British empire in India, using the armies of the EIC to conquer large areas of it, including Bengal, the area known to several Album characters a century later. The EIC asserted the right to collect taxes directly from Bengal's landholders in 1765.[17] It also operated a total monopoly of trade in India, enforced by its armies. Part of the scandal that was the EIC lay in the fact that its armies were paid for by Indians themselves; British taxpayers contributed nothing. The scandal surrounding Clive epitomised 'the larger structure of imperial greed and exploitation', in Dirks's view. Clive was questioned by a parliamentary committee about his acquisitions, often in the form of huge 'presents' from Indian princes but 'was unabashed in his extraction of loot ...'[18] His fortune was estimated in 1760 to be £1.2m, the equivalent of £75m today.[19]

Kilvert's interest in and knowledge of India is clearly demonstrated by the 18 January 1871 *Diary* entry about his visit to the Royal residence of Claremont in Surrey, significantly in the company of his brother-in-law, a Madras army surgeon, Samuel Wyndowe, an Album character. Kilvert noted that Claremont belonged once to the Earls of Clare 'before it was bought by Lord Clive'. He also noted luxuries there introduced by Clive such as 'a richly coloured superb deep Persian carpet' in the bathroom. The windows of Clive's bedroom, visited by Kilvert and Sam, used to rattle during gales but Clive used to wedge them tight with guineas, 'being more plentiful with him than anything else'. He left the guineas in place, later purloined by chamber maids. Kilvert was obviously aware of Clive's vast wealth and its origins.

Men gravitated to India to make money and to forge careers and this was the motivation in part of Frederick, another son of Dr. John. Born in 1839, he was junior by two years to his brother William. His life was summarised by Emily Kilvert:

> Frederick, the second son was a very nice fellow and very kind to us children and we were all very sorry when the news came to Langley Rectory of his having broken a blood vessel. He was very ill for a long time and when he got better he went to Barbadoes for his health and got much better. I remember so well some of us, myself among the number, going down to Chippenham Station to say goodbye to him as he passed through on his way up to Town. After some time there he came back to England, but it was considered better that he should live in a warmer climate so he went to India and got an appointment in the Uncovenanted Service.

Fred's photo appears early in the Album, after those of two of his sisters and their husbands. Looking serious, he sports a luxuriant moustache and sideburns. Little can be seen of his clothes because his photo is a vignette – head and shoulders only. Inscribed at the top of the back of it is 'Fred. Kilvert Oct. 1883', probably in his own handwriting, since it differs from Anna Maria's. This date is odd because his service record makes no mention of a leave at this time that would have enabled him to return to England. His photo shows a man in his early / mid-forties, which certainly fits with the date of 1883 because he was born in 1839. Two faint words appear at the bottom of the photo, which might be 'Bath Bird'. 'Bird' could refer to the Bath photographer, Frederick Bird, although the photo was actually taken by Henry Lambert.

Emily knew that Fred's chances of getting-on were limited in the Uncovenanted Service (US), which was the lower echelon of the Indian Civil Service (ICS), recruited almost entirely from persons born in India whether European, Eurasian or Asian. The superior Covenanted Service was known as such because its members entered into a covenant with the Secretary of State for India. Openings into it came through attendance at Haileybury College, the vast neo-classical training establishment set up in 1808 by the EIC for its civil servants. Edward Lockwood spent three years there (1851-4), thereby joining the ranks, as he put it, of 'the embryo Bengal administrators known as the "Heaven-born"', which indicated his sense that he was about to 'get on' in spectacular fashion. The popular phrase 'Heaven-born' designated those fortunate ones who had obtained EIC appointments.[20] Lockwood had been a pupil earlier at Marlborough college, attended 1861-1866 by Kilvert's brother Edward. Edward was sent there partly because it was Evangelical but in addition it 'provided cheap education for sons of impoverished clergymen, precisely the kind of people ... disproportionately attracted to the pursuit of patronage'.[21] The Kilvert parents perhaps saw the College as Edward's gateway to a job in the ICS.[22] Many College pupils went on to Haileybury, to the professions, and to Addiscombe, the EIC's military college, near Croydon. This was true also of Cheltenham College found in 1841 (two years before Marlborough). Sam Wyndowe of the Album went to Cheltenham. Bourne summed up the impetus behind going East:

> Englishmen went to India, at least until the 1890s, not because they wanted to or because they liked the country or because they liked the work it gave them, but because they found in its 'spacious households' a 'refuge from the sordidness of poverty'.[23]

Emily Kilvert was living in Langley Burrell when she received news that Fred had broken a blood vessel so it was some time after 1855 because the Kilverts moved there that year. He was ill for 'a long time' afterwards and then went to Barbados for his health. The next known milestone in his career is his arrival in India to take up an appointment as Deputy Collector at Garhwal on 14 July 1867. Emily gave, as the reason for the move, the need to live in 'a warmer climate'.

Sir Monier Monier-Williams, who was born in Bombay, the son of Colonel Monier-Williams, surveyor-general of the Bombay Presidency, gave a vivid first-hand account of what it meant to be a collector in 1850. He wrote: 'In the eyes of the people of his district he is every inch a king. He speaks like one, acts like one, and really has the power of one'. His title of collector did not adequately explain his duties. 'He not only collects the revenue, but has high judicial powers, and the whole welfare of a small territory is committed to him. He superintends police, civil engineering, road-making, rural economy, municipal government, sanitation, education, every conceivable matter'. Monier-Williams further illustrated the kingly behaviour of the collector in his description of dining in his presence. 'I repair', he wrote, 'to his drawing-room and dining-room' after hearing the collector's 'brief and business-like order for dinner'. He continued:

> The collector and his wife, beaming with hospitality, make me sit down at a well-appointed dinner-table. I have a French menu placed before me. I eat a dinner cooked with Parisian skill, I drink wine fit for an emperor, and am waited on by a stately butler and half a dozen stately waiters in imposing costume... I am evidently on enchanted ground.[24]

Fred's post as Deputy Collector was the bottom rung of the preferment ladder. It paid a salary of 250 rupees per month, £25 a month or £300 a year (£12,000 in today's terms). He worked in this capacity from July 1867 to October 1870 in Garhwal and Kumaon, districts of northwest India. By May 1871 his post was Assistant Superintendent in Terai, a region of northern India adjoining Nepal. He went home on leave on 15 August 1871. He remained Superintendent in Terai until December 1874, earning 400 rupees per month. He was Assistant Commissioner in Terai and Kumaon from August 1878 until December 1881. It was during this period that being a member of the US made promotion problematic for Fred. US officers had been deemed eligible to become Assistant Commissioners in July 1876, but his name had been omitted from a list of such officers put forward for the promotion.[25]

One letter backing Fred's promotion speaks of him as 'an excellent officer'. On 1 April 1882 he became Extra Assistant Commissioner, 3rd grade, retaining this rank until November that year, but in May 1883 he was again an Assistant Commissioner. From June 1885 to May 1889 his posts were Senior Assistant Commissioner and Superintendent in locations where he had earlier served. For the rest of his service (1889-1894) he was Assistant Commissioner, second and first grade, in towns in the state of Uttar Pradesh. Part of his job entailed service in law courts because *Allen's Indian Mail* reported that he was a magistrate in Kumaon in 1870 and (later) that he was to go to the North West Provinces in that role. Much of his work as Commissioner and Collector involved long, gruelling journeys through the heat and dust of the countryside.

Since the Calcutta Chief Justice, Sir Arthur Buller, was 'an old friend of my people at home', as Edward Lockwood put it, it comes as no surprise that he began his career in 1857 as a magistrate. In addition, because officials senior to him had been killed in the Mutiny, he was promoted quickly, soon finding himself Chief Magistrate on a salary of £3,000 (£120,000 today). Luck played some part in his getting-on but he also had patronage and the prestige of Haileybury behind him. On his journey out to India in a P. and O. steamer he was understandably aware of the growth of a feeling of self-importance. To him, 'the Indian Civil Service was the finest in the world for persons of mediocre talents like myself'.[26] Fred's talents may also have been mediocre but his position was totally different. With neither patron nor training,[27] he could find a foothold only in the US and began at the bottom. Even at the pinnacle of his career he was earning nowhere near the salary that Lockwood attained at the start of his. Fortunes could differ widely in British India. However, since Fred paid no taxes and servants were cheap, it is possible that he could live in the kingly way, on 'enchanted ground', like Monier-Williams's collector.

Fred had sought out India partly as a health cure. (Lockwood was very clear-sighted about India's drawbacks: a mean temperature of 80°, mosquitoes, cholera, and fever.) There are signs that Fred's health suffered while he was there. Illness may have been the reason for his not being in touch with his mother in early 1870. Kilvert recorded on 28 February 1870 'Aunt Marianne uneasy because Fred has not written for 3 mails', i.e. for three months.[28] (The much reduced time it took to convey mail and passengers in the P. and O. steamships greatly increased the desire for news of India. Furthermore, many more ships were in use: 516 ships arrived in Calcutta in 1839, compared with only 246 in 1832.) Fred's service record noted that he was 'Absent in excess of authorised leave on 15 August 1871'. His service record also notes that he had 'a furlough to Europe on medical certificate from 2 March to 28 November 1874'.[29] It was during this leave that he married Emily Mary Ellis in a service performed by Kilvert at St. Mary's Bathwick on 15 August 1874. The day before, Fred had brought his intended from Bath to the Kilvert home at Langley Burrell for lunch, followed by croquet and tennis on the Vicarage lawn 'in a drizzling rain'. This friendliness on the Kilverts' part towards a member of Dr. John's family is a reminder that Emily Kilvert had always remembered Fred as 'a very nice fellow'.

Fred's bride was the daughter of James Walter Elley Ellis, originally of Devon, a Cambridge-educated barrister. He had married Emily Treslove of Bathwick, who was herself a barrister's daughter, in 1840. Emily Ellis was born in 1842 at North Tawton in Devon. By 1871, she had moved from Bathwick to live at 2 Royal Crescent, Bath, with her recently widowed mother and two of her sisters (one other one had married). The two sisters, Katharine and Harriet, aged twenty-five and eighteen respectively, were unmarried, as twenty-nine year old Emily was. Two servants were employed. A neighbour at Royal Crescent at that time was Mrs. Middleton of the Album (see chapter four). The path of Emily had been crossed years before by another Album character – Henry Hewitt – in whose Bath social circle she often figured. In his diary entry for 31 March 1864, he wrote: 'Walked with Miss Ellis to Hampton Rocks – down Bathwick Hill home' (Hampton Rocks is a beauty spot on Bathampton Down). It appears he was invited to her home on 4 April that year for his diary entry read: 'Ellis – didn't feel inclined to go'. However, on 31 May he recorded: 'Took a bunch of roses to the Ellis's'. He and his father went to tea at the Ellis home on 4 June, while on 8 June he had been invited to a picnic there but again declined to go. These diary entries suggest that Emily Ellis might have married Henry Hewitt ten years before Fred Kilvert did. When Henry was courting her in his vague intermittent way she was twenty-three; when she finally married she was thirty-two.

Emily's photo is a vignette, like that of her husband. Two words, which could be 'Bird Bath', appear on it as they do on his and by the same hand that dated his. Her photo too was taken not by Bird but by Lambert. A cameo brooch sits beneath the white collar of Emily's dress. There is a slightly exotic look to the other object at her neck – a necklace of two strands, made of some white material which could be ivory (although it might be fabric of some kind). Her hair is drawn tightly back into a chignon. It is hard to make out what composes the cap that surrounds it, but it too imparts a foreign air. Could it and the necklace reflect Indian influence? Whatever their nature and origins, we need to remember that Emily would have chosen them carefully as part of the image she wanted her CDV to project. She looks, somewhat seriously, even sadly, to her left; Fred looks to his right, which means, given their arrangement in the Album, that they look away from each other. Had their photos been changed over, they would have faced each other as other married couples in the Album do, e.g. the Rev. and Mrs. Smith, Sam Wyndowe and Mrs. Wyndowe.

It is worthwhile to examine the *Diary* entry about Fred's low-key wedding, which Kilvert found very strange, because it throws a light, though a dim and uncertain one, both on Fred himself and on the family that continued to live at 12 Darlington Street after Dr. John's death. Kilvert underlined several times how strangely early the wedding was. First, he noted that he slept in Bath 'to be ready for Frederick Kilvert's wedding tomorrow morning early'. Then he noted that he performed the ceremony 'at 9.15 immediately after the 8.30 morning service'. The best man didn't appear until 'the end of the ceremony' because he 'overslept himself'. In addition, the wedding breakfast had the air of being very basic and hurriedly put together. 'One missed the wedding cake at the head of the table,' Kilvert commented; 'Instead of it appeared some loose wedges of cake on a dish'. There was little sense of occasion about it too because it took place at one o'clock, which meant that the wedding party were 'all separated for three hours'. Kilvert's summary of the occasion shows just how odd he felt it to be: 'The wedding was ostentatiously early and quiet and studiously as unlike a wedding as possible'. His choice of 'ostentatiously' and 'studiously' indicate his sense that a deliberate effort had been made to keep the numbers of those attending down to a minimum, as well as to keep the affair away from public attention.

One is bound to speculate about what and who lay behind this policy of secrecy. It is hard to believe that Fred and Emily, and Emily's mother, would opt for a secret wedding. Nor can one imagine that Fred would do so if he did not have the approval of his mother Marianne. She was still alive at this time and living at 12 Darlington Street. She did not die until 31 March 1878. If she herself had not attended the wedding that fact would tend to confirm some antipathy on her part to it. The marriage certificate shows that neither she nor any of Fred's sisters were witnesses, which certainly seems odd. The four witnesses were Emily's mother and sister Katharine and two men, Mr. Williams and Mr. Hunt. No member of Fred's family was there to give formal assent to the proceedings. Was Kilvert being discreet or deliberately evasive by referring vaguely to 'the wedding party' without identifying its members? The marriage certificate described Emily as 'spinster of Caerbadon House'; she was thirty-two. Fred's occupation was recorded as 'Indian Civil Service. Uncovenanted.'

It is noticeable that Kilvert, in order to ensure that he was available early to perform Fred's wedding ceremony, slept overnight, not at Marianne's but at '8 Edward Street', as he recorded. This was not the address of a relative or friend but that of a lodging house in a street of lodging houses. A transcription error may have resulted in '8 Edward Street'; at 9 Edward Street at this time lived his friend Marianne Awdry, widow of Peter Awdry, Chippenham solicitor. Since Kilvert had his (non-wedding) breakfast at the Sydney College home of his sister Thersie, only a few hundred yards from Darlington Street, it is strange that he didn't sleep there.[30] The reason may have been that he considered it tactless because Thersie and her husband had not been invited to the wedding. One wonders whether it was tact which determined that he chose to say nothing in his diary about Marianne as the influence behind the secret wedding, even though he knew, or suspected, that she was. Plomer, the editor of the *Diary*, who showed a relish for family controversy, would not have omitted any comments by the diarist on this score.[31]

A further strange dimension of Fred's wedding is the wedding breakfast, which took place, not at his mother's home but at 'Mrs. Ellis' house in Cleveland Walk', as the *Diary* records. The reason for this may simply have been a desire to include the bride's mother in such celebration as there was, in which case the responsibility for providing 'loose wedges of cake' instead of a whole cake would have been hers. Economy seems hardly sufficient to explain this minimal provision since Mrs. Ellis was wealthy and her Cleveland Walk home, Caerbadon House, was one of a number of small mansions in a wide, elegant street lying near the top of Bathwick Hill.[32] She came to live there some time after the 1871 census; the 1873-4 *Bath Directory* shows her there and subsequent ones record her up to 1879. Her husband had died on 27 December 1870, leaving an estate worth half a million pounds. Kilvert made no reference to Marianne and her daughters at Mrs. Ellis's house.

After their wedding, Fred and Emily went out to India and their son (and only child) John was born at Naini Tal, Bengal, in September 1875. He entered the medical profession like his grandfather, after whom he had been named, becoming M.R.C.S. and L.R.C.P. He died in 1904. He and his mother had returned to Bathwick by 1891, Fred remaining in India. In 1901, Fred had returned and was living with Emily at 'Fieldside', Somerset Road, Ealing. She died there on 17 December 1902, leaving over £3,000 to Fred, who died on 26 December 1905 at Budleigh, Devon. In spite of poor health, he had survived twenty-seven years in the 'cursed East'.

Kilvert officiated too at the wedding of Eliza – the last of Dr. John's daughters to be married. She was forty-one years old. Even her eldest sister Anna Maria had married before her and another sister, Antoinette, who was only three years older than Eliza, had married twenty-four years before at the age of twenty. It is not hard to see why Eliza failed to 'get off' earlier. Her Album photo shows a plain, rather masculine-looking woman standing, back to a window, with one arm resting on a padded chair. Her large bustle thrusts out her tiered skirts. Her wedding took place on New Year's Eve 1874, a few months after that of her brother Fred. Kilvert's *Diary* entry records his awareness that her wedding bore the same features as his. It seems to have been kept as secret as possible partly by taking place as early as possible, as Fred's had. 'Up early and went to Bath by the 8.30 train to marry Eliza Kilvert and Mr. Russell,' Kilvert wrote. The train was late so he 'ran up Darlington St ... and got there by 9.30'. It had been assumed by Eliza's family that he was not going to make it on time so the parish curate had been asked to deputise. He was 'unordered' when Kilvert appeared. As at Fred's wedding, the wedding party was very small: Anna Maria Gwatkin (Eliza's sister) and her husband, the bride and groom, and Kilvert. 'This was the whole wedding party,' the diarist observed incredulously. Eliza's sister Lucy and her husband had been invited but were prevented 'by illness and the stress of the weather'. Choosing New Year's Eve for a wedding was strange enough but attendance at this one was made more difficult by the fact that it was bitterly cold – '17 degrees of frost,' Kilvert noted.

Kilvert could not stress enough how pitifully small the wedding party was: it moved across the road to the church 'quite promiscuously, by twos and threes' (one two and one three would have comprised the entire group!). His subsequent emphases register a clergyman's unease that a joyous occasion like a wedding should be concealed almost as something to be ashamed of. 'Literally not another soul was in church beside Stiles the clerk and the pew opener and his wife. The day of the wedding had been kept so very quiet, that no one knew when it was to be, not even the Bampfyldes next door and such friends'. Kilvert was able to find kind words for the bride's clothes, if not for her beauty:

> Eliza wore a travelling dress of dark blue cloth trimmed with brown fur, and a dark velvet bonnet and she looked very warm, sensible and comfortable... She behaved very nicely and well all day, perfectly simple, natural, unaffected and self-unconscious.[33]

'I like what I have seen of Russell,' Kilvert wrote in his diary. One of the things he liked about Russell was his eager response to Kilvert's question at the Ceremony: 'Wilt thou take this woman to be thy wedded wife?' Russell 'burst in with great and sudden emphasis, "I will!"' Eliza then 'looked up at him reproachfully'. Francis John Roberts Russell was born in Ireland. He was a member of the Royal College of Physicians of Ireland, a Licentiate of the Midwives Society, and a Licentiate of the Society of Apothecaries (as Dr. John was). When he registered with the Medical Register, as doctors had regularly to do, on 5 June 1874, just before he married Eliza, he was living at 85 Goldhurst Terrace in London.

It is difficult to assess what Kilvert knew about Russell, apart from knowing he was a doctor. Did he, for example, know that he was a Catholic with roots in Ireland? Emily Kilvert did because she wrote in her 'Recollections': 'he belonged to the Roman Church'.[34] She certainly knew that in 1912 when her 'Recollections' were written, and perhaps earlier.

Emily could look back on half a century, not only of anti-Catholic, but also of anti-Irish prejudice. Fears of both were aroused by the passing of the Catholic Emancipation Act of 1829 and by the doubling of Irish immigrants from 300,000 in 1841 to 600,000 in 1861. One effect of this latter development was the restoration of the Catholic Church hierarchy, which was seen as an attempt to convert Britain from its Anglican faith. The Oxford Movement of the 1830s and 1840s contributed to these fears. Thus 'anti-Catholicism was an integral part of what it meant to be a Victorian'.[35] Anti-Irish prejudice was also an integral part of this outlook. Frank Neal, after noting 'the general hostility to Catholicism which was endemic in Victorian Britain', observed that the Irish were synonymous with Catholicism. He also referred to 'the widespread antipathy towards Catholicism among the educated classes'.[36] This antipathy played a prominent part in the story of the Album characters, Fred and Mrs. Koe, that is the subject of a later chapter.

This antipathy surfaces in *Kilvert's Diary* in entries which together show Kilvert attempting to maintain a balanced position towards the Irish Question. During a dinner party on 14 January 1872 at the home of the Rev. Venables, the diarist admitted to being 'convulsed by Captain Adam's stories of the manners and customs of the Irish'. In other entries, however, he expressed sympathy for Irish people he himself met, as on 14 September 1872 when he journeyed from Bristol with 'a good-humoured sleepy Irish Squire and a family of the fairest noblest looking boys I ever saw ... and a fair noble-looking mother'. He was doing his best here to reject the stereotypical view of the Irish as a physically degenerate race. He was also moved by the sight, during his visit to Liverpool in June 1872, of 'ragged Irish bare-footed women and children' and of Irish emigrants on the docks.

Is it possible that Kilvert was aware that Russell's Catholicism was the reason for the secrecy of the marriage between him and Eliza, that it was the reason for the absence from it of Marianne, of Lucy and her husband Thomas Parsons, rather than, in their case, 'illness and the stress of the weather'? Notable absentees too were members of Russell's own family who, as Irish Catholics, perhaps disapproved of his marriage to a Protestant. Kilvert, although hostile to Catholicism (see *Diary*, vol.2, p.437), sometimes prayed in a Catholic church (see *Diary*, vol.3, pp.230, 357). It was possible for him to warm to Russell as another human being, to forget his religion, and to rejoice that a Catholic and a Protestant could marry in spite of prejudice. (On one occasion when he prayed in a Catholic church, his prayer was for 'brotherly love, and the union of

Christendom'.) Is the sub-text of his *Diary* account of Eliza's wedding unstated criticism of the prejudices of her family that could keep them away from a happy occasion? And could he not, as a Christian and as a sensitive man, bring himself to voice that criticism of relatives in his diary? When he expressed his approval of Russell, was the sense of it 'I like what I have seen of Mr Russell', even if (some) others do not?

Russell and his photographer[37] had together chosen a pose that underlined the former's importance and authority. He is comfortably seated and looks confident and relaxed, full face to the camera, legs crossed, arms folded. His hair, parted in the middle, is long and visible at the back of the left side of his head (unless it is a sideburn, though a sideburn is not visible on the right side). His moustache is luxuriant. His dark, three-quarter-length coat contrasts with light-coloured trousers. (Most urban men's clothes were dark from around 1850.) No backdrop diverts attention from the solid central figure, apart from the edge of a dark curtain. Because Russell had become 'family' by marrying Eliza, his photo comes early in the Album – fifth if we assume a photo of Marianne ('Mamma') was originally the third, next to Russell's bride, which is ironic given the tensions surrounding their wedding.

After his marriage, Russell returned to his practice in London, and a son called Oswald was born to Eliza in 1876 when she was forty-three. Having a doctor husband who was a specialist in childbirth would have been comforting for her. The 1881 census shows the family at 48 Lupus Street, Westminster, by which time Oswald was five. Kilvert visited them at this address on 23 June 1876, noting that Frank went out to see a patient while he was there. Marianne, who had recently been ill, was staying in the house at the time. Frank was not at home at the time of the 1881 census. However, Eliza's age then is recorded, on testimony presumably supplied by herself, as forty, whereas she was actually forty-eight. The explanation for this could simply be that the enumerator made an error, were it not for the fact that the 'error' is apparent too in the 1891 census. Eliza's age is given there as forty-five, which means she had aged only five years since 1881. Though she may have sought to slow down the ageing process, she could not finally escape it; she died in 1908. Her son Oswald, five years old at the 1881 census, was fifteen at the 1891 one, so he had aged according to natural processes.[38] There is an anomaly too regarding Frank's age in census returns. He had given his age as forty-six to the 1891 enumerator but at the 1901 census, when he was a boarder in the Newport, Monmouthshire, home of Dr. John Lane (born in Ireland as he had been), his age is recorded as fifty-two, only six years older than at the census ten years before.

Kilvert had obviously seen a parallel between the two weddings of Dr. John's children because his attitude to them both was the same. He felt it was wrong that the legitimate desires of family, friends and parishioners to attend were being denied, and the shock he registered was the shock which other people of the time would have registered. He must have speculated about the family's reasons for declining to celebrate the weddings in the conventional way. Dr. John himself was long since dead, but his two children were being married in the church where he had worshipped, and in the parish where he had lived, for thirty-seven years. Would he have approved of keeping the weddings so secret that even his friends and next-door neighbours knew nothing of them and to which they were not invited? Such a way of proceeding was a slap in the face for the institutions of family and community, the institutions underpinning the Album itself.

Kilvert's *Diary* entry for 17 September 1873 shows that he knew the difference between a secret wedding and a merely quiet one. It was a family wedding, just as those of Fred and Eliza Kilvert were, and he performed the ceremony just as he did then. However, the atmosphere was quite different. He made a point of noting that it was 'a very quiet wedding'. No bells were rung and his sister Fanny was 'the only bridesmaid'.[39] The bride was his cousin Lizzie Kilvert, daughter of his uncle Francis, brother of Dr. John. None of Dr. John's family were present. Kilvert's sister Thersie 'came up for the wedding'. As usual, the artistic talents of ladies had been deployed to embellish the ceremony: wreaths made by the bride and her sister 'were quite lovely, scarlet geranium and white clematis'. Kilvert brought them home and hung them on the walls of the breakfast room. 'Dora made the bouquets, the bride's bouquet and all, and arranged the breakfast table with her usual perfect taste'. Kilvert himself went to his friends, the Awdrys, and borrowed 'a dozen of the new fish-globe glasses for roses, to decorate the breakfast table'. It was all a far cry from Fred and Emily Ellis's Spartan, perfunctory and apologetic wedding breakfast. At that of Lizzie Kilvert, all was love, ease, openness, simple, homely pleasures and mutual support.

Eliza's sisters were invited to her wedding: Anna Maria was present and Lucy too was to have been one of the guests. Kilvert chose to mention this latter fact; since he made no reference to invitations being extended to sisters of Fred at his wedding, it seems they were not invited, something which perhaps he found too painful to record. He was rather inclined (or determined) to refer simply to 'the wedding party'. We know that none of Fred's sisters were witnesses. Nor was Marianne. It is possible that both his sisters and mother were in the wedding party which went to the bride's house, although Kilvert's failure to acknowledge the fact does seem significant, given the other strange circumstances surrounding Fred's wedding. Why was the wedding breakfast at Caerbadon House so basic? Was it some kind of protest on Mrs. Ellis's part against the secret wedding and the non-attendance of the bridegroom's people? If it was, it would have been very hurtful to her daughter whose wedding day it was. Kilvert made a point of registering that his branch of the family approved of Fred's bride: 'We all like what we have seen of Miss Ellis'. Perhaps this observation, paralleling the approving one he made of Dr. Russell, bore the implication: 'no matter what Marianne's branch of the family think of her'.

If Marianne had some objection to Miss Ellis, what could it have been? It has been suggested earlier that a possible objection to Dr. Russell as husband for Eliza could have been that he was a Catholic. No such obvious reason presents itself in the case of Miss Ellis. (Her family has not been found in nineteenth-century lists of Catholics.) Fred had after all secured for himself a girl from one of Bath's wealthiest and most respectable families, daughter not merely of a solicitor but of a barrister[40] – just as Eliza had secured a husband who was not merely a doctor but an M.D. Furthermore, Fred would have been as hurt as his bride to find that their wedding day had become the arena for inter-family hostility. Was it coincidence that, two days after registering 'We all like what we have seen of Miss Ellis', Kilvert's diary entry (for 7 August 1874) contained a passage replete with heavy emphasis on the joys of family harmony: 'This evening Fanny, Teddy and I dined at Monkton, a nice family party, "in a friendly way", said the note of invitation, and it was very pleasant and friendly'. Had conversation already turned in the Kilvert home, when Miss Ellis came to lunch, to who would and who would not be at her wedding? And was the diary entry about the 'nice family party' at the home of the Awdrys at Monkton an oblique commentary on that conversation? The real reason for the tension underlying Fred's wedding is just as mysterious as that underlying the distance which Kilvert's family always maintained to Dr. John's. Its pivot in both cases seems to have been Marianne. What a pity it is that we cannot see her in the Album, 'the very shadow of the person lying there fixed for ever' (Elizabeth Barrett Browning's words quoted in chapter one), for that would enable us to at least reach beyond the shadow to its substance. And what kind of significance, if any, do we attach to the fact that no photo of Marianne has survived among the Album pictures so carefully preserved, ordered and reordered by her daughter? A further interesting question, in the period when the stereotype of Irishmen represented them as drunken, idle, backward, irresponsible, and cunning children of their native bogs, is what Marianne's attitude was to her son playing the part of Dunbilk, 'a not over refined, rattling, rollicking Irishman', intent on 'bilking' (i.e. cheating) respectable families of their hard-earned money. Even his friend Captain Hawksley castigated him (out of his hearing) for his 'bog-trotting impudence'. We don't know for certain whether Marianne had accompanied her husband to the Bath Theatre. The fact that he attended makes it more likely that she did too and that they enjoyed together, with the rest of Bath's respectable citizens, Tom Taylor's satirical portrait of an Irish rogue.

CHAPTER FOUR
Soldiers, spouses and spinsters

Inevitably in this story of the Kilvert Album some people will figure as major characters and some as minor ones. Members of Dr. John's immediate family will naturally be found among the former. Other individuals will be major figures because they have a more important story to tell, because their lives, careers, and achievements have more intrinsic interest. Some individuals are cast in minor roles simply because their lives cannot be illuminated by substantial primary sources such as biographies, letters and diaries. About some, it has been possible to come up with only a handful of basic facts. This chapter is one of two which give comparatively brief accounts of characters who had a place in the network of relatives and friends in Anna Maria's extended family. All of them would of course have had importance to that family, although the importance would have varied over time. Limited though these accounts are, each makes a significant contribution to the ethos of the Album society, which this book sets out to convey. In addition, each individual, couple or family represents links which helped to bind that society together.

India, the common denominator of some many Album characters, helps to explain why Mrs. Middleton, born around 1799, found a place in it. Her photo pictures a woman in her mid-sixties, which means it was taken around 1866. A short, round figure, reminiscent of the compiler's Grandmamma and of Queen Victoria, she sits, left hand resting on a closed book on a table and her right hand on her knee, draped curtain behind her and a carpet under her feet. She is clothed completely in black, even wearing black lace mittens, with black ribbons securing her bonnet. A black lace shawl is part of her ensemble. She resembles the royal widow of photos taken soon after Prince Albert's death in 1861 because her husband too had recently died in March 1866.

Her name was Mary Ann Middleton (née Ochterlony) and she was a lady of considerable means, because her address in 1861 was 25 Royal Crescent, Bath's most elegant terrace. Six servants looked after her and her husband then: there was her fifty-year-old Kent-born bachelor coachman, William Brown, Thomas Daniel, her thirty-year-old footman, who was a local man, a thirty-six-year-old, unnamed lady's maid (also born in Kent), and two housemaids, one of whom, like the cook, was born in Wiltshire.

Mary Ann's husband, Henry Johnson Middleton, was almost ten years older than she. He was born 29 July 1791 in Southampton. His father was Nathaniel Middleton (1750-1807) and his mother was Frances Ann Morse, born in Jamaica. Their first-born, Hastings Nathaniel, was born in Cawnpore in 1781 and several other siblings were born in India. Henry's career exemplified graphically how fortunes could be made there. He had become a 'writer' (i.e. a clerk) with the EIC in 1807, the year his father died, but didn't go out to India until July 1809. By February 1812, he was Assistant to the Collector of Sarun. He was a Collector in his own right between October 1812 and October 1814 in Sarun and Shahabad. Posts as Assistant Secretary and Accountant to the Commissioners in Bihar and Benares followed between 1816 and 1818, when he became Collector in Juanpore. By 1820, he was Assistant to the Civil Commissioner of the Delhi Territory.

A clue to the ethos in which Henry had been raised is the fact that his brother had been named Hastings after the first Governor-General of India, Warren Hastings (1732-1818). Warren Hastings had gone out to India in 1750 as a clerk with the EIC. He quickly began to immerse himself in Indian culture and to learn Indian languages. He collaborated with Clive in wars against hostile Indian princes but was appalled by corruption in the EIC and by the excessive demands made for money and territory on those Indian princes who became allies of the British. The reforms he introduced were based on knowledge of and respect for Indians' way of conducting affairs.

William Dalrymple in his book *White Mughals* characterises Hastings as 'the most enlightened of all British Governors-General' and shows his influence on a group of soldiers and administrators of the period. One was General William Palmer whose career 'had flourished under Hastings, who had shared his love of, and interest in, all things Indian'[1]. When Resident in Lucknow, Palmer had taken an Indian wife and the couple named their third son Hastings. Palmer became increasingly disturbed by the attitudes and policies of Lord Wellesley,[2] the new Governor-General appointed in 1797, who furthered and deepened the idea of racial hierarchy, which had begun to appear in the 1780s. Palmer wrote to Hastings complaining of 'the system of oppressing [Indians] adopted by the present government', of how they were barred from the best positions in administration, and 'treated with mortifying hauteur and reserve. In fact they now have hardly any social intercourse with us'.[3] At this time too, Hinduism found itself under attack from Evangelical leaders in the EIC for being a religion of gross superstition.

Palmer was a close friend of James Kirkpatrick, Resident in Hyderabad, another Briton who had 'gone native' by marrying a Moslem and taking an Indian wife, thereby incurring the disapproval of Lord Wellesley. Sir David Ochterlony, father of Mary Ann, was an army general, veteran of several Indian wars, and became Resident in Delhi. He became entirely Indianised. Among the targets of the growing criticism of such Britons was their adoption of Indian dress and their growing of beards. Lady Nugent, wife of the British Commander-in-Chief, criticised Ochterlony for his 'immense whiskers'. Dalrymple summed up the new mood:

> All over India, as the eighteenth century gave way to the nineteenth, attitudes were changing among the British. Men who showed too great an enthusiasm for Hinduism, for Indian practices or even for their Indian wives and Anglo-Indian children, were finding that the climate was growing distinctly chilly.[4]

Mrs. Middleton, with an Indian mother and an Indianised father who favoured Warren Hastings' stance towards India, no doubt deplored this change in temperature.

On the military front, the new, ruthless mood of the period is typified by Lord Wellesley's treatment of Tipu Sultan, prince of Mysore, who was perceived as a threat to British interests in India because he was over-friendly to the French. His Seringapatam fortress was attacked in

1799 by an army of British and sepoy troops. The peace terms offered to Tipu were designed to humiliate him: 'Tipu was required to give up half of his remaining kingdom, pay an immense fine, and send four of his sons and four of his generals to be kept as hostages by the British. Tipu refused to accept'. In the ensuing battle he was killed. The orgy of pillaging in which the victorious troops indulged illustrates the extent to which conquest at this time was focused on acquisition of wealth. Tipu's possessions were auctioned, the army shared £1m in jewels and other treasures as 'prize money', and the 'gilded tiger's head from the Sultan's throne was sent to the British monarch at Windsor Castle'. Gott's account of this episode ends thus: 'No Indian ruler had illusions about what lay ahead. The British were in an expansionist mood. Indian princes had to decide whether to accept the bribes the British offered to join their camp, or to resist'.[5] This was the India in which the Album people made their careers, their marriages, and raised their children.

Although 1820 was the first time Henry Middleton had been based in Delhi, he had obviously met Mary Ann Ochterlony beforehand because he married her on 22 February 1817 at Patna, Bengal. The marriage record shows that her father David Ochterlony[6] was present at the ceremony but no mention is made of her mother, which is no doubt explained by the fact that she was an Indian woman, one of David's thirteen wives. (The story of this relationship is told in chapter six. There is an almost complete lack of information about Ochterlony's marital affairs and his Indian children because the subject was taboo in Victorian times.) Henry Middleton obtained a regular series of promotions, staying no longer than three years in any one post (his average was two years). From 1820 he was Deputy Superintendent of Delhi, Superintendent of Ajmere, Secretary to the Board of Revenue in the Western Provinces, Commissioner of Revenue in the Divisions of Bauleah (1831) and Dacca (1832), finally becoming Civil and Sessions Judge at Moorshedabad in 1835. His long leave in England (three and a half years – February 1828 to July 1831) may have been occasioned by illness, especially since he retired 'On Annuity' on 1 May 1836.[7] He had given twenty-six years of service to the EIC but as a Covenanted employee, unlike Frederick Kilvert. The wealth he accrued in his EIC career is clear from the fact that when he died on 16 March 1866, his estate was valued among 'Effects under £60,000', worth £2.5m today. When his wife died on 18 June 1878, her personal estate was valued at £25,000, or £1m today.[8]

The Middletons' neighbours in the Royal Crescent in 1861, by which time Henry was on the retired list of Bengal Civil Servants, were on one side a seventy-year-old female 'Landed Proprietor', living alone apart from a lady's maid, a cook, a housemaid and a house-servant, while on the other side was a forty-four-year-old gentleman described as 'Captain, Royal Navy, not employed' (who nevertheless managed to employ six servants to look after himself, his wife, and two infant daughters). In 1871, the immediate neighbours in the Royal Crescent of the now widowed Mary Ann Middleton were a female landed proprietor of seventy-one and her fifty-year-old daughter, both widows, looked after by four servants, and a sixty-nine-year-old 'Retired contractor / Magistrate', with three unmarried daughters aged 35-44, plus six servants. Mary Ann Middleton herself is described as a 'fundholder'. With her as a visitor was an unmarried lady who had also been born in India.

That the experience of getting-on in India could be infinitely variable is illustrated by the case of Thomas Child, whose photo does not appear in the Album, although that of his daughter, 'M.G. Child', does. He was born around the same time as Henry Middleton (1798 as opposed to 1794). Thomas was born in Thornbury, Gloucestershire and, like Henry Middleton, met his wife (Harriet) in India. She was born in Dinapore, where W.D. Arnold, author of *Oakfield* (see next chapter), was stationed with his regiment in the 1840s. A soldier who was there in 1858 pursuing rebels after the Mutiny described it as 'though not a large station for Europeans, it is nevertheless a good healthy one'.

Thomas Child's career parallels in some ways that of Fred Kilvert, outlined in the last chapter. The former was a surgeon in the Indian Army[9] and, like the latter, served for years at a modest level; he certainly did not make a fortune like Henry Middleton. Thomas's home in 1861 was Ellern Croft House, a substantial mansion set apart from its neighbours on the fringe of Wotton-under-Edge, where we find him, retired at the age of sixty-three, living with Harriet and their daughter Mary Grace, aged nineteen and unmarried. Mary's photo appears in the Album opposite that of the child, Maggie Lancaster. No special link has been found between the Lancaster family and Mary Grace to explain that juxtaposition. They were perhaps simply friends within the social circle of Dr. John, whose daughters Lucy, Anna Maria, and Eliza may have been particular friends of Mary Grace before they got married and left her behind. Dr. John obviously had something in common with Thomas Child in that they were both surgeons. In her photo, Mary Grace looks to be in her mid-twenties so it was taken around the mid- to late-1860s. The photographer was Henry Lambert of 10 Fountain Buildings in Bath. He was at these premises from 1862 until 1888. He also took the photo of 'Grandmamma'. Mary Grace sits at a table, looking sideways with a sweet, pensive expression, one hand on an open book on the table, the other on her knee. There is something else on the table – perhaps a basket. Behind is a vaguely classical backdrop. She wears a dress of dark, rich material, spotted with light-coloured patches.

The census returns on her and her family tell a sad story. In 1861, Mary Grace, who had no siblings, was still only nineteen and lived with her parents, both then in their sixties, in the pretty but small and isolated market town of Wotton-under-Edge, Gloucestershire, where she had been born. Bath and the friends of Dr. John's circle were thirty miles away. Her immediate neighbours made a stark contrast with those of Mary Ann Middleton in the Royal Crescent. One neighbour of Ellern Croft House, was a sixty-year-old wheelwright. Another was a carpenter and his twenty-year-old son, also a carpenter. There were two other women neighbours – a woollen cloth worker and a seamstress. These humble folk lived in cottages beyond the extensive grounds of Mary Grace's home. 1871 came and Mary Grace was still unmarried. The neighbours around Ellern Croft House were then a turnpike toll renter (retired), a seventy-five-year-old wool spinner, and a farm labourer. The Childs lived in grand style, maintaining three servants in 1861 and 1871. Even though the family was well-to-do, its social circle was perhaps limited where it had settled and offered Mary Grace little opportunity for getting off. In 1881, when Thomas and his wife were in their eighties, there were four servants so that little of the domestic labour could have fallen on Mary Grace, now aged thirty-nine and still unmarried. In 1901, with both her parents dead, Mary Grace was living in Portishead, near Bristol, with two ladies, one in her forties the other in her fifties, both of whom had experienced marriage, as she had not, though they were widows then.

It is difficult to see that Mary Grace Child could have taken much of a part in Anna Maria's extended family. She always lived in Wotton-under-Edge until the 1880s. Access to Bath by train would have been possible but not easy. The Gloucester to Bristol Railway, originally established in 1844, went through Charfield, three miles from Wotton (which had no station). Mary Grace would then have had to change trains in Bristol for Bath. With the last of Dr. John's daughters married by 1874, she would have become even more peripheral, effectively buried in the Gloucestershire countryside, and a social failure because she had not secured a husband.

Wotton-under-Edge is almost as near Cheltenham as Bath, although no evidence has been found connecting Mary Grace to our next minor characters, who follow her in the Album – the Vander Meulens – who lived in Cheltenham. Col. Charles Jowett Vander Meulen (the name is originally Dutch and means 'from the mills') was in the 73rd Regiment. He was born in St. Albans in 1791 and his mother's name was Jowett. Originally there was a business background. In a list of names of 'Directors of Companies, Persons in Public Business' appears this entry: 'Vander Meulen and Jowett, Merchants, 10 Tokenhouse Yard'.[10] A reference, dated 1 January 1817, in 'Deaths and Marriages in London and Middlesex' noted the death of Josiah Jowett formerly of the banking house of Vandermeulen and Jowett of Leeds.[11]

The army, rather than business, was the chosen career of Charles Jowett Vander Meulen, whose CDV was taken by George Alder, born in Cheltenham in 1829. He had a studio there in 1854-6 and 1865-70, before moving to Croydon. Vander Meulen stands, stiff and serious, one hand on the back of a chair, the other by his side, in a dark suit with a watch chain across his waistcoat. A domestic interior has been suggested in the studio, along with the commonly found classical backdrop. The *Gentleman's Magazine* reported on 7 April 1837 his promotion from Captain to major in the 73rd Foot Regiment,[12] and from major to lieutenant-colonel on 8 April 1842. The Regiment served in various parts of the Empire: the Mediterranean (1829-39), Canada (1839-41); it was in Britain from 1841 to 1845, when it was sent to the Cape of Good Hope. The 73rd Regiment became involved in the Kaffir Wars in South Africa's Cape Colony, recovered from the Dutch in 1806, to the north of which was the land of the Xhosa people, also referred to as Kaffirs. The British policy in 1809 was to expel the Xhosa from their land by force to an area further east and to reallocate their land to European settlers. A small, ill-prepared rebellion by the Xhosa against this policy was easily suppressed. Bolstered by stronger forces, the British began to expel the Xhosa in 1811. Under the command of Colonel Graham, a policy of extermination was pursued. He told a correspondent:

> The only way of getting rid of them is by depriving them of the means of subsistence ... the whole force is constantly employed in destroying prodigious quantities of Indian corn and millet which they have planted ... taking from them [their] cattle ... and shooting every man that can be found.

The Xhosa fought another war to resist the British in 1835-6. The war in which Colonel Vander Meulen took part began in 1846. Since the 1835-6 war, white settlers had been forbidden to move into Xhosa land, but their demands for fresh land were renewed in 1844. The Xhosa raised a large army to resist encroachments and initially defeated British forces. The defeated British commander was replaced with General Sir Henry Pottinger, who had experience of Indian wars. He stated that 'by devastating their country, destroying their kraals, crops and cattle, [the Xhosa] ... must finally be humbled and subdued'. The army's medical officer, Sir John Hall, described Pottinger's policy as 'a disgrace to the age we live in'. The Xhosa chief was persuaded to negotiate but was seized and imprisoned, and was interviewed in 1847 by the new Governor of Cape Colony, General Sir Harry Smith, who told him:

> I am your Paramount Chief, and the Kaffirs are my dogs. I am come to punish you for your misdoings and treachery. You may approach my foot and kiss it, but not till you repent the past will I allow you to touch my hand.

General Smith formally annexed the Xhosa land and it became a part of Cape Colony.[13]

This then was the war and the colonial outlook that Colonel Vander Meulen experienced from 1846 to 1853; his services won him the South Africa (1853) Medal. His long service in various colonies made him a figure akin to Peterkin Gay, one of the three heroes of R.M. Ballantyne's novel *The Gorilla Hunters*, published in 1861 when the suppression of the

Indian Mutiny was a recent event. Peterkin introduces himself as a navy lieutenant, who has 'been all over the world', adding 'I've been fighting with the Kaffirs, and the Chinamen, and been punishing the rascally sepoys in India, and been shooting elephants in Ceylon ...'[14] Kilvert gave a copy of Ballantyne's book to Hugh Thomas on 23 March 1872 for his birthday. Hugh was the son of Evan, who belonged to the Thomas family, of which the Llanthomas ones were one branch. Ballantyne's novels embody the aggressive imperialism of the period, underpinned in his case by fervent Evangelicalism. While Kilvert would not have condoned the savage treatment meted out to the Kaffirs, he shared with Ballantyne a belief that native people in Cape Colony and elsewhere were superstitious savages, who could only be raised up by means of white man's education and religion.[15]

Before joining the 73rd Regiment, Charles Vander Meulen was a lieutenant with the 48th (Northants.) Regiment in Australia and on 16 May 1818 he married Margaret Edwards Wild, step-daughter of Lieutenant John Wild of the same regiment, at St. Philip's, Sydney, New South Wales. She is not however the rather exotic lady with flowers in her ringleted hair,[16] voluminous skirts and lace shawl, who sits, left hand on a table, facing inwards towards him on the opposite page. That lady was Charles's sister-in-law. The CDV was taken by Richard Dighton of Cheltenham. On the back of it, Dighton declared himself to be an 'artist', as some photographers of the period were wont to do. He was the grandson of the famous eighteenth- century caricaturist and portrait painter Robert Dighton, whose eldest son Richard was also an artist. It was Richard junior (1824-91) who took Mrs. Vander Meulen's photo. He too was an artist: his earliest known work is a watercolour equestrian portrait of the 3rd Earl of Sefton (1844). Cheltenham Art Gallery and Museum has a collection of watercolours and drawings by all three members of this family. It also has a number of CDV collections by Richard junior.

Watering places such as Bath, Brighton, Bournemouth and Cheltenham have long had a reputation as resorts for retired colonels. At the time that Anna Maria was beginning to compile her album, Col. Vander Meulen was living, not with his wife, but with his sister, Rachel, at Carlton Villa, Hewlett Road, Cheltenham. Strangely, he was surrounded at

Carlton Villa by working people. On one side, there was a plumber and a carpenter, while on the other, at Carlton Cottage, was an elderly widow whose unmarried daughter, aged thirty-three, was a teacher. Coincidentally, the brother of the teacher was George Bartlett, a CDV photographer of Cheltenham, who had described himself for the purposes of the 1861 census as an 'artist'. On the backs of his CDVs he styled himself as 'Artist and Photographer'. It is in this way that Bartlett (and Dighton) can be seen in the tradition of portrait painting which photography continued. When the Colonel died on 1 October 1865, his estate was valued around the £5,000 mark, £200,000 today. The date of his death means we can place the time his photo was taken at around the early 1860s. His home then was Sydenham Villas, Cheltenham.

The executors of the Colonel's will, which is dated 12 August 1865, were two soldiers who were his friends: Charles Thompson, Brevet Major in the 64th Regiment, and Captain Standish de Courcy O'Grady. No mention is made in the will of Vander Meulen's wife, who has not been found in censuses, probably because she was with him on his overseas postings. Nor is it known when she died. Two thousand pounds were bequeathed to their daughter Rachel. The remainder was to provide an annual income for life to the Colonel's sister, Rachel Butler Vander Meulen. She died in 1884, aged ninety-two.

The Lancaster family is another with a military background. It has been possible to identify its members through Maggie Lancaster, the three-year-old, posed standing on a chair, her arm through the handle of a basket, and looking appealing and vulnerable. On the table nearby is a ball. The photo must have been taken in 1868 because she was born on 7 March 1865 in Ealing, London. The 1871 census shows her as a pupil in the home of Marianne Awdry, aged forty-four, at 9 Edward Street, Bathwick. There were several branches of the Awdry family in Wiltshire at this time and Kilvert was especially friendly with those who lived at Monkton House in Chippenham. *Diary* entries frequently record the Awdry daughters Bella, Margaret and Georgie from Monkton visiting the Kilvert home at Langley Burrell, for example on 16 May 1870, 19 May 1870 (NLW edition). On 27 May 1870, Kilvert went with his sister Fanny to a croquet and archery party at Monkton House. The men of the Monkton Awdrys were solicitors (other Wiltshire branches boasted clergymen) and Marianne, of Edward Street, Bathwick, had married Peter Awdry of the Monkton branch, who was a solicitor. She was living with him and their children at The Grove, Chippenham, in 1861 but he had died by 1871 and she was making ends meet then by taking in paying pupils, one of whom was Maggie Lancaster. Marianne's daughter Julia, aged nineteen, could help with the teaching and there was also a twenty-two-year-old governess, Mary Arnaud, living in. There were two other pupils, both boys, one from Kent and one from Clevedon, Somerset. In addition to caring for the pupils, Marianne had the task of raising her younger children: Ada (4), Peter and John (both aged 6), Emma (11), Graham (13), and Lucy (14). By 1881, Marianne was still at 9 Edward Street living with her four unmarried daughters.

Although Maggie had no girl pupils to play with at Edward Street, there were Marianne Awdry's daughters. Maggie perhaps found in Marianne a surrogate mother to replace her own, Christiana Elizabeth, who had died in Bath aged thirty on 10 May 1870. Maggie's second name was Christiana, shortened, it seems, in her mother's case to 'Cana', the name in the caption below her Album photo. Christiana Elizabeth's maiden name was Medley and she was born in March 1840 in St. Thomas's Vicarage in Exeter, daughter of John Medley, first Bishop of Fredericton, New Brunswick, Canada. She had gone out there with her family at the age of five. Her brother, Captain Spencer Medley, served for many years with the Royal Navy, eventually settling and dying in New Zealand. An additional military dimension of the life of Maggie was that her father, Henry John Lancaster (the 'H. Lancaster' pictured in the Album), was a captain in the Royal Artillery when her mother married him on 4 May 1864. He appears in the *Bath Directory* in 1870 living at 9 Norfolk Buildings, Bath, a mile from Bathwick. He was manager then of the Great Western Loan and Discount Company located at 11 Bridge Street, which leads into Pulteney Bridge over the Avon. Various businesses – watchmaker, grocer, pianoforte / music seller, teacher of Hindustani, butcher, engraver – were Henry's neighbours there according to the 1878/9 Directory. Maggie was living with her father at Portsea, Hants., in 1881, listed as a 'scholar'. She married in October 1888.

Her photo and that of her father were taken by Edwin Flukes, who had a business at 41 Milsom Street in Bath from 1860 to 1874. On the back of their pictures is the Royal Crest and the words 'South Kensington Museum To the Science and Art Department'. His advertisement in the 1860-1 *Bath Directory* refers to his 'Photographic Rooms' incorporating 'the Glass Room', which provided 'pure and uninterrupted light where Portraits of Unsurpassed Excellence are taken from 10 till 5'. He had a work of his called 'A Frame containing Four Photographs' in the 1863 London Photographic Society Exhibition. He also took the picture of the Rev. W.R. Smith, husband of Kilvert's sister Thersie. We have only the head and shoulders of Henry Lancaster, showing his Dundreary whiskers and dark jacket of thick material. Cana Lancaster's picture was taken in Regent Street, London, by a photographer called Hay and on the back of it is the Royal Standard. A photographic partnership was established in 1855 at 79 Princes Street, Edinburgh by two brothers David Syme Hay and George Heron Hay. They advertised then 'much improved portraits ... taken in a few seconds'. In 1856, they were being praised in the *London Times* (16 December) for their 'untouched photographs rivalling in clearness and delicacy the finest productions of their class'. George Hay had a studio at 191 Regent Street from 1865 until 1870. Since Cana Lancaster died in 1870, her photo must have been taken in this period. Cana's picture has faded badly, especially round her head, but we can make out a rather plain woman with a long face in her late twenties. She wears a long dress in some dark-coloured material flecked with lighter-coloured patches like that of Mary Grace Child. The design worked into the end of Cana's sleeves seems to echo that of her fabric belt. The long chain hanging from her neck might have had a crucifix on its end but the left of her clasped hands makes it impossible to tell. Behind her is the kind of embossed wainscot that appears in other Album photos.

It has been noted earlier that Dr. John's next door neighbour in Darlington Street were Captain and Mrs. Bampfylde, who are the remaining Album characters with whom this chapter is concerned. The Bampfyldes were not only neighbours of Dr. John but also friends, as Kilvert confirmed when he expressed amazement that 'friends' such as they had not been invited to the wedding of Eliza, Dr. John's daughter. The CDV of Captain Bampfylde was taken at the 35 Milsom Street studio of Mrs. Henry Richard Williams, who had previously operated at 8 Fountain

Buildings from 1858 until 1862 when the arrival of the photographer Henry Lambert at no.10 may have prompted her removal to Milsom Street, which was also a more central and more prestigious location.[17] Captain Bampfylde, a tall man, stands looking directly at the camera, with one hand on the back of a chair, the other resting on the top of a cane, behind is the embossed wainscot and curtain found in other Album pictures. He has the full moustache and sideburns of other Album men. Mrs. Bampfylde is seated next to a table on which is a vase of flowers. One arm rests on the table while the other holds on her lap an object that cannot be clearly identified. A large black lace shawl lies over her dress, her wide skirt is trimmed with flounces. Her photo is on the opposite page to that of her husband, though they do not look at each other.

Captain Bampfylde's grandfather had obtained a degree in Civil Law at Balliol College, Oxford, in 1810. His son was the Rev. Charles Francis Bampfylde, Rector of Dunkerton, a village very near Bath. He too had gone to Balliol. He was living with his three daughters (his wife had died) at Dunkerton in 1841. In 1851, then aged sixty-four, he was still there, his three unmarried daughters aged from twenty-eight to eighteen. His second son was Francis James (the Album's Captain Bampfylde) and he was born on 30 May 1827. He married Catherine Thompson at Guildford in 1850. Francis James did not follow his father into the Church but chose the army for his career. (His wife was the daughter of a surgeon in the Royal Artillery.) The will of Francis's father tells us that Francis had already received his share so that he could purchase a commission in the army. The system of purchasing commissions had existed for many years. Every officer had to start at the lowest commissioned rank – ensign in infantry regiments – and this would have been Francis's first rank as it was that of William Kilvert, Dr. John's son, who had died in Calcutta. Francis's regiment was the 49th infantry. The cost of a commission as ensign was £450 or £20,000 in today's terms. Securing that first opening as an officer in the army in mid-century was an expensive business.[18]

Knowing that the will of Francis's father was dated 6 February 1851 helps us to estimate when the newly-wed son and his wife left England for India. Their first son, Francis George, was born in 1852 and was born 'At sea' according to the 1861 census, thus confirming that the family was on its way to India then. Francis senior may have become a captain by this time; one had to serve two years as ensign before promotion to captain. The only entry in *Allen's Indian Mail* relating to Francis records that 'Captain Bampfylde' was to go to Murree, a hill station in Punjab (now in Pakistan) for the period 15 July to 29 October 1854. Presumably he went there with his young family – Francis George (aged two) and Catherine (aged only a few weeks)[19] – to escape the summer heat in the plain. The dangers of raising a family in India is illustrated graphically by the record of deaths on the same page of *Allen's Indian Mail* as that which recorded Captain Bampfylde's departure for Murree: one third (eight out of twenty-four) of them were of children under twelve, most were infants. Francis and his family were back in Europe by autumn 1856 because a son, Charles Agar, was born in France at this time. The Bampfyldes escaped not only the diseases of the 'cursed East' but were fortunate too to escape the Mutiny, which broke out six months after they left India.

The 1861 census shows Francis living at 11 Sion Hill, in the socially superior district of Lansdown in Bath. His photograph shows him aged around forty so it must have been taken in the mid-1860s. He had by then left the regular army and his occupation was given as 'Captain and Adjutant of Volunteers'. The Volunteers were companies of amateur riflemen raised from 1859 onwards when war with France seemed a threat. Kilvert took much interest in the activities of Volunteer companies wherever he lived.[20] There were four Volunteer Companies in Bath in the 1860s: 1st (Bath) Company, 2nd (Bathwick) Company, 17th (Lyncombe) Company, 18th (Walcot) Company. Francis belonged to the Bath one.[21] The 17th was commanded in 1860 by Captain William Hewitt, father of the Album's Henry, who often drilled with them. His diary entry for 19 July 1860 also recorded that '1st and 2nd Company [were] photographed. Front rank kneeling, rear rank standing'[22]. Evidently, the Volunteers too wanted their 'likenesses' taken.

Francis Bampfylde's family in 1861 consisted of Francis George (9), Catherine (7), Georgiana (6 – and born in India like her older sister), Charles (4), Frederic (2). Frederic had been born on the Isle of Wight so the family had spent some time there; one of the family's four servants also came from there.[23] Wealthy people lived around Francis on Sion Hill at this time: one neighbour was a retired Indian Army major;

another was a female 'landed proprietor'. Four pupils at a nearby school had all been born in India. Francis remained at 11 Sion Hill until 1863 when he moved to 10 Darlington Street, next door to Dr. John. The 1871 census tells us that Francis's son, Francis George, was an Oxford undergraduate and that living with the family was Mrs. Bampfylde's father John Thompson, 'widower 83 half-pay assistant surgeon Royal Artillery'. By 1881, Francis, now a major, had these children at home in Darlington Street: Georgiana (26 and unmarried), Alice (20 and unmarried), Harry (16), and James (15). Two servants were employed. Neighbours were a clergyman, a publisher / bookseller, three people who lived on dividends (two from railway shares). At Dr. John's former home now lived another doctor. Some time after 1881, Francis left Bathwick and went to live in Sevenoaks, Kent. He died at Gibraltar on 16 March 1890: personal estate at death £15,299 (over £800,000 today).

Mrs. Bampfylde did not have far to go to have her CDV taken. From her Darlington Street home she went half a mile to 29 Henrietta Street where the Theweneti brothers had a studio from 1860 to 1868. One brother was Edward Lawrence Theweneti, the other was Michael. One other Album photograph was taken by the Thewenetis – that of Mrs. Middleton – and this gives rise to the interesting fact that there was an Anglo-Indian dimension to the Album photographers. As we have seen, Mrs. Middleton was born in India, married there, and spent a considerable part of her life there with her ICS husband Henry. (Album characters who had been born in India or had spent a considerable part of their lives there are referred to here as 'Anglo-Indians', which was the practice in some of the literature of the period [e.g. the *Calcutta Review*]. It is also the practice in some accounts of India to use 'Anglo-Indian' to mean those of mixed race such as Mrs. Middleton.) The Theweneti brothers were, it seems, photographers with a significant number of Anglo-Indians of the former kind among their clients. In a city like Bath, in which families with Indian connections preponderated, every photographer there would have had some as clients. However, the fact that the Album photographers Joseph Perkins and Henry Lambert had the leading Anglo-Indian Younghusband family as customers suggests that they were especially favoured by families with that background. The Younghusband Collection, among the India Office Select Materials in the British Library, consists of CDV portraits bequeathed by Dame Eileen Younghusband.[24] They are contained in a leather-bound album with metal clasps similar to the Kilvert one. The portraits are of members of the Younghusband and Shaw families in the 1860s. Dame Eileen (1902-1981) was the only daughter of Sir Francis Younghusband (1863-1942), born in India, son of an Indian Army general. Some of the twenty-one portraits were taken by the Theweneti brothers, Perkins and Lambert. The Thewenetis took the CDV of Mrs. Younghusband (Annie Shaw). In addition, among the India Office materials is a photo taken by Perkins of Lieutenant George Younghusband (1831-1858) of the 5th Punjab Cavalry, who was killed in the Indian Mutiny.[25] A memorial at St. Peter's Church, Freshford (a village only two or three miles from Bath), tells how 'he fell mortally wounded near Futteghur on 2 January 1858 and died on the second day aged twenty-six years'. Three of the Lieutenant's brothers were also soldiers in the Indian Army.

When we examine Album CDVs taken by the Perkins studio in Bath we see that Anglo-Indians of Dr. John's extended family were also its clients: Mrs. Wyndowe (i.e. Emily Kilvert), Colonel Cholmeley, Henry and Caroline Hewitt, born in India (whose father, Captain William Hewitt, served in India). Furthermore, Henry recorded in his diary that his maternal grandfather, Colonel Cotgrave, also an Anglo-Indian, went to have his CDV made at Perkins accompanied by Henry.[27] Only two other Album people were photographed by Perkins – L.S. Falkner and Mrs. W.R. Smith. The former did not herself come from an Anglo-Indian family but she was friendly with the Bettington family of Bath, which was friendly with the Anglo-Indian Hewitts. Mrs. W.R. Smith was the sister of an Anglo-Indian – Emily Wyndowe. A similar pattern is observable in the case of Henry Lambert.[28] The Album CDVs he took were those of the Anglo-Indians Fred Kilvert, his wife Emily, and Mary Grace Child, whose father was an Indian Army surgeon. The only other Album picture Lambert took was that of Grandmamma, whose two grandsons – William and Fred – were Anglo-Indians. We could sum this situation up thus: three Album photographers – the Thewenetis, Perkins, Lamberts – took pictures *only* of the Anglo-Indian characters or of the people closely associated with them who appear in the Album.

A further interesting aspect of the Anglo-Indian dimension of Album pictures concerns their order. The pictures of the Rev. and Mrs. W.R. Smith are followed, logically enough, by those of Dr. Wyndowe and Mrs. Wyndowe – a Kilvert sister and her husband following another and her husband. The latter husband and wife were also Anglo-Indians and after their pictures comes that of another Anglo-Indian (and a relative of Mrs. Wyndowe), Colonel Cholmeley.[29] Kilvert himself separates Colonel Cholmeley from another Anglo-Indian – W.B. Macrone, who is followed by L.S. Falkner, a friend of another Anglo-Indian, Henry Hewitt. A similar pattern comes later in the Album. The picture of the Anglo-Indian Mary Grace Child is followed by the military figure of Colonel Vander Meulen (though he did not have an Indian background) but then come the Anglo-Indians Caroline and Henry Hewitt, Captain and Mrs. Bampfylde. Anna Maria must have had some principle directing her ordering of the photos in the album: experience of India, or of life overseas, seems to have been one element in it.

This chapter has focused on Album soldiers, particularly Indian Army ones, and their wives and daughters. The military interests of some who had known army life in India were perpetuated and given expression by Bath's Volunteer Companies. Even some of the Bath photographers had helped to link Anglo-Indian Album people by promoting contact, cohesiveness, and reinforcement of shared values and experiences – the 'connectedness', mentioned in chapter one, to which a family album bore witness. This chapter has also shown the extent to which professions other than the army enabled Album men, their forebears, descendants and friends, to get on in the competitive world of mid-Victorian England. Captain Bampfylde's grandfather was a lawyer, as was Peter Awdry, whose wife knew Album people. The fathers of Captain Bampfylde and of Cana Lancaster were in the Church, as was the Rev. W.R. Smith. Henry Lancaster had become a businessman after army service and the forebears of Colonel Vander Meulen were in business. The involvement of so many Album characters in medicine is further reinforced by the army surgeons Thomas Child and the father-in-law of Captain Bampfylde.

The career of Captain Bampfylde's second son, Charles, born in France in 1856, makes a fitting postscript to this chapter because it illustrates both how a descendant of an Album character got on in the second half of the Victorian period and how colonial service remained a key factor in an Album family. He was educated at Sidney College, Bath, where he would have been in the overall charge of the Rev. W.R. Smith, who was Principal of the College from 1868 to 1874.[30] Charles then became a cadet on the training-ship *Worcester*.[31] In 1875, aged nineteen, he joined the Sarawak Civil Service, transferring in 1882 to work for the British North Borneo Government. In 1884 he re-entered Rajah Brooke's[32] service and was appointed Acting Resident of Sarawak Proper in 1885. When he retired, he became political agent in England for the Sarawak Government. He co-authored with the Rev. S. Baring-Gould[33] *A History of Sarawak under two White Rajahs* in 1909. When Charles died on Christmas Day 1918, he was a Fellow of the Royal Geographical Society.

An additional postscript is needed to highlight what this chapter has had to say about the plight of the unmarried woman, poignantly illustrated by Mary Grace Child. In some ways she is reminiscent of 'Poor Elizabeth', daughter of Kilvert's aunt Mary, referred to in chapter one. However, whereas Elizabeth cared, for a relatively short time, first for her mother and later for her brother, before escaping to a Chippenham hotel, Mary Grace had to look after her ageing parents for over twenty years, trapped in the countryside. The case of Marianne Awdry, which this chapter has also looked at, shows that teaching was the only avenue, apart from being a governess or a nurse, open to a lady (in this case a widowed one) who needed to earn some income to be independent.

CHAPTER FIVE
Getting on in India:
Samuel Wyndowe and Edward Kilvert

The foregoing accounts of Anglo-Indian society enable us to understand some of the forces that could cause the changes in an individual's personality and outlook dreaded by Kilvert. William Delafield Arnold, however, indicated in *Oakfield* a force of change that began to exert influence even before arrival in India, that occurred on the journey there: 'an Englishman,' asserted Arnold's hero, 'leaves his morals at the Cape'. In this vulnerable state, the average Englishman possessed neither strength nor inclination to resist the corruption of Anglo-Indian society. Those who came from Britain were 'thrown into a society [with] an evil and low-principled tone ... which forced back all expressions of tender feeling and made people ashamed of affection, industry, common honesty, even professional duty'. Everything in them retreated in the face of India's 'coarse, animal, worldly existence'.[1]

Arnold's repeated emphasis on worldliness and materialism underlines the extent to which for many men India was about getting-on. The theme figured strongly in an article in the 1844 *Calcutta Review*, which characterised the English in India as 'foreigners – boy-foreigners, ... ignorant of Indian life', whose dominant motivation was pursuit of wealth. The Anglo-Indian, it said, 'left England young, healthy and poor, and came back old, decrepit and rich'[2]. The essence of this statement is that men went out to India *intending* to be changed, that they went in order to get on but paid a price for it. The *Review* article also made other interesting observations about Anglo-Indian society. Money went much further in India because everything was cheap: servants, clothes, carriages, housekeeping, and there were no taxes, 'We have the cholera but no taxes'. In addition, a more liberal morality prevailed. At home there was always a struggle to keep up appearances whereas in India one could be more open and informal.[3]

We have seen that Kilvert was aware that fortunes could be made in India from his knowledge of Lord Clive's history. An even more telling *Diary* entry is that of 1 May 1875. Austin, an old Langley Burrell farmer, told Kilvert that his uncle had gone to India as an army private, then changed to the EIC's service and risen to be Assistant Commissary General. "'Why," I said, "if you had gone you might have become Governor General of India." The old farmer grinned. "I might have been a clerk," he said.' Kilvert's brother-in-law, Sam Wyndowe, had gone out to India not as a private, like old Austin's uncle, but as an officer and a doctor. His background was military. His father, also Samuel, was initially a lieutenant in the 1st Royal Dragoons and had been slightly wounded at Waterloo in 1815. On 4 July 1819 he married Miss Ann Thomlinson, daughter of the late Colonel Thomlinson, 18th Regiment of Infantry. The home of Sam senior was Blencogo, Cumberland. He first placed his son (born 1830) at a school in Huntley, near Gloucester in 1841, but transferred him in August 1843 as a day boy to Cheltenham College, a school which from its founding in 1841 had a military bias. One of its founders was a Captain Iredell and it was originally divided into Classical and Military sides. A large number of its pupils in the 1840s to 1860s went on to the EIC's military college Addiscombe.[4] Another Album character who experienced the ethos of Cheltenham College was the Rev. William Smith, husband of Thersie, Emily Kilvert's sister. He went there as a boarder in 1846. It was William's son Percival who first brought Kilvert's notebook diaries to the attention of William Plomer their editor. The official College history explained that the ideals behind it heralded a new modern society based on science and commerce, one in which merit rather than patronage counted:

> A new era in literature, and new requirements in extended commerce, new demands in almost every branch of knowledge, began to bring about what may be termed ... a revolution in the domain of education. Science put in her claim for consideration, and modern languages became a necessary part of the times, and mathematical training ... forced its way to the front. Competitive exams in accordance with national wants struck

a death blow to nepotism, nominations, and old hereditary claims to lucrative posts. A more practical age requires a sterner test.[5]

It is relevant here to note that Marlborough College, founded 1843, was soon to offer some of its pupils, one of whom was Edward Kilvert, brother of the diarist, a modern curriculum of this kind.[6] It was confirmation that society was changing and in ways that Album characters welcomed. Dr. John was endorsing it in the support he gave to the PMSA. It was a society in which the middle-class professions of medicine, law, the army, and the Church that figure extensively among the Album people could flourish. Kilvert himself both welcomed this society and was excited by it.[7] Significantly, a number of Cheltenham College's headmasters and masters had been at Dr. Arnold's Rugby.[8] Dr. Henry Highton, Cheltenham Principal 1859-62, was one. He was a pioneer of the electric telegraph and a writer on scientific subjects. An Evangelical flavour informed the College, partly as a result of the Rugby influence.[9]

The steady drift of Cheltenham College pupils to Addiscombe College meant inevitably a steady drift towards India. Sam Wyndowe, who left Cheltenham College in 1845, did not go on to Addiscombe.[10] His medical training took place at St. George's Hospital, London, where he was dresser (surgeon's assistant) to Frank Buckland, son of the famous geologist, William Buckland. Frank became Assistant Surgeon to the Life Guards in February 1854, which appointment, coming a month before Sam Wyndowe's army appointment, may have influenced the latter. Buckland, a keen naturalist, became well known to the Victorian public for his series *Curiosities of Natural History*. He has been referred to as 'the David Bellamy of Victorian times'. After completing medical training Sam took up a post as assistant surgeon in the Indian Medical Service of the Madras army on 24 March 1854. In 1855 he was appointed to a cavalry regiment, the Nagpur Irregular Force. The *Calcutta Review* stated that 'assistant surgeons in Madras are, on their first arrival, made to do duty at the General Hospital, and to keep case books, until they are reported duly qualified for the general duties of the army'.[11]

Sam's service record contains a special section headed 'Services in the Field':

> Served with Nagpore Irregular Cavalry in the Sambalpore and Raepore Districts 6th December 1857.

In Chanda Districts from 5th May to 16 June 1858. In Chundwana Districts from 6th November 1858 till February 1859.

Engagement with rebels 30th December 1857 near Sambalpore, horse shot, received medal for Indian Mutiny. Received expression of approbation from Her Majesty's Government ... also thanks of the Government of India. See letter no.270 dated India Office London, 2 July 1861 from the Secretary of State and letter no.1216 dated 29 October 1860 from the Secretary of the Government of India Military Department.[12]

Behind Sam's very full whiskers in the Album's vignette photo of him was a man perhaps in his mid-thirties, which means it was taken (in Paris actually) in the 1860s. The back of his photo records that it was taken at the Maison Mayer and Pierson, Boulevard des Capucines, Paris. Pierre-Louis Pierson ran a studio in Paris from 1844 that produced hand-coloured daguerreotypes. He became partner in 1855 with the brothers Léopold and Louis Mayer, who had been named 'Photographers of His Majesty the Emperor' by Louis Napoleon III the year before Pierson joined them. Emily Kilvert recalled first meeting Sam in the house of her uncle Walter Coleman when he was 'home on sick leave after the Indian Mutiny'. (He had two years' leave in total 'on medical certificate'.) The date was early 1860. Emily, aged seventeen, was not looking her best: 'I had on a very soiled print dress,' which she was hiding under a long cloak. She was in the drawing-room and suddenly heard 'a manly footstep' and in walked the man who was to be her future husband. '"Sweet seventeen" blushed and looked like an idiot,' Emily ruefully recorded.[13] She did not comment on the manly beard of truly Sikh proportions which Sam is wearing in the Album photo. Did she learn soon afterwards that he was something of a Mutiny hero, commended in letters from the British Government and the Government of India?

It was at this time (1860) that Sam was appointed to civil employment in the Central Provinces and on 15 June 1864 became Professor of Chemistry at Madras Medical College. In 1867 he was resident surgeon at Hyderabad (Kilvert received a letter on 2 February 1874 from Emily in Hyderabad saying that Sam was 'in his office writing lectures'). Kilvert was fascinated by another letter from Emily which he was reading on 10 May 1872. It told of her journey with Sam from Bombay to

Hyderabad, and gave what the diarist called 'a capital description' of the moment when their horses refused to go any further and were replaced by bullocks. It was

> ... in the midst of a violent thunderstorm at midnight, the pouring rain, the intense stifling heat of the carriage, the wailing hungry baby, the lightning-lit barren dreary landscape and the motionless figures of the Sowar horsemen who were escorting them.

Kilvert enjoyed an account such as this for its power to bring home the sheer strangeness of life in India. Compensating Sam and Emily for the ordeal of their journey was 'their arrival at the Residency'. Some description of this astonishing building would almost certainly have appeared in Emily's letter.[14] It had been built between 1797 and 1805 by James Kirkpatrick, the Resident at Hyderabad who had gone native at the time when British and Indians could live together in harmony, as chapter four noted. William Dalrymple wrote of the Residency:

> It was one of the most perfect buildings ever erected by the East India Company. It had a grand, domed semi-circular bay on the south front, reached through a great triumphal arch facing the bridge over the Musi. On the north front a pair of British lions lay, paws extended, below a huge pedimented and colonnaded front.[15]

Sam Wyndowe's senior position at Hyderabad Medical School would have meant that he and Emily attended Residency functions.

Sam could not accompany Emily when she returned home in April 1875 Kilvert recorded, adding 'But he will be here by the winter when he has served the time for his second rate of pension'.[16] We know what he was being paid from the 7 February 1870 *Diary* entry: 'Sam is to have half pay £1000 per year whilst in England'. This must have seemed a princely sum to Kilvert, who was being paid £100 a year at the time. Sam had become surgeon in 1866, surgeon-major in 1873, and brigade-surgeon in 1879. On 5 August 1878 Emily, then living in Norwood, London, was telling Kilvert in a letter that Sam was 'in low health in India and they have lost an investment of £1000' (£40,000 today). Sam survived thirty years in India, retiring in 1884, with the rank of Deputy Surgeon-General. Between 1882 and 1884 he was Superintendent of the Hyderabad Medical School.[17] In 1901 he was living with Emily in Kensington. The extent to which India had penetrated the society in which he moved can be gauged by the fact that his daughter Annie married Colonel Walter Phillips, Commanding Officer of the 28th Punjab Regiment.

Edward Kilvert is not pictured in the Album but he is relevant to the story of the Album characters firstly because he was one of Dr. John's brothers, secondly because he spent time in India, and thirdly because his life story illuminates something of the outlook of his generation. *Kilvert's Diary* makes only two references to him. One mentions how his cradle was upset when the diarist's father was fencing at home with his brother Francis and the latter fell to the ground. It was thought that Edward had been killed. The other entry records the burial of his wife Emma next to him in Widcombe cemetery on 3 January 1879. Kilvert, with his strong sense of history, showed awareness on 2 October 1870, when he heard of the death of his aunt Mary, Edward's sister, that 'My father is left alone now of all his brothers and sisters, the last survivor of that generation of his family'.

Edward was born in 1807 and, being only ten when his father died, he would have come, as all his siblings did, under the influence of his brother Francis, from whom he probably received his early education. He graduated from Oxford's St. Alban Hall in 1843.[18] The Halls at Oxford were often cheaper than the Colleges and it may have been the case that Edward went on 2 April 1840 to St. Alban Hall, at the age of thirty-two, because university fees could not be afforded sooner. Halls seem to have been more ready than Colleges to accept mature students. Frank Perry's *The Church in Madras* states that 'While at Oxford he was influenced by the Tractarian teaching and became what was known as a moderate High Churchman'.[19] His faith was strong enough to send him to India in the face of its dangers to spread the Gospel. Appointed Assistant Chaplain on 2 January 1846, he set sail for India on the 26th on board the *Tartar*. His first post was at Secunderabad, which oddly he took up only in 1847 (perhaps after some training). He moved to Bellary also in 1847, where he stayed three years. After Trichinopoly (1850) and Vellore (1852), he settled at Jaulnah, which was his final posting.

The EIC had for years resisted introduction of missionaries but after the renewal of its Charter in 1813, the position changed. Prior to this, it had been tolerant of native religions; its chief purpose was trade. Evangelicals seized the opportunity to introduce more missionaries after

1813 and started a public campaign to whip up support for the policy. The second Bishop of Calcutta, Reginald Heber, was an Evangelical, and took up his appointment in 1823. He was an inspiring figure in this period to Evangelical families like the Kilverts, who were devoted to the Church Missionary Society (CMS). Emily Kilvert gave full details of 'Mama's missionary working parties' in her *Recollections*. By 1831, there were fifty-eight CMS preachers in India. Stokes has emphasised the importance of Evangelicalism in connection with India: 'Evangelicalism, the rock upon which the character of the nineteenth-century Englishman was founded, owed much of its impetus to the India connexion'.[20]

The presence of more missionaries produced 'a discernible difference in attitude to Indians ... after 1813'. [21]Because they feared that Christianity was being forced upon them, sepoys had mutinied at Vellore in 1806.[22] The Governor of Bombay was warning in the 1820s of dangers resulting from what he called 'religious zealots' and from policies designed to 'Europeanise native people'. Lawson noted that in this period 'missionary zeal took on special significance for Company rule in India'. It and political groups such as the Utilitarians 'believed that in westernising India the spiritual lives of those "in trust" would be improved'.[23] Ferguson contrasted the EIC's 'amoral' rule of the eighteenth century with the Victorian vision: 'The Victorians had more elevating aspirations. They dreamt not just of ruling the world, but of redeeming it ... the aim now was to improve other races'.[24] That Kilvert had assimilated this doctrine is evident in the *Diary* entry for 27 October 1874 when Mr. Barne, the CMS lecturer who regularly spoke at Langley Burrell Church, illustrated 'the number of the heathen' to be converted by declaring that 'if 5000 should pass through Langley every day it would take 400 years for all the 800 million to go by'.

Modern Indian writers have taken a realistic view of the Victorian policy of 'improvement'. The EIC's monopoly of trade undermined that of India itself, destroying its merchant class, forcing Indians to depend on agriculture. In 1840, Sir Charles Trevelyan reported to a Commons Select Committee: 'We have swept away their manufactures; they have nothing to depend on but the produce of their land'.[25] In addition, taxes were imposed on the people. Ramkrishnan Muckerjee commented: 'With this blood money of India was built the Industrial England ... the edifices of the great Victorian Civilisation'.[26] As more and more Indian territories were annexed, so more and more land taxes flowed into the British exchequer. The right to levy taxes (in Bengal) was first granted to the EIC in 1765. One consequence was the Great Bengal Famine of 1769-70, in which ten million Indians died. Famines were common and regular in other British territories thereafter:[27] 'Imperial disruption and taxation, coupled with drought and famine, marked the start of the British Empire in India; it was a pattern to be sustained over the next 200 years.'[28] Kilvert commented on the Bengal famine of 1874 in a lecture to Langley Burrell parishioners on 4 November 1874,[29] showing once again the interest he took in Indian affairs.

The citizens of Bath were receiving news of the 1860-1 famine in Agra and the Punjab from their local newspaper, the *Bath Chronicle*. The 2 May 1861 issue quoted a report from the *Calcutta Englishman*, dated 12 March:

> Col. Baird Smith, the Special Famine Commissioner, has arrived at Agra to meet the Central Committee. We cannot at present hold out any certain hopes of improvement in the state of things in the North-west, where food is still being distributed.

The 2 May *Chronicle* also reported on a local initiative designed to help famine victims. The Bath Indian Famine Relief Fund committee had held a meeting on 4 April. The committee included the mayor, eleven army generals and colonels, and various clergymen, including the Rev. Scarth, vicar of St. Mary's, Bathwick. The public were urged to make donations to the Fund.

To illustrate what he called the 'humbug' of civilising Asia, Arnold in his *Oakfield* has a lengthy discussion between Middleton, noted for his frankness and 'strong earnestness', and a missionary, the Rev. Wallace. The view of the former is that approaches to India should begin with physical improvements, then intellectual ones via education, and only then spiritual ones. Wallace, however, insists that prospects for India depend on the prospects of the Church. Middleton asks him what he meant by the 'Church', because if he meant chaplains, of whom there were only thirty in Bengal, then their influence would be completely insignificant. And he asks Wallace directly: 'has Christianity had any effect upon this country; I do not mean in individual cases, but at all, nationally?' He himself doubted whether, if a whole army of missionaries were sent out by the CMS, it would have '*any* effect upon the natives' (Arnold's italics). Even if they did have any effect, their converts would only become money-worshipping, godless men like the British. The dead weight of EIC tradition denied the possibility of spiritual revolution in India: 'There is an utter want of nobleness in the government of India, it still retains the mark of its commercial origins'. It could not have spiritual purposes and ideals when its main aim was revenue collection. 'No amount of Sunday services will break the force of the spirit of commerce'.[30]

We can obtain an idea of Edward Kilvert's duties from the following summary by a missionary who was his contemporary:

> ... preaching the Gospel, superintending schools, circulating Bibles, distributing tracts, arguing with Brahmins, mingling with the thousands who were congregating at annual festivals, and warning them of their sin and danger.

This summary came from the 1850 tract, *India and the Hindus*, written by the great-great-grandfather of Andrew Ward. Ward noted that many Europeans preferred Moslems to Hindus because they could better understand their beliefs. (Kilvert showed interest and some sympathy for the Hindu practice of sending their dead 'adrift down the sacred [Ganges]'.) Missionaries could hope to make more conversions among Hindus in spite of their caste system, superstitions, and 'barbaric customs', whereas Moslems were more opposed to Christianity. However, Hindus were, Ward wrote, critical of Christianity because it was 'hopelessly simple-minded' and of Anglo-Indians' 'gluttony, drunkenness and lechery'. They also recognised that Anglo-Indians were not regular church-goers.[31]

Edward Kilvert's career in India as a missionary began in the period when Arnold was out there experiencing disillusion and despair. There are signs that Edward's career there was blighted by a spiritual breakdown, resulting mainly perhaps from what he witnessed or heard about during the Mutiny (which Arnold predicted in *Oakfield*). The details of his movements and of his leaves supplied by *Allen's Indian Mail* lend weight to this interpretation. The Mutiny began on 10 May 1857, towards the end of the thirty days' leave he was granted on 15 April 1857. It is not known whether this leave was taken at home or in India. Suppression of the Mutiny lasted from 1857 to 1858. The *Mail* reported on

26 March 1860 that Edward Kilvert, Chaplain of Jaulnah, had 'private leave for three months, from date of quitting his station'. The wording here – 'private', as opposed to 'official' leave, and 'quitted his station' – is suggestive of a form of breakdown, which the *Mail* was discreetly declining to make explicit. *The Church in Madras* was similarly inexplicit, noting that after Edward retired in 1861, 'His health did not allow him to do any permanent work in England'.[32] The leave he took in March 1860 had been granted on 21 February. However, on 12 May 1860 the *Mail* stated that it had been cancelled 'at his own request'. Did he request the leave because he badly needed a break from India, but cancelled it because he was determined to carry on? A year later (21 May 1861) came the announcement 'the Rev. Edward Kilvert, Chaplain of Jaulnah, is permanently to return from the service'. The record of his leaves shows a pattern of disturbance in the period leading up to and in the aftermath of the Mutiny, which would have been a traumatic time for men in his position. 'The establishments of Christians and missionaries were among the first targets of popular fury'.[33] Edward himself would not have met with that fury at Jaulnah (modern spelling Jalna) because it lies in the state of Maharashtra, over five hundred miles south of Bengal, the seat of the Mutiny. Niall Ferguson wrote of the Mutiny year: '1857 was the Evangelical movement's annus horribilis. They had offered India Christian civilisation, and the offer had been not merely declined but violently spurned'.[34] Missionaries like Edward would inevitably have experienced a sense of rejection. He returned to England an invalid as many did who sought India as a land of promise. William Arnold fared even worse because, like his eponymous hero, he contracted a disease in the 'cursed East' that was to kill him. He was on his way home when he died at Gibraltar on 9 April 1859.[35]

The spirit of progress that pulsed through Victorian Britain made its impact on Cheltenham College where Sam Wyndowe was a pupil and, combining with missionary zeal, gave rise in British India to a policy of 'improvement'. Though suffering the ill-health common among Anglo-Indians, Sam prospered in his work of developing medical services. The career of Edward was, however, cut short by a complete breakdown in his health. He was permanently changed by India and not for the better.

CHAPTER SIX

Getting on in India: India and change

So far the efforts of Dr. John and two of his sons to get on have been examined. The issue of getting daughters off is the second aspect of middle-class parents' 'great domestic problem', referred to earlier. The problem was particularly 'great' for Dr. John because he had six daughters although one died in infancy. All the others married apart from one.[1] Emily Kilvert provided details of the eldest, Antoinette, based on a traumatic childhood memory. She was chasing her sister Dora round a table and the fleeing Dora collided with a maid carrying a 'steaming bronze tea-urn'. Boiling water splashed over her neck and arms. 'I shall never forget the poor child's screams,' wrote Emily. Antoinette was staying in the Kilvert home at the time and helped to keep Emily and her siblings quiet for Dora's sake by settling them to draw at the dining-room table. Emily noted that she had no 'distinct remembrance' of Antoinette beyond this childhood memory, except that she called her 'Anty' and that she died 'within the year' (1852) after marrying the Rev. Thomas West when only twenty-two. 'I have always heard that she was the flower of the family,' Emily added.[2]

Emily also remembered Anna Maria, who did not manage to attain marriage at twenty-two like Antoinette. When Anna Maria married in 1870 she was forty-three and her husband, Theophilus Gwatkin, was a widower aged fifty-six with children of twenty-one, eighteen, and fifteen. The fact that he had been born at Meerut, India, in May 1814, son of an army general, was further reinforcement of the Indian links in Dr. John's family, as well as of the links to trade, because Gwatkin was a wine merchant and ships' chandler in Liverpool. The snobbery that disapproved of doctors like Dr. John carrying on the 'trade' of selling their own medicines has already been noted. A similar snobbery manifested itself among higher social groups towards marriage which involved what Best called 'the fatal touch of trade'.[3] Dr. John's family, descended from a Bath coach-builder, did not entertain this prejudice, nor did John's brother Francis, who made a point of praising 'honourable commerce'. Kilvert too approved of people earning a living through 'Honest Work'.[4] Furthermore, the industrial economy of mid-Victorian Britain encouraged the development of the professions: engineers, architects, accountants, lawyers, surveyors, civil servants, teachers, dentists and doctors, soldiers, clergymen. The Kilvert family mixed regularly with members of several of these professions and that meant that they were mixing with gentlemen.

Kilvert, who himself had four sisters, was aware both of women's desire to marry and of social expectations that they would do so. He was friendly with the Langley Burrell family of John Smallcombe, who was a landowner. Emily Kilvert referred to the family as people she remembered from her wedding day in 1865. Smallcombe and his wife had a daughter whom Kilvert called 'Bee', probably a transcription error for 'Bec' for her name was Rebecca. On 20 May 1870 his concern for her appears in his remark 'Poor Bee looks very waxen white and ill'.[5] She was then twenty. Five years later (12 May 1875) Kilvert called on her family, then living at 8 Pelham Place, London. They were out but he called two days later and found Bee in. He described her as 'an old friend' and stressed how 'radiant and beautiful' she was. He was relieved that she was 'unspoilt ... perfectly unchanged' by her London life.

> "I have not a friend in London," she said, a little sadly I thought. "Plenty of acquaintances, but not a single friend. Men come here and put up their eye glasses and say Haw Haw, and they haven't slept since they saw me last, but I don't care for any of them".

Here we seem to be in the London world depicted by Trollope in his *The Way We Live Now*, published 1875 but being written from 1873 onwards. In it, we meet upper-class men who talk of love to girls but don't mean a word of what they say. A major theme of the novel is the marriage market. Lady Georgiana Longstaffe, who is nearly thirty, is terrified of being left on the shelf; she sees other girls 'having chances' while she has none. She constantly complains 'If I don't marry what's to become of me?' She puts her position (that of all spinsters) to her mother – doomed to live with parents with 'no chance of a home of my own to live in'. In desperation, she threatens to 'run off with the first man that will take me' even if he is a tradesman. Bee Smallcombe was also nearly thirty when she got married though it was four and a half years after Kilvert was commiserating with her unmarried state. On 14 October 1879 (by which time he was dead) she married George Trowsdale in Chelsea; he was twenty-seven and she was twenty-nine. He was a clergyman. 'Of course it is a come-down to marry a curate,' Lady Georgiana's mother observed, 'but a clergyman is always considered to be decent'.[6]

Three of Kilvert's sisters married and two of them appear in the Album; the one who married a clergyman will be considered later. Here the focus will be on Emily, who married Samuel Wyndowe. The Album pictures her, large hat and black lace shawl on her knee, in a rustic seat, the leaves and blossoms of a studio plant behind her. It was an appropriate setting for a woman who had a passionate love of Nature. Kilvert expressed fear that Bee Smallcombe would be changed and 'spoilt' by life in London. A much greater fear that Emily and her family would be changed by life in India haunts the *Diary* passages that deal with them.

Kilvert's fear rested on understandings about conditions in India that he had already built up before Emily's marriage to an Indian Army surgeon in 1865. Such understandings derived from stories he heard from families who had relatives there,[7] from Dr. John's family, from journals, novels and newspapers. We also know that the Indian Mutiny was a topic of discussion at his uncle Francis's school when Kilvert was a pupil. In addition, Kilvert's family was wholly committed to missionary work and converting the 'heathen' of India to Christianity was both an inspiring future challenge and, in the lives of those who had devoted their lives to it in the past, a source of pride. On 20 March 1871, Kilvert was reading the life story of George Cotton, former Headmaster of Marlborough College, who became Bishop of Calcutta. Kilvert's deep interest in India is also signalled by the book he was reading on 18 November 1878 – 'on the sofa in the library all day reading *The Dilemma*'. The book, by George Tomkyns Chesney, had come out in 1876.[8] It is a lengthy (three volume), searching analysis of British administration in India and of its responsibility for, and reaction to, the Mutiny. The idea that 'India was truly the paradise of the middle classes' (Bourne's observation, quoted earlier[9]) is subject to severe scrutiny in *The Dilemma*. That Kilvert would read the book is another sign, not only of his intellectual calibre, but also of the seriousness of his desire to understand the India that his sister knew.

Kilvert was prepared to accept Chesney's realism but, like many Victorians, he romanticised India and Britain's rule there. The famous Eton teacher and scholar William Johnson (1823-1892) typified the pride and patriotism felt in the period towards the Raj. He wrote to his brother in 1863: 'I am reading a book which ... contains enough to make an Englishman happy – *Dalhousie's Administration*'. Dalhousie was Governor-General of India (1848-56) and was responsible for important reforms as well as for annexing several profitable Indian provinces. A.N. Wilson referred to him as 'a modernizer, an improver, a moral policeman'.[10] Johnson admired Dalhousie as one of those 'who killed themselves making empires', who possessed courage that scholars like himself lacked. In a later letter, he expressed the desire to write Dalhousie's biography. An entry in his *Journal* (25 September 1868) shows him musing romantically about some of his Eton pupils stationed in isolated hill forts in India pining for their lost youth. And when he resigned from Eton at Easter 1872, he toyed with the idea of going to live in India 'to worship the Union Jack'.[11]

The Dilemma concerns Olivia, a young woman newly arrived in India, and her ability to avoid being changed by the deadening influence of its British society. Captain Sparrow sympathises with her because, as a lively-minded woman, she would inevitably be bored with endless picnics and 'nothing to do but yawn'. Boredom of this degree would undermine an individual's moral character and aspirations. Olivia has a better chance than most young ladies introduced to this way of life because she is older than them, has spent time in various European countries, is intelligent and possessed of an independent, liberal outlook. She is, for example, prepared to judge sepoys (Indian soldiers) on their merits, unlike Mrs. Polwheedle, the brigadier's wife, who characterised them as 'thieves with black faces'. The novel's hero, Lieutenant Yorke, an officer in a native regiment, is pleased by Olivia's interest in his men. Young ladies usually showed none, especially in the brief period of spinsterhood before they 'got off'. Olivia is different: 'She had come to India [wanting] to know all about the country and its people'. Her sensitivity and sincerity make her 'different from most of our young ladies'.[12] Her outlook is the one that eighteenth-century visitors to India tended to have: 'a great many Europeans responded to India in a way that perhaps surprises and appeals to us today, by crossing over from one culture to the other, and wholeheartedly embracing the great diversity of late Mughal India'.[13]

Chesney's novel starts: 'At the beginning of the cold season, there takes place the annual importation of young ladies from England'. At the time, this importation from England was mockingly referred to as the 'fishing fleet'. However, Olivia's main aim in coming to India was not marriage. Chesney observes at one point that by the age of twenty-one 'most English girls in India are wives and mothers'. Lady Georgiana in Trollope's *The Way We Live Now* did not consider India as the source of a husband but was well recognised for that reason in the society in which Album characters moved.[14] *Punch* was making comic play with this fact in an article of 4 July 1857 under the heading 'The Matrimonial Market', which presented a letter supposedly from a mother of ten daughters. She confesses that she 'exports' one or two of them to India every year. Some had managed to get married, 'others have not been so fortunate', and had returned to their 'disconsolate mother', the strain and cost of which was very heavy. Return tickets from India were unavailable and 'vessels will not make a reduction on taking a quantity'. The mother urged Mr. Punch to support the recently announced Suez Canal scheme, which would shorten the journey to India by one half, thus reducing the cost. He, however, deplored packing young ladies off to India like 'living merchandise', labelled 'On Sale or Return'. The mother who 'exported' her daughters to India was buoyed up by the belief 'Better be married at Bombay, than remain single in London'. Perhaps the parents of Bee Smallcombe believed it 'Better to be married at London, than remain single in Langley Burrell'.

Kilvert had a love of ocean-going ships, as can be seen in the *Diary* entry recording his visit to Liverpool on 20 June 1872 in the company of Anna Maria, and would have known that the P. and O. Company, whose steamers took people to and from India, was founded in 1840, the year of his birth. He made frequent references to people going out to or returning from India. Sometimes it was visits there by celebrities like the Prince of Wales but usually he was concerned with relatives and friends. He noted that his former lover, Ettie Meredith Brown, was to sail for India to be married; her husband-to-be was William Henry Wright, a professor at Muir College, Allahabad. One *Diary* entry in which Kilvert's anxiety surfaced regarding the changes that Indian experience wrought is that of 1 October 1874 when he met George Warlow in Clifton: 'I had no idea he was in England. He returns to India next spring.' The entry reiterates the idea that Warlow was unrecognisable to Kilvert. He was 'a perfect stranger', Kilvert wrote, and expressed 'ignorance of his identity' and 'could not recognise a feature in his face', even though he 'looked well'. Evidently the diarist was disturbed that a man well known to him could be so completely changed physically and wondered at the causes.[15]

Kilvert's fear of India's mysterious and somewhat sinister power to change people appears almost obsessive in the case of his sister Emily. She had gone out to India shortly after she married Sam Wyndowe on 25 July 1865, and returned after nearly five years on 26 April 1870. Kilvert was bidding her farewell again on 24 February 1872; she sailed with Sam from Southampton on 29 February on the *Ceylon*. She returned with one of her daughters on 27 April 1875 (Sam had to stay on). In 1870, anxious to see her as soon as possible, Kilvert was eagerly speculating on 18 April about where Emily's ship would be: 'well past Suez and on the English side'. While still in Clyro, he had a letter from his sister Dora about her reunion with Emily and he was relieved to hear that 'Emmie is brown but scarcely at all changed'. That she was home safe was his other concern: 'Long expected, come at last. Thank God'. Eight days later he received a letter from Emily herself which stated that she found her family at Langley Burrell 'so very little changed. My father and Dora the most so.'

Emily kept in very close touch with her family in England as the *Diary* entry for 27 July 1874 confirms: 'This morning we had our usual weekly Indian letter from Emmie'. Mail from India was taking a month to reach England at this time so the frequency with which Emily wrote letters home is notable. It indicated that she had the leisure for letter-writing but perhaps also an awareness on her part that her family was always anxious for her welfare. Her brother seemed glad to have the 'weekly Indian letter', and the comfort of believing, vis-à-vis Emily and Sam's marriage, 'What a happy marriage that has been, and they seem so fond of each other'. This belief helped to ease his anxiety over their safety in India.

Emily's letters supplied Kilvert with the stories of Indian life that he enjoyed passing on to others. As we have seen in the example of her difficult journey to Hyderabad, he relished her sensitive and precise descriptions partly because they enabled him to picture her life in that strange, exotic country so far away, and partly because he was a writer himself. Another particularly good example is the *Diary* entry for 2 July 1872:

> A letter from Emmie this morning. She gives a beautiful description of a landscape and scene she saw whilst waiting in the carriage one evening for Sam. The lofty rock, the abode of the fakir. One Tree hill, the little temple crowning the hill, the mango grove on the plain and the procession of girls moving across the sandy plain, singing.

Reports about and by Emily were of some reassurance to Kilvert but he had to see for himself whether the sister he had known remained the same or whether India had made her a stranger whose personality, manner, values rendered her alien, less lovable, like a fairy-tale character bewitched by some malign force. The *Diary* entry (16 May) recording the brother's reunion with his sister is filled with joy and relief:

> Dear old Emmie ... such a happy meeting and she not the least changed except perhaps that she seemed a little fuller in the face. The old manner, look and voice just the same, so natural, so familiar, and she looked so bright well and happy. A little sunburnt, but she will soon get her rosy cheeks again. Thank God for bringing them all safe home.

The phrasing here – 'the old manner, look and voice just the same' – suggests that the basis of Kilvert's fear was that Emily would be literally unrecognisable, as George Warlow was. This is confirmed in an entry, omitted from Plomer's edition of the *Diary*, which records the reunion of Emily with her brother Edward. Kilvert wrote: 'Neither Emmie nor Teddy knew each other [in] the least, and could hardly be persuaded of each other's identity.' The diarist acknowledged that Teddy had changed a lot since Emily had last seen him but was surprised that 'he did not recognise her as she is so very little changed'.[16]

In Kilvert's account of Emily's homecoming from India on 27 April

1875, the harping on the issue of change is again dominant: 'there was Emmie, looking perfectly unchanged by her three years' absence ...' The 'change' that he most feared with regard to his sister was that from life to death. His cousin William had not returned from India; Lechmere Thomas had not returned from Ceylon. Kilvert would have been aware too, as most Victorians were, that children were especially vulnerable to India's climate and diseases. The figures for deaths printed in *Allen's Indian Mail* underline this clearly. In 1863 (the year William Kilvert died at Calcutta from 'diarrhoea'), of the fourteen who had died in April, eight were children while of sixteen who had died in May, three were infants. The last chapter noted that Emily, wife of Frederick Kilvert, returned from India when her son John was five and did not return, perhaps out of anxiety over the threats it posed to children's health. Cholera, dysentery, smallpox and malaria were among 'the myriad Indian hazards' noted by Ward, who also added that 'India was regarded as a spiritually and socially, as well as physically dangerous place for children'.[17]

Apart from fearing the dangers of India's climate, diseases and violence which threatened his sister, her husband and children, Kilvert was also troubled that India was transforming them into Indians. He referred several times to Emily and her family as 'the Indians'. It was an aspect of the central fear that they were becoming totally different, un-English, people. It was of course particularly noticeable in Emily's children. They suffer from England's cold, are devoted to their ayah (nurse), Annie has learnt how to dance 'like an Indian dancing girl' and has learned Indian words. It is quite clear that Kilvert harboured an irrational fear that his sister and her family were coming to resemble Indians in their skin colour. In May 1870, he was relieved to find that Katie, the eldest daughter, was not brown but 'much fairer than I expected', just as he was relieved that her mother, though 'brown' and 'a little sunburnt', would soon recover her 'rosy cheeks'. Langley Burrell people had already decided that Sam Wyndowe was an Indian. Kilvert noted on 29 February 1872 that his neighbours said they 'supposed [Sam] wasn't a darkey' but in such a way as to confirm that they supposed he was!

Emily's youngest daughter Mary (known as 'Mayndie'), although born in England in June 1871, accompanied her parents back to India in February 1872.[18] On 3 May 1875 when she had come home again,

Kilvert was expressing concern that she was (as a result somehow of being reared in India) 'a tiny child of her age'.[19] Four days later he was observing that she 'has more Hindustani than English, and chatters away to the ayah in Hindustani but makes havoc of English grammar'.[20] He then gave examples of her pidgin English. She was four then and her English grammar should have been well developed.

Later that month, at a children's party, Mayndie was 'in great form and sang to the assembled company her celebrated Indian song which she learnt from her ayah'. Kilvert then quoted a verse from it and explained some of its words: '"Butcheon" means a child, "Dood wallah" a milkman, and "Jungali" anything wild'. Mayndie's command of Hindustani was placing a distance between her and her mother because 'Even Emmie cannot translate the song and we forgot to ask the ayah to interpret it before she went'. The closeness of child to ayah in their shared Indian language was another source of anxiety to Kilvert.

Ironically, Kilvert himself was being changed by the 'Indians' in his own family. He adopted Indian words, referring to a pram as a 'chota gharry'. He liked to pass on Emily's Indian experiences to others, telling a Clyro farmer about her '[Indian] adventures'. He told another friend of her expedition on elephant back to hunt deer. The excitement and exoticism of India had been part of Emily's experience since she was a child, long before she married an Indian Army surgeon. She recalled a brightly coloured picture over the fireplace on the wall of the Harnish nursery: 'one of an elephant with a howdah on its back and its Mahout in scarlet and gold seated astride its neck'.[21] Kilvert also grew very fond of the children's ayah, who was largely responsible for their Indian manners. When she was about to return by herself to India on 27 May 1870, he was particularly touched by her devotion to them: 'She seemed very sorry to ... leave the children ... [and was] crying bitterly'. He added 'I am quite sorry she is going'. He liked her constant good humour. Although she ate with the other Vicarage servants in the kitchen, he treated her as a lady: 'I made her a low salaam and polite speech'. He liked the fact that she was a Christian (a Catholic) and sympathised with her because she was homesick and suffered from the English cold weather. He admired her 'fine erect carriage learnt by carrying ... burdens on her head'. She and a local man, John Gough, who had been in the army in Bengal, tried to converse but the ayah was from Madras and they had few words in common. Kilvert met her again in 1875 when Emily and Mary returned home with her. He had found much to like in her, in spite of concern that his nieces were being changed under her influence. However, it was clear that she loved them and they loved her. She was an aspect of India that he could trust, someone from the East, whence came 'all evil things', and found in her nothing but good.

Kilvert's response to the ayah typified that of generations of Englishmen who had gone to India as merchants, soldiers and administrators. He was fascinated by her Indian ways, which had some of the exoticism that excited Emily Kilvert in her childhood. He couldn't help liking the ayah though she was making his nieces into Indians. Particularly noticeable in this context is this *Diary* entry: '[Annie], *instructed by the ayah*, stands on the dining room table and sideboard and "nautches" – dancing like an Indian dancing girl' (my italics). The picture this scene presents is astonishing enough in itself: an infant English girl dancing on the table and sideboard in the dining-room of a Victorian rectory belonging to a sixty-five-year-old Evangelical clergyman. However, the fact that she was 'dancing like an Indian dancing girl' takes the incident into the realm of fantasy.

We can travel into that realm on the word 'nautches', used by Kilvert to convey what Annie was doing when she danced. He could have learned this Indian word from the ayah, from Annie's mother, or from Sam Wyndowe. How much he knew of its background would have depended on who his informant was. 'Nautch' is an anglicised form of the word 'nach', meaning 'dance' or 'dancing', found in Hindi and Urdu. The kind of dancing it represented had been part of Indian tradition for centuries. Joshi explained that until the mid-nineteenth century some Indian castes placed their daughters at a very young age in Hindu temples. These girls, known as devadasis, helped priests in the performance of sacred rituals and sang and danced in temples.[22] ('Deva-dasi' literally means 'slave girl of the gods'.) 'They enjoyed high social and economic status and were looked upon by royalty as well as ordinary people as cultured and respectable'. For women in British and European religious communities, celibacy was the rule, whereas devadasis were allowed to have sexual relations with priests and with feudal lords and princes, who paid for their upkeep.[23]

The British settlers who arrived in India in the eighteenth century were much taken with Indian dancing girls, some of whom migrated from temples in order to entertain the new white masters. It was the arrival of settlers which led to the abandonment of the religious element in the lives of devadasis and they became ordinary prostitutes, as Nevile explained: 'Nautch represented cultural interaction between the natives and the early English settlers in India. Its professional exponent, the nautch girl, held the white sahib spellbound for nearly two centuries'. The wealthy British 'nabobs' of the Clive era often adopted the lifestyle of native princes, to the extent of maintaining 'troupes of nautch girls and musicians for the entertainment of their guests'.[24] Understandably, beautiful Indian girls and their sensual dancing had special appeal for the soldiers of the EIC armies. The girls would often 'shed their stiff reserve and cool propriety, displaying their seductive charms'. The phrase 'with hands tossing and twisting above her head', which Kilvert used about Annie's dancing, showed he was alert to a style of dancing poles apart from the formal and decorous Lancers, cotillons and quadrilles he was used to. Chatterjee wrote of 'the charm and sweetness' of nautch girls and of the way 'British men were fascinated by these entertainers, who were quite distant from the stiff, corseted prude [sic] Victorian women'.[25] One particularly erotic dance was the Kaharka nautch, described thus by an English gentleman:

> While rendering it the nautch girl would tie a sash round her loins, through which she pulled up her gown... Twisting a turban saucily round her head she would let her long black hair fall on her back and around her bosom and then dart forward with animated gestures.[26]

There was eroticism not only in the dancing; nautch girls' songs had as themes 'either the amorous escapades in the lives of gods or conventional romantic tales, usually about the lover's yearning for the beloved'.[27]

If Sam Wyndowe, an officer in the Indian Army since 1854, had been Kilvert's chief informant about the nautch, he may well have included in his account a few hints about its sensual nature, based upon his experience. It seems certain that Kilvert would have known, as a man of the world, a good deal about what nautch dancing stood for, just as he knew about the obscene 'stereoscopic slides "The Diversions of Satan",' made for an Indian prince which, as Kilvert put it delicately, 'were not pronounced enough to suit his taste'. These were shown to Kilvert on 7 June 1872 by another Indian Army officer, Major Thomas of Llanthomas. An element in the diarist's concern about his nieces becoming Indians was undoubtedly the nautch dancing of Annie. She was not that far from the age (seven) when devadasis began their service in Hindu temples, service that began with dancing but soon led to prostitution. The nautch, witnessed by generations of British in India, would inevitably have figured in talk of experiences there and it seems almost as inevitable that Kilvert, with so many Anglo-Indian men in his circle of friends, would have heard it mentioned. Furthermore, a group of devadasis had 'created a stir in western Europe and UK' when it did a dance tour in 1838.[28] Dr. John Shortt read a paper, *The Dancing Girls of Southern India*, to the Anthropological Society in London in 1868 and it was published in 1870, the year in which little Annie was doing her nautches. Kilvert could therefore have learned much about the subject from sources other than his sister and her husband.

If Emily Kilvert had talked to her brother about the nautch, her account would have been more likely to have focused on its religious origins and formal, artistic properties. British women had written extensively on the subject in diaries and journals. Their view alternated between two extremes: 'The more liberal ones found the nautch tasteful, the music sweet and lyrical, the women beautiful and supple', while others saw it as proof of a 'decadent oriental culture'.[29] Unsurprisingly, the nautch became a target for Evangelical visitors to India such as Mrs. Sherwood (1775-1851), author of the famous and influential children's book *The Fairchild Family* (1818, 1842, 1847). She wrote of Englishmen with 'mothers at home who cared and prayed for once blooming boys ... slowly sacrificing themselves to drinking, smoking and the witcheries of the unhappy daughters of heathens and infidels'.[30] Missionaries had increasingly joined with English-educated Indians as the century went on to condemn the nautch and the devadasis, who were 'temple prostitutes and clear evidence of the barbarity of Hinduism that needed to be eradicated'.[31]

Sir David Ochterlony, father of the Album character, Mrs. Middleton, who was introduced in chapter four, was a British soldier seduced by the 'witcheries' of a heathen daughter. When Kilvert was voicing his fears that his sister and husband would be changed by India, he did not have in mind the kind of change which had overtaken Ochterlony. He had gone there in the eighteenth century when 'the boundary between ruler and ruled was inconspicuous and both would mix freely with each other'.[32] Giving oneself up to either the Hindu or Muslim culture of India was once a common pattern among British merchants and army officers, as Dalrymple pointed out: 'Virtually all Englishmen in India at this period Indianised themselves to some extent'.[33] He also told of five thousand British captives in Algiers in 1626 whose fate disturbed the authorities in Britain because they might be forced to accept Islam. Some did under duress but many willingly accepted it. These Britishers, among whom were some women, had been taken prisoner when their ships were captured by Barbary pirates. Almost two centuries later, Kilvert's father was recalling an episode in 1816, when he was twelve, which concerned the British admiral, Sir Edward Pellew, who undertook to release Britons imprisoned in Algiers. His fleet bombarded Algiers, destroying much of it as well as the enemy's fleet, and 'releasing no fewer than three thousand Christian slaves from a hideous bondage'.[34] To Robert Kilvert, it was impossible to conceive that their residence in Algiers could be anything but 'bondage' and that at least some of them might have relinquished Christianity for Islam. His outlook was the product of the change in attitude, outlined in chapter four, which was apparent by the early nineteenth century, when any kind of 'going native' was regarded with horror.

Mrs. Middleton's father, Sir David Ochterlony, was one who completely adopted the Muslim faith and way of life. Tradition stated that his thirteen wives (some sources called them 'concubines') used to parade, each on her own elephant, behind Sir David when he took the evening air in Delhi. Among his wives was Mubarak Begum, the youngest of them and said to be his favourite.

> She was originally a dancing girl slave who later converted to Islam and was taken on by the general. Being far younger than he and also because of her skill in singing and dancing she had great influence on the ageing general. In no time she began to direct things within the walls of the residency.

Mubarak Begum incurred the hostility of the British and the Indians because of her haughtiness. She signed her letters 'Lady Ochterlony'.

'People treated her as a nautch girl due to her background'.[35]

Dalrymple confirms this view of Mubarak Begum, not only as Ochterlony's favourite wife, but also of the way she was 'accused of giving herself airs', and offending the British. According to Dalrymple, she was brought from Poona and 'presented or sold ... to General Ochterlony when twelve years of age'.[36] This part of her background as well as her talents as a nautch dancer meant that the mosque she built for herself is still known in Delhi as 'the Prostitute's Mosque'.

Ochterlony was faced by a dilemma concerning his two daughters by Mubarak Begum, one of whom was Mrs. Middleton. Dalrymple told how moving his letters were (written around 1803) in which he considered whether to bring the girls up as Christians or Muslims. Ochterlony noted that they were 'uncommonly fair' (no sign of Mrs. Middleton's racial origins is visible in her Album photo) but that would not guard them from racial prejudice in Britain, especially when it became known that they had mixed blood. If, on the other hand, he raised them as Muslims and they became wives of Muslims, he admitted that 'I own I could not bear that my child should be one of a numerous harem'. Dalrymple commented that this was 'rather rich coming from Ochterlony', who had himself a harem of thirteen wives.[37]

Mary Ann did not end up in a harem and married, as we have seen, not an army officer but an EIC official. Nor did she become (or at least remain) a Muslim. Her will and other sources indicate a strong Anglican orientation. Her will refers to her son, the Rev. Henry Ochterlony Middleton, born at Cawnpore in 1820. She made a number of charitable donations to Anglican bodies.[38] Her two daughters, both spinster ladies, devoted themselves to good works, notably St. Peter's Church, Plymouth, rebuilt between 1878 and 1882 through their liberality, beginning with £6,000 in 1878. Mrs. Middleton's orthodox, respectable life in Bath makes an intriguing contrast to her beginnings in Delhi as the daughter of an exotic nautch girl of highly dubious reputation. However, the story of the British in India is full of such contrasts. A final interesting point about that nautch girl is that she 'fought against the British during the great Indian rebellion of 1857, demonstrating the drastic breakdown in British-Indian relations caused by racism, segregation and oppression. By then, the India that Ochterlony had made his home no longer existed'.[39] The

William Kilvert — late 92nd Highlanders

G. R. & Cᵒ. PATENT.

Grandmamma

BY APPOINTMENT

FRED.ᴷ C. BIRD

PHOTOGRAPHER AND PORTRAIT PAINTER

38. MILSOM STREET

BATH

*Duplicates of this Portrait may always
be obtained. It can also be enlarged up*

G.R.& Cᵒ. PATENT.

E. F. Kilvert

F. J. R. Russell.

G. R. & Cº PATENT.

G.R. & Cº PATENT.

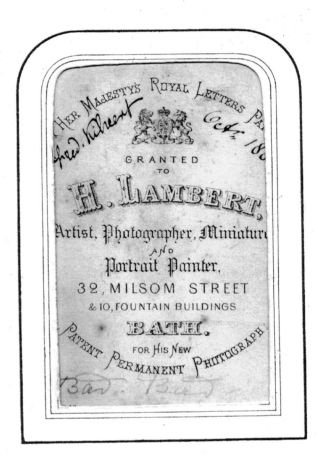

G.R.& C!: PATENT.

Fredk Kilvert

G. R. & Co. PATENT.

Mrs Fredk Kilvert

G.R.& C? PATENT.

G.R. & C? PATENT.

J. R. Parsons.

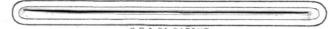

G. R. & Cº PATENT.

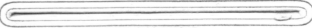

G. R. & Cᵒ PATENT

H. B. Parsons.

G.R. & C.º PATENT.

L. G. Parsons.

G. R. & Cº. PATENT.

Revd W. R. Smith

G.R. & Co. PATENT.

G.R. & Cº PATENT.

G.R. & Cᵒ PATENT.

Mrs S. J. Wyndowe

G.R. & Co PATENT.

Col.ᵐ Montague Cholmeley

G. R. & Cº PATENT.

W. B. Macrone

L. S. Falkner

G.R.& Cᵒ PATENT.

G.R. & Cº. PATENT.

Katie Buée

Fred.ᴴ Koe

G. R. & Cº PATENT

H. Lancaster

Maggie Lancaster

G. R. & C? PATENT.

M. G. Child

G. R. & Cº PATENT.

G. R. & C? PATENT.

Caroline Hewitt

Henry Hewitt

G. R. & Cº PATENT.

Captn Bampfylde.

G. R. & Co PATENT.

Mrs Bampfylde

Fanny Lawrence

G. R. & Cº. PATENT.

Arundel Rogers.

G.R. & Cº PATENT.

Revd L. R. Hamilton & Daughter

G. R. & Cº PATENT.

Mrs Middleton

G. R. & C⁰. PATENT.

G.R. & Cº PATENT.

G. R. & Cº PATENT

G.R. & C? PATENT.

G. R. & Cº. PATENT

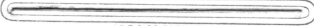

G. R. & C? PATENT.

*Above, 12 Darlington Street, Bath-
wick, the home of Dr John Kilvert.
Right, plaques to Dr John and his wife
Marianne (Mary Anne) at St Mary's,
Bathwick, and Dr John's gravestone.
Below, 10 Darlington Street, home of
Captain Bampfylde, and, bottom, 35
Henrietta Street, where Marianne's
mother, Mrs Becks, lived*

Left, 12 Sydney Buildings, Bathwick, a property in which William Bueé had an interest; right, 2 Adelaide Place, Bathwick, home of Captain Hewitt, father of Henry and Caroline

Left, 7 Darlington Place, Bathwick. William Macrone's mother and daughters lived here. Right, Tyning House, Widcombe. William Macrone's sister Josephine lived here

Left, 11 Sion Hill, Bath. Captain Bampfylde lived here in 1861. Right, 29 Royal Crescent, Bath, home of the Bethell family from 1856

*Top, 16 Royal Crescent, Bath. Mrs
Bethell (mother of Jane) lived here in
the 1870s. Above, 25 Royal Crescent,
where Mrs Middleton lived. Above
right, 9 Edward Street, Bathwick.
Maggie Lancaster lived here as a child.
It was the home of Marianne Awdry.
Right, Caerbadon House (now
Brandon House), Bathwick. Mrs Ellis
(mother of Emily) lived here*

Above left, 2 Park Lane, Bath, the home of Lucy Stringer Falkner. Right, the Blackheath home of Mr and Mrs Koe, 15 Bennett Park. Below is Ellern Croft House, the home of Mary Grace Child at Wotton-under-Edge, Gloucestershire

Above, Milsom Street, Bath, in 1910, showing the upstairs premises occupied by the photographer Frederick Bird in the 1870s and by his son when the picture was taken. Below, the street in 1884

Picture credits: This page Colin Johnston, Bath Record Office; the Koes' house in Blackheath, Giles Toman; and all the other photographs, John Toman

India that replaced Ochterlony's was the one Emily Kilvert knew. When she and her family returned to England, Kilvert expressed relief that her husband Sam was also unchanged. A number of sources throw light on the way Indian life could change men, particularly army officers. In *The Dilemma*, Chesney traces Lieutenant Yorke's struggle to remain uncorrupted by Anglo-Indian society while endeavouring to get on. The novel continually contrasts the worlds of army officers and of civilian administrators (like Frederick Kilvert and other Album characters) in terms of their benefits, rewards, privations, and career prospects. Children were, Chesney noted, generally a hindrance to a man's career. Like most army officers, Yorke has gone to India to get on and he constantly frets at his poor prospects. He seeks to get on by studying native languages and military science. He believes that by learning Hindustani he will understand Indians better and has faith in the sepoys under his command in the 76th Native Infantry.

Having fallen in love with Olivia, partly because of her superior moral qualities, his desire to get on is all the greater, since he hopes to marry her, but doubts she will ever become 'the bride of a penniless subaltern'. Nevertheless, he reflects that 'Surely his patient efforts to qualify for preferment would be rewarded before long. Everybody said that India was a country where any man could win success without interest or favour, merely by deserving it'. His attempt to cheer himself up gives way later to depression: 'All the education in the world won't get a fellow on the Staff'. When Olivia encourages him by underlining his deserts, he replies that deserts matter little – 'a little interest' [i.e. patronage] 'is worth any amount of brains in these times'.

Surrounding Yorke are demoralising influences which he tries to resist, one of which is snobbery. It centres partly upon which regiment a man belongs to. The Horse Artillery is regarded as 'crack branch of the service'; native regiments are held in low esteem, seen as much inferior to British ones. HQ staff are admired as 'swells' who get 'tremendous salaries'. Wide differences in pay exacerbated snobbery. The monthly pay of an ensign – the rank on which William Kilvert started – was 208 rupees, one twentieth of the 4,166 rupees received monthly by the Commissioner of a district. Mrs. Polwheedle typifies the obsession with rank and status. Acutely conscious of her position as the wife of a brigadier, she sneers at native regiments and cannot see that Indians' concern with caste, regarded by her as 'nonsense', parallels her own concern with rank. Olivia, on the other hand, is prepared to judge sepoys on their merits. She admits she expected them to be 'insignificant-looking creatures', whereas they are 'fine fellows'.

The subaltern's apartment in which Yorke lives is a twenty-foot square room with whitewashed walls, a thatched roof, and a small verandah on which were two cane-backed 'lolling chairs'. Earthenware jars suspended one above the other served as a water-filter. Boxes of beer and soda-water were stacked by the verandah wall. The fate of many young officers like Yorke was to drink themselves to death.[40] According to the 1844 *Calcutta Review*, ladies occupied their time in making and receiving visits, writing letters, and reading novels; some did household tasks, others entrusted such tasks entirely to servants. Boredom was the bane, not only of women in this society, who had few duties, but also of army officers. The hot season left them particularly idle because then the ladies headed for hill stations where it was cooler: 'For even the most stalwart British ladies and their most resilient children the hot season was unthinkable without their shutters, tatties, punkahs, frequent baths and vast, dark bungalows'.[41] The civil officials and officers faced 'hot weather dullness. Nothing but billiards and rackets for a fellow to do'. In the cold season there were bachelor parties, ladies' parties, cricket matches, and some hunting. *The Dilemma* emphasises that cholera is an ever-present danger. One of the 'dilemmas' of Chesney's book is that though India was a place of promise, a means of getting on, it was hostile to Europeans. A young doctor, new in India, says he is keen to gain some experience of cholera and an experienced doctor wryly reassures him that he was bound to encounter it soon.[42] In *The Dilemma* we hear of one regiment that has suffered 100 deaths from it.

Chesney's account of life in India covers the 1848-68 period. Another account (based as his was on actual experience) is *Oakfield* by William Arnold, published in 1853. He was a son of the famous Dr. Arnold, pioneering educationist, headmaster of Rugby School, who wrote: 'India is of all fields of honourable action that this world offers, to my mind the fairest'.[43] His son opted for a life of action in India, going out in 1848 after obtaining an EIC cadetship. He himself is Oakfield, the central figure of his novel. From the start he hated the life. He found the coarse language of the mess of the 38th Regiment stationed at Dinapore 'so revolting as to be even strange to me' (he'd experienced it at school). He was like his father in temperament: full of ideas, earnest but impetuous, melancholy, and taking everything too seriously. Oakfield wrote to his sister: 'Social Reform is becoming the cry of the world; and I fancy it must be the cry of wise men in India as much as anywhere else'. He defined 'Social Reform' as 'forming society anew ... on a foundation of common sense and intellect, not of animalism and violence and hazard'. Its other foundations were 'truth and justice' and 'Christ and his gospel'. In India, reform meant changing 'its immorality to a state of comparative Christian earnestness'. These were the values that permeated the social group in which Album characters moved. Underlying the desire to get on lay their belief that India, backward and superstitious, posed a challenge to a successful, dynamic, industrial and Christian nation like the British. Indians too must be encouraged both to get on and to embrace Christianity. For Evangelical families like the Kilverts, converting India to the gospel of Christ was a divine mission.

Oakfield's stance early in the book is that every European was engaged in 'the grand work of civilising Asia'. However, before long he has recognised that European society in India also needed to be changed because it was 'gross in its lowest phases, and false and Mammonish in its highest'. He deplored its 'loose language, its money-loving, its rank-loving'. Army officers were 'in nine cases out of ten ... mere animals' and were quite unable to show courtesy to native Indians. A native regiment was 'the very worst specimen of Indian society', the staff and civil service were generally better morally than the army, and the élite of the two was positively good. Boredom was one of the great evils of European society, members of which steered a middle path between their duties and 'the vacuum of literally doing nothing'. Getting on was, in Oakfield's view, the driving force of this society. He remarked to a fellow officer: 'Both at home and in this country, they think more of allowances and position and so on than anything else'. Arnold's novel shows in detail the changes, wrought by India, that threatened men of religious and moral conscience.

CHAPTER SEVEN

Henry Hewitt in Bath and Australia

Henry Hewitt's story is above all a story of getting on and of Empire. Born in 1839, he was descended from families who had lived in India for many years. His mother Caroline (born 1808) came from the Cotgrave family. Her grandfather John Cotgrave had married Martha Vigors in India in 1769. Caroline married William Vigors Hewitt (born 1800) on 1 June 1826 at Masulipatam, Madras, the first trading post (1611) established by the EIC. Both Caroline and William were from military families. Her father, Richard John, was a lieutenant colonel in the Madras Engineers. Son of General William Hewitt, William himself was a captain in the Bombay army. India destroyed his health because he was invalided home around 1837-8 with his wife and three-month-old Caroline. Henry told how the family nearly died at sea when their ship, the *Earl of Eldon*, caught fire 1,100 miles from land. They survived in an open boat, saving the family Bible, which later accompanied Henry to Australia.[1] 'Mrs. Hewitt may have been something of a religious fanatic,' Helen Vafeas speculated, 'which may have contributed to her separation from her husband soon after Henry's birth on 30 November 1839'.[2] After that, he had responsibility for the children's upbringing. Caroline (senior) always referred to her husband as 'my cousin Hewitt' because they were first cousins.

The family were together in Somerton, Somerset (between Glastonbury and Yeovil) in the 1841 census: husband William, Caroline, daughter Caroline (aged four) and Henry (aged one). By 1851, the separation of husband and wife is visible. Caroline (senior) was then a visitor in the Somerton home of John Pyne (76) and his daughter Anne; neither of the Hewitt children were present because they were away at school.

Caroline was at a young ladies' school at 20 Richmond Terrace, Clifton, Bristol, in 1851 along with eleven other girls. Head of this establishment was forty-year-old unmarried Jane Barrett, helped out by two 'school assistants'.[3] Caroline was to remain unmarried till the end of her days. In 1871, she was living (aged thirty-three) with her father at 3 Church Street, Widcombe, Bath. One servant was employed and their neighbours were a retired doctor on one side and a retired schoolmistress on the other. William Hewitt had lived in Widcombe earlier (1850-7) and then, from 1857-9, at 2 Adelaide Place in Bathwick, before moving to Church Street, Widcombe. He died on 28 December 1878 and Caroline moved to South Bersted, Sussex, to live with Harriet Manson, aged forty-nine, another spinster, who had been born in Bombay and whose income came from an EIC pension. Caroline's income was from dividends. Her brother Henry, who rarely corresponded with his sister after he moved to Australia in 1864, wrote that she 'grew up to be a cranky old maid, although rolling in money'.[4] He could see little value in the lives of women who failed to get married. The 1891 census shows Caroline living alone, apart from one servant, in South Hayling, Hants.

Although Caroline's mother had a husband, she lived most of her life as a spinster. We have already seen that in 1851 she was living as a lodger in someone else's home. This pattern continued for the next thirty years. The Somerton home she lived in from 1861-1871 was that of Clement Edkins, a surgeon.[5] She was still in Somerton in 1881 but this time in the home of another surgeon, Edmund Valentine, aged forty-six.[6] She is listed as a 'widower'. She died on 1 January 1883, leaving £228, around £10,000 in today's values.

Captain William Hewitt had placed his daughter Caroline in the Clifton young ladies' school. The school he chose for son Henry is even more characteristic of his outlook. Bruce Castle School in London was an off-shoot of Hazelwood School that was established in 1819 in Edgbaston, Birmingham by Thomas Wright Hill, originally a brassfounder. Its headmaster later was his son Rowland (1795-1879), famous for his sweeping postal reforms, which have tended to eclipse his educational achievements. Hazelwood became a beacon for the new middle class, eager for an education which reflected the industrial and technological society that was emerging and that contrasted with the (mainly) classical curriculum of the public schools. Hazelwood was unique partly because it provided lessons in science. Pupils were surrounded by models of steam-engines, air pumps, electrical machines, and microscopes. A roof-top observatory contained telescopes. Walls were covered with maps, then comparatively rare. Unique also was Hazelwood's atmosphere. Of Thomas Wright Hill his grand-daughter wrote: 'My grandfather inspired his sons and pupils with a longing to acquire knowledge'.[7] Thomas Wright Hill was a close friend and admirer of the Birmingham chemist (and Unitarian) Dr. Joseph Priestley and Hazelwood was driven by his ideas on education.

All the serious journals of the day were united in praise of Hazelwood in the 1820s. Its fame, 'known and revered throughout the world',[8] could easily have reached William Hewitt even in India because James Silk Buckingham, a notable writer and reformer, wrote a long article about it in his *Oriental and Colonial Review* in 1824. In every respect Hazelwood was radical and before its time, but nevertheless continued to attract Tory and Anglican parents. Hey called it 'the most remarkable experiment in secondary education that Great Britain had ever seen'.

Hazelwood's success was such that a new establishment, the Bruce Castle School in Tottenham, conducted on the same lines as its predecessor, opened in 1827, becoming so popular that Hazelwood closed in 1833. Rowland Hill and his brother Edwin took charge of Bruce Castle while their younger brother Arthur (1798-1885) kept Hazelwood going. When it closed, he too moved to the new school, becoming its headmaster as Rowland's health failed. It was in 1850 that Charles Darwin was anxious to choose the right school for his sons so that they could 'get on'. He was writing on 4 September 1850 to his friend W.D. Fox: 'I cannot endure to think of sending my Boys to waste 7 or 8 years in making miserable Latin verses'. Darwin himself had endured such a curriculum at Shrewsbury School as a boy and wanted for his sons the kind of education available at Arthur Hill's school. His letter continues: 'We have heard some good of Bruce Castle School ... kept by a brother of Rowland Hill of the Post-Office'. Darwin felt nervous at the 'awful experiment to depart from the usual course', i.e. public schools.[9]

Nevertheless he and his wife visited Bruce Castle School to see what it was like on 6 September 1850. It is fascinating to think that Henry

Hewitt was a new pupil in the school as Darwin and his wife were shown round it. He is one of 49 pupils, aged 9-16, listed there in the 1851 census. Arthur Hill (aged 52) is listed as the head of the household, living with his sister-in-law Theodosia Maurice. Countries about to become independent and eager to become democracies knew of Bruce Castle, which explains why some of Henry's fellow pupils came from Peru and Mexico. Others were from the USA, Australia, France and the Philippines. Of the 49 pupils, four had been born in India.

After Bruce Castle, which he left in 1853, Henry spent some time at the Grammar School in Bath, according to Vafeas. Her account of his years in Bath, the sources of which are the diaries he kept from 1860 to 1864, are invaluable not only for the insights it provides into his life and personality, but also for the detailed picture of contemporary social life there shared by the Album characters. A member of his Bath circle was the Album's Lucy Stringer Falkner, who was a sister of Frederick Falkner, cousin of Kilvert's father. Relatives of Lucy were to be the means by which Henry Hewitt was able to emigrate to Australia, as will be explained later. His Album photo could have dated from 1862 when he recorded that he gave his likeness to close friends and family before he left for six months in France, or from 1864 before he left for Australia. He noted that he 'paid Miss Perkins 13/- for 11 of my cartes', which shows how expensive they were (the weekly wage of a local agricultural labourer was about eleven shillings at this time). Only a Joseph Perkins has been identified running a photographer's business in Bath at this time. Brian Smith noted him at 9 Milsom Street (1856-8) and at 12 Bridge Street (1860-74).[10] He took the photos of Kilvert's sisters Thersie and Emily, Col. Cholmeley, Lucy Falkner, and Caroline Hewitt. Miss Perkins may have been Joseph's daughter or sister.

In his Album photo Henry stands very erect, one leg bent across the other, looking not at the camera but sideways as though to a distant future. One hand holds a top hat (characteristically he is the only Album man, apart from William Kilvert, to be photographed with this mark of fashion) while the other rests on a rustic chair similar to the one (in the same studio) in which Emily Kilvert sat for her photo. The image he presents corresponds to the self-portrait he wrote on the back of his 1860 diary: 'A young man of fashion and figure and worth / But of no great pretension to fortune or birth'. His diaries were, in Vafeas's words, 'a daily record of social activities and occasionally work' but were not 'a means of personal expression or self-examination'. They provide 'an outline of a gentlemanly life of ease in the England of the 1860s' and clues to his decision to leave the country to go to work on an Australian sheep-station. The Bath years were for him a period of pleasure-seeking marked by no great urge to get on. 'If 1860 and 1861 were idle years the following three years were idleness perfected,' Vafeas noted.[11] Henry's father's friends were largely military men and Henry associated with their sons and daughters. He might easily have become a soldier himself but it seems it would not have paid enough for him. Furthermore, he was later to show a distaste for army life, although as a young man in Bath he did join the local Volunteers, the corps of amateur riflemen. His father commanded the 17th Somersetshire Company. During 1859-1860, Henry did drill most mornings and evenings.

The Volunteer movement incorporated a number of values for middle-class mid-Victorians such as the Album group. It was a manifestation of the increased leisure time they enjoyed and was praised for promoting physical fitness and manliness. One commentator of the time credited the Volunteers with 'fostering a love of outdoor life that has been utterly wanting among the great middle classes for a century'.[12] The movement acted too as a kind of social cement: although led by gentlemen, it attracted working-class men into the local corps, which had the features of a social club. To be a member was to be both respectable as well as patriotic. Queen Victoria herself regularly attended Volunteer reviews. A later chapter notes the involvement of another Album character in one of the Bath Volunteer companies.

To back her claim that Henry's circle of friends 'operated like an extended family', Vafeas noted that he and his sister Caroline often slept at friends' houses, sometimes with their father. (The circle of Album characters, of which Henry was a part, seems also to have operated as an extended family.) It was rare too when Henry and his family did not eat with friends. Always fond of women, he frequently accompanied various young ladies to social functions. On 9 April 1860, he took a Miss Cameron to a Fancy Dress Ball. Earlier (28 February) he had taken her to 'a jolly little party'. He accompanied Miss Susan Reeves to Watercolour

Exhibitions and to the Royal Academy in London. A diary entry for 31 March 1864 reads: 'Walked with Miss Ellis to Hampton Rocks[13] – down Bathwick Hill home'. (His courting of Miss Ellis was summarised in chapter three.)

Henry's endless social round, late hours (4 a.m., 4.30 a.m., 5 a.m.), love of smoking, which he was going to 'give up' all his life, and unserious attitude to work led Vafeas to observe that 'overwhelmingly his concerns were purely hedonistic'. His father adopted a policy of locking the front door at 10 p.m. unless his son was at a party, His father gave him an allowance of £1 a week but it was never enough and he was always borrowing from friends. He had been set to study law in afternoons with J.J. Falkner, a Bath lawyer. During 1860, he decided to pursue a legal career, following the example of several of his friends. He went to London, living at first with his father in James Street but then went into lodgings. In October 1860, he joined the law firm of Pilgrim and Phillips but was half-hearted about his studies. His diary entries sometimes record: 'Cut the office'. He did have some serious interests. He read Dickens, Trollope, and Bulwer Lytton, went to lectures on 'Electrobiology' and 'Electromagnetism', collected fossils and dried ferns. However, he gave himself up, as he had in Bath, to the social round. 'Henry "did" everything, including the Strand, various ladies ("did Miss Hamilton"), a different church every Sunday, even hospitals; "did the Middlesex hospital".'[14] On 30 October 1860, he recorded that he and a friend 'did Stone's Rooms, Olympic, Cyder Cellars, Evans, Piccadilly Saloon, Haymarket. Home at 6'.[15] On 24 January 1861, he noted: 'Went out with South and got *beastly drunk*' (his emphasis). He liked company and friends often slept at his lodgings. 'Henry was developing into a "problem son" and a poor relation with no prospects'.[16] He returned to Bath for an Easter break in April 1861 and at the time of the 1861 census was lodging in the Bradford-on-Avon home of Edward C. Eversley (57), who had been born in the West Indies and was a retired army officer, perhaps a friend of Henry's father.[17] Henry's occupation is given as 'solicitor's clerk'.

He was tiring of life as a solicitor's clerk. Back in London on 15 April 1861, he noted in his diary: 'Office again – idle as ever'. On 3 May, his articles expired.[18] Two days later, his father called to see Mr Phillips, who might have found it hard to give Henry a good report. On 18 November he himself told Phillips he had decided to give up law. From here on, he continued to drift. He and his friend Sheean went sailing in a yacht off the Pembrokeshire coast and went over to Ireland. From October 1862 to May 1863 he, his father and Caroline went to Hyères in the South of France, a centre for English tourists, where the social round continued; called in to Paris on the return and 'did' all the sights. He studied book-keeping in a semi-idle gentlemanly way in London in February 1864. He now began to relish an adventurous life in the Colonies and took to noting when friends departed for or returned from foreign places. On the cover of his 1864 diary are notes on average sailing times to Australia: 97 days, though some ships had done it in 65 days.

He had sounded out in 1863 a contact in Australia with a view to emigration. The Bettingtons were family friends in Bath and Henry had written to James Brindley Bettington, his senior by two years, stating that he wanted to acquire 'colonial experience' at Brindley Park, a large estate in Hunter Valley, New South Wales. James Brindley Bettington (senior) was also a wealthy Sydney merchant. Henry's family were acquainted with the great aunt of James (junior) in Bath. Lucy Stringer Falkner's sister, Sarah, had married John Bettington in 1841. James Bettington welcomed Henry's proposal and he booked his passage on 15 November 1864 on the *Granite City*. On 3 December, he sailed. Vafeas considered his departure 'puzzling' because he neither saw his mother prior to it nor was seen off by his father and sister Caroline, although they often visited London. William Hewitt may have been hurt by his son's failure in his law career and disapproved of his colonial foray. Vafeas thought that Bruce Castle School 'had probably fostered in Henry a positive attitude to emigration'. Henry himself noted in 1899 that Sir Rowland Hill, brother of Arthur, the School's headmaster, used to come to the school at weekends. Sir Rowland helped to found in 1833 an association for colonising south Australia.[19]

Lucy Falkner was descended from the Falkners who had come to Bath in the late eighteenth century with Kilvert's grandfather from Shropshire. Her father, Francis Henry, had married in 1807 Sarah Stringer of Astbury Hall, and Lucy (born 1827) was the sixth of their seven daughters. Originally involved in a Bath wine business, Francis was later a partner in the banking house of Falkner and Falkner. The family lived in Lyncombe, adjacent to Widcombe where William Hewitt lived at different times. Lucy's life, which can be traced through census records, epitomises the plight of the unmarried woman of the time. She had to witness the marriage of each of her sisters in turn. When she was fourteen in 1841, she was at home with two of her brothers and two of her sisters. In 1851, only one sister remained at home with Lucy. Lucy was living in 1861, when she was thirty-three, with her unmarried brother Frederick, her sister Catherine and her husband the Rev. Joseph Beckett and their child Rose. By 1871, Lucy's mother and father had died and Frederick was head of the household; the only other occupants were Catherine and Rose, a cook and a parlour maid. The source of Lucy's income at this time is given as 'Colonial Grants'. She herself was head of the household at the time of the 1881 census, when she was living, still with Catherine and Rose, at 2 Park Lane, adjoining Royal Victoria Park, in the Walcot parish of Bath. In 1891 her situation was the same. Catherine had died by 1901 and Lucy lived with her unmarried niece Rose. Lucy died in Bath in spring 1917 aged ninety. Her Album photo, which seems to date from the late 1860s, shows her full face to the camera, one hand resting on a chair back, a curtain behind her, a black lace shawl over her full-skirted dress.

Henry's position as an emigrant had parallels, according to Vafeas, with characters in colonial literature – useless gentlemen who, having failed in England, can find no occupation or purpose in life – and she contrasted life in India with life in Australia: 'Service in India for the British Raj was respectable and secure; Australia was for convicts and failures'. She believed that Henry would have taken a more positive view of his position, that 'he fitted the romantic literary image of impoverished gentleman emigrating to seek his fortune'.[20] On arrival in Sydney in March 1865, he spent the first week in the home of John Blaxland, whose wife Ellen was another sister of Lucy Stringer Falkner of the Album.[21] The Blaxland and Bettington sheep-stations were adjoining and after sojourn at the former, Henry moved to the latter – Brindley Park – to begin his apprenticeship on the land. In the Australian Arcadia, everyone was supposed to be equal but the Blaxlands and Bettingtons and other Hunter Valley families saw themselves as aristocrats in a society that duplicated the class structure of the English countryside. It is likely that Henry saw himself as leading a leisurely life on a country estate.

While in Bath, he had courted his cousin Leila Cotgrave and wrote her a letter on 18 February 1866 saying that of all letters from England he liked hers best, adding that his sister Caroline wrote him 'much nicer letters now' than when he first arrived in the Colony. (Vafeas's detailed account of his life gives little evidence of correspondence between brother and sister. Caroline may have been disappointed at Henry's failure so far to get on.) After reassuring Leila that he had 'no whiskers' (he has moustache and beard in his photograph), he thanked her for the letter she had sent him from her brother Tom, a soldier in India. It was suspected that, like characters in *The Dilemma*, he had taken to drinking heavily and Henry reassured Leila that the hot climate of India may have caused drink to have had a greater than normal effect upon him. Drink was, he added, 'the besetting sin' of Australian life. The idea was prevalent in New South Wales, although not as hot as India, that heat could undermine the morality and the health of settlers.

Henry stayed at Brindley Park, presumably as a store-keeper, until 6 February 1867 when he relocated for a year to a cattle-station at Condobolin, three hundred miles away. Here he spent time rounding up cattle, branding calves, surveying land, and driving cattle to other stations. His life as a cowboy in the rough, primitive society of the outback was a long way from Bath's fashionable extended-family circle. The diaries he kept from 1869-71 are increasingly taken up with work, unlike his earlier records of socialising. He had settled down too in another important way, having married Minnie (Maria) Hallen, daughter of an architect (and related to the Bettingtons), on 16 December 1869, after his return to Brindley Park the year before. He made clear in a long poem that his view of a wife was that she should be the docile, self-sacrificing 'Angel in the House' of Coventry Patmore's popular poem (1854-1862). Their home was a rudimentary wooden cottage, extended by Henry's own hands. A daughter (Leila) was born on 10 October 1870 and a son (Henry Vigors) in 1872. Henry became a magistrate that year. However, tragedy struck on 27 August 1873 when Minnie died after giving birth to another daughter (Minnie); Henry was now a widower with three young children.

Henry was lonely after Minnie's death and wanted someone to look after him and his children. In 1875, he married Mary Simmons, a well-educated Evangelical woman who had gone to Australia (not seeking a husband) as a governess. She was twenty-five to his thirty-six. He loved poetry;[22] she disapproved of it as light and frivolous. He was fond of drink; she disapproved of that too. Vafeas speculated that she probably thought of 'reforming' him. 'Henry's decision to marry Mary was a watershed in his life. It was a double betrayal of class and Empire'.[23] It was a betrayal of the former because Mary was a farmer's daughter, with no connections and no money; local gentry disapproved of the marriage. It was a betrayal of the latter because Australia was a colony of Empire where notions of caste had to be upheld. Henry's father was so outraged by the marriage that when Mary wrote to him, he returned her letter with a note saying: 'I do not wish to hear from you; I wish to hear from my son'. Vafeas saw the marriage as typical of Henry. He had no 'great ambition or vision; a life of gentlemanly ease was his desideratum'. His marrying a farmer's daughter was attributable in part to the influence of Australia's democratic outlook.

Nevertheless, Henry was still very much the traditional English gentleman, a fact that Vafeas underlined when his (and Mary's) infant son Roger was accidentally drowned aged twenty months: 'Henry habitually kept his deep feelings to himself ... those who show lack of restraint ... reveal their lack of "British breeding". The military tradition, the tradition of the British Empire and the Raj had shaped Henry for life'.[24] His stance towards the Boer War was also the product of his Empire background. Even after living for thirty-five years in Australia, he still spoke of the English imperial cause in South Africa as 'ours', although at the same time he showed the aversion to military life he had had from his youth. He urged his son Will not to volunteer and became very cynical about the British campaign against the Boers: 'He knew from listening to his father's and uncle's experiences in India that British imperialism meant suppressing natives'.[25] (Nevertheless, one of his grand-daughters remembered him as 'a pukka sahib'.)

One who cherished the 'Angel in the House' ideal of women was not going to be sympathetic to the movement for women's suffrage. When agitation for it began in Australia, he saw it as evidence of a world turned upside-down. He readily settled into old age even when not old in years.

In 1912, he was writing 'I feel myself utterly useless, and worn out ...' His (and Mary's) son Tom was killed on the Somme on 29 July 1916. In the War's aftermath Henry was depressed and resigned. He didn't idealise his son as 'a glorious Anzac; he thought of him as a soldier who had died fighting for the British'.[26] His feelings about Australia were always ambivalent. The country had disappointed him, but his children were Australians; he, however, was still an Englishman in his heart. In 1922, he renewed correspondence with Caroline, his sister. He died, aged ninety-two, in 1931, and his last thoughts were of Somerset. He had returned there in 1884, during which time he went on a cruise to Norway with his cousin Leila (née Cotgrave).[27] His last thoughts must have embraced memories of some Album characters, a link reinforced by the inclusion in Vafeas's book (opposite p.6) of his Album photo taken by Miss Perkins of Bath. Of his (and Mary Simmons's) decision to leave England, Vafeas wrote: 'they shared a restlessness, and the courage ... to cut oneself loose from all that is familiar, known and secure, to embark on a long and dangerous journey and, on arrival in the distant land, to begin anew'.[28]

Henry Hewitt as a young man enjoyed a carefree existence in the fashionable Bath society of the early 1860s but never completely fitted in there and began to drift. He did not choose India as an arena for such talents as he had and, after contemplating the army as a career for a while, rejected the world of the military families by which he was surrounded in Bath. The home of Henry, Caroline and their father in the late 1850s / early 1860s was 2 Adelaide Place, which lies directly behind Darlington Street, Bathwick, where the mother and sister of William Macrone lived from 1854 until 1881. William Hewitt and William Macrone would have been able to reminisce about experiences in India. Henry mixed in his youth with the children of Anglo-Indian families, one of whom was that of Colonel Hogg. He was the son of Sir James Hogg, Administrator-General of Bengal and Chairman of the EIC. Colonel Hogg retired from the army and became Conservative M.P. for Bath in 1865.[29]

Steeped in army society and traditions as William Hewitt was, he nevertheless showed some capacity to envisage other careers for Henry by sending him to the progressive Hazelwood School, comparable to Cheltenham College in that it had a modern outlook, reflecting the period's technological society. For his daughter Caroline, William chose inevitably a typical ladies finishing school. Henry eventually sought to get on by emigrating to Australia, identifying himself with useless gentlemen who, having failed in Britain, ended up in the colonies. His life in Australia, as store-keeper and cowboy, and his marriage, were disappointments to his father and sister. Sociable and easy-going, he was probably a likeable character, though in some ways a black sheep of his family – and of the extended family of the Album, most of whose members would not have considered his Australian career as an acceptable form of getting on.

CHAPTER EIGHT

Album characters and the Indian Mutiny

Neither Henry Hewitt nor his sister Caroline witnessed the cataclysmic event that reverberated throughout its British history – the Indian Mutiny. The event reverberated throughout the middle and late Victorian period in Britain. It would have reverberated throughout the lives of the Album characters, several of whom were actually involved in it. The name of a Hewitt relative of Henry and Caroline would be forever associated with its beginning on 10 May 1857 at Meerut, forty miles north-east of Delhi.

Lieutenant-General William Henry Hewitt, uncle of Henry and Caroline, with over fifty years' army service behind him, was aged seventy and in poor health (Ward, who referred to him as 'Bloody Bill', noted his 'obese and arteriosclerotic' condition) when he commanded a force of Native and British troops at Meerut in 1857. The numbers of the two units were finely balanced – about 2,000 of each. Towards the end of April, eighty-five sepoys had refused to use the cartridges for the new Enfield rifle because it was rumoured that they were coated in beef or pork fat. To Hindus, to whom cows were sacred, they were a threat to their caste status, to Moslems, who adjured pork, they undermined their religious status. Sepoys needed to bite off the fat-impregnated paper surrounding the cartridges before inserting them into their rifles. The issue of the cartridges was the Mutiny's immediate, though not sole cause.

A full review of its causes cannot be undertaken here. However, some of the findings of Dr. Surendra Nath Sen, who devoted the first forty pages of his book to causes, may be given. One of the ways in which 'the Englishman did much to alienate the Indians' was the 'systematic exclusion of the natives from official employment of a superior character'.[1]

Another was the treatment of sepoys. They were paid only a pittance, far less than their British counterparts. NCOs often cursed and struck them. Officers regarded them as 'inferior creatures', according to one anonymous British commentator, who went on: 'The sepoy is sworn at. He is treated roughly. He is spoken of as a "nigger" or pig'.[2] Young officers in particular 'fresh from school, often called natives "niggers".'[3] An educated Indian loyal to the British thought that the hauteur of European officers caused a rift between them and their native subordinates. A British officer, Lieut. Shannon, observed: 'I think that a cause of the mutiny may be that in every British mind in India contempt for the natives is deeply rooted'.[4] The Englishman, I.T. Prichard, summed up the situation in a book written after the Mutiny: 'The population of this country had no love for us. It would have been strange if they had. What did they owe to us? Nothing.'[5]

Some Indian scholars have viewed the Mutiny as the First War of Independence, though it is doubtful whether a nationalist movement existed in 1857. The Mutiny was not nationwide but limited mainly to Bengal. Chesney noted in *The Dilemma* that the Bengal army had lacked discipline for a long time. Fraternisation between British officers and sepoys declined over a long period and the former began to lose confidence in the latter. Joseph Sramek noted a growing distrust of sepoy regiments from the 1830s onwards. The reasons for this were concerned with 'shifting British interpretations of caste away from class towards race and eventually religion.' Protestant missionaries increasingly came to interpret caste more as a matter of religion than a marker of social or racial status.[6]

Minor cases of insubordination in the weeks before 10 May 1857 should have alerted the British to the threat of mutiny. General Hewitt was oblivious to this threat. Eighty-five Meerut sepoys were found guilty at a court-martial of refusing to use the new cartridges and were sentenced to ten years' imprisonment with hard labour, a very severe sentence. They were paraded chained before their comrades, causing further antagonism. Hewitt, who had hoped the men might be executed, rejected pleas for mercy. When their comrades went on the rampage, the General was slow to react, issuing no orders to his strong force of British troops to attack the mutineers. The latter stormed the jail, releasing the sentenced men. Some British officers, and their wives and children were killed. Hewitt could, and should, have made efforts to prevent the mutineers from marching off to Delhi but didn't. After the Meerut affair, the first outbreak triggering the Mutiny that followed, he was relieved of command and came home in disgrace, dying in Bath at Westfield House on 16 April 1863.

Kilvert was sixteen when the Mutiny broke out and newspapers and magazines of the day brought the shock and horrors of it into every home in the land. One of his contemporaries at uncle Francis Kilvert's school on Bathwick Hill recalled its being discussed along with other disturbing events. When the diarist was given an account by his Langley Burrell parishioner John Gough of arriving with his regiment in Cawnpore forty-eight hours after the massacre there, he would not have been hearing of its horrors for the first time. The very fact that he felt compelled on 22 January 1873, sixteen years after the event, to incorporate Gough's account into his diary indicates both that it still haunted his memory and still seemed of some relevance. The Mutiny of 1857 was the first in which large numbers of white women and children were killed. Inevitably part of Kilvert's anxiety over the situation of his sister Emily and her family in India would have derived from memories of the Cawnpore massacre, which had happened only eight years before she and Sam Wyndowe had gone out to India for the first time. Hearing Gough's account would have revived Kilvert's fears about her family.

The Victorian mind and memory had been seared by the massacre of women and children at Cawnpore. Gough explained why:

> He said the scene was horrible, so horrible, shocking and disgusting that it could not be explained or described. Women's breasts had been chopped and sliced off and were still lying about with their other parts which had been cut out. Women were cut to pieces and mutilated in a vile and shocking manner. The most devilish and beastly ingenuity had been at work in mutilating the persons and violating and dishonouring the parts of the poor creatures. A child's head had been cut off and was lying on the ground with the lips placed by a devilish jest as if sucking the breast of a woman which had also been chopped off.

Alison Blunt emphasised that the savagery and horror of the Mutiny 'came to be embodied in the fate of British women' through newspaper accounts, pictures in journals, and parliamentary debates.[7] It is noticeable that in Kilvert's diary entry based on Gough's account, the massacre is referred to with a capital 'M', as though in his mind it ranked in importance with the Mutiny itself. His awareness of it would have been shaped by the *Illustrated London News* (*ILN*) that was regularly read in the Kilvert home. Emily Kilvert told how she remembered the pictures in it of the Duke of Wellington's funeral.[8] In her examination of the responses of the contemporary press to the Cawnpore women, Blunt noted that the *ILN* painted 'a ghastly picture of rapine, murder, and loathsome cruelty worse than death'. The *Times* dwelt upon images of British women raped and dragged naked through the streets. *Blackwood's Magazine* wrote of 'outrages on women and children' and of 'devilish and cruel atrocities'. The *ILN* asked how, in the light of the atrocities committed, those who called for mercy for mutineers could justify their claim. *Punch* (12 September 1857) had a satirical poem, 'Pity the Poor Sepoys', on this theme:

> Oh! be not too hard on the poor mutineers,
>> Though your women and children with torment they slew,
> Though we dare but whisper their deeds in your ears,
>> Don't punish them more than 'tis needful to do.
> Do not hang your black brothers – to woman and child
>> Though they did all that devils could ever invent –
> If by means more affectionate, gentle, and mild,
>> You can others deter, and cause them to repent.

Women's journals showed conflicting reactions to the perpetrators of atrocities. *The Englishwoman's Review* called for 'heroic vengeance' whereas *The Lady's Newspaper* recommended mercy on the grounds of racial and cultural differences between British and Indians: 'we are wrong in judging these dusky children of the sun by the same rules that would be just and right with home communities. We are a Christian, they a heathen, nation'. Some of what Kilvert called the 'furious, almost ungovernable' reaction of Gough's comrades resulted from their finding that 'Numbers of the poor women had jumped down the great well with their children to avoid the horrors ... being perpetrated on the bodies of women'. A soldier's account quoted in the *ILN* stated that 'the [women] having been stripped naked, beheaded, were thrown into a well; the [children] having been hurled down alive upon their butchered mothers'.[9] Such accounts made the well notorious at the time, a place of horror; later it was covered and made into a grave for victims.

Andrew Ward drew attention to the sexual element in the Victorian reaction to the Massacre, to 'the effect that the sight of the ladies' naked and mutilated bodies had on even the most hardened British soldiers of nineteenth-century India'. This element is implicit in the *Diary* entry about Cawnpore that was based on the account given to Kilvert by the hardened soldier Gough: the entry dwells on women's breasts and their 'other parts'. Kilvert shows many times in his writing that he too entertained what Ward called 'Arthurian notions of the inherent purity and virtuousness of English womanhood'. The 'paramount mission' of Anglo-Indian men was to keep their women safe; events at Cawnpore meant that they had signally failed, and their savage response was driven, not only by 'grief and outrage', but also by 'humiliation and guilt'. As Kilvert listened to Gough's testimony of what he saw at Cawnpore, his thoughts would have been on his sister and her children and their vulnerability. 'The image of fair English women in the clutches of dark sensualists trespassed dangerously into untravelled regions of the Victorian imagination'. Kilvert's preoccupation with the extent to which the skin of Emily and that of her children was in danger of turning from fair to dark acquires greater resonance in the light of these understandings. In Ward's view, memories of Cawnpore's slaughtered women and children 'festered in the minds of every Anglo-Indian' ever afterwards.[10]

Stories of the Massacre and of the Mutiny in general had great resonance for Victorians because so many had relatives and friends in India. This was the case with many people known to the Kilverts. Kilvert's uncle Francis had been curate as a young man to the Rev. Harvey Marriott of Claverton; Marriott's father had been an employee of the EIC. Kilvert's father was also a close friend of the Rev. Marriott. Sir Hugh Inglis, father of Sir Robert Inglis, patron of uncle Francis (he had married from the latter's grand Clapham house in 1822), was a Director and three-times Chairman of the EIC. Among *Diary* characters with India links was the Rev. Henry Dew, Vicar of Whitney, one of whose brothers served in India during the Mutiny. Henry Pearson, father of Mrs. Venables, wife of Kilvert's Clyro vicar, had been in the ICS. The Mutiny had brought tragedy into Venables's family. His cousin Rowland wrote to him on Easter Day 1858 telling him that another cousin, Edward, was at Lucknow (scene of a long and bloody siege during the Mutiny) with General Frank's division. Edward hoped to be home by June but his hope was vain because he died of wounds suffered in the fighting.[11] In a letter dated 17 September 1857, the Rev. Venables himself wrote that he hoped 'it is not true that [Nana] Sahib has escaped by committing suicide'.[12] Nana Sahib was leader of the Cawnpore mutineers and he allegedly ordered the killing of the British women and children. Blunt stated that the newspapers of the time represented him 'in dehumanised and often demonic terms',[13] and had the reputation in England of being 'the most bloodthirsty of the rebel leaders'.[14]

Nana Sahib, whose actual name was Dhondu Pant, was born in 1824 and brought up in Cawnpore in the territory of the Indian prince Baji Rao II, by whom he was adopted. Baji Rao died without an heir. Lord Dalhousie, Governor-General of India, had introduced the so-called Doctrine of Lapse, whereby any princely state under EIC influence would automatically be annexed if its ruler died without an heir. Indian tradition held that a prince without an heir could choose a successor. Nana Sahib had expected to succeed Baji Rao when he died in 1851, and would have received from the EIC a pension of £80,000 had he done so. However, the EIC stopped the pension after Baji Rao's death. Nana Sahib was outraged and sent a representative to England in 1853 to plead his case to the British Government. The plea fell on deaf ears.

There is some uncertainty as to whether the Cawnpore massacre was deliberately ordered and, if so, by Nana Sahib, or whether it resulted from the tense and confused conditions prevailing in the region during the fighting. According to Gott, 'there is no evidence that Nana Sahib himself gave orders for this massacre'. It may have occurred in reprisal for stories of atrocities committed by British troops on Indian villagers as they advanced to relieve Cawnpore. Nana Sahib's fate is unknown because he disappeared after the town was recaptured. One story told how he sought refuge in hills in Nepal. Jules Verne's novel *The End of Nana Sahib* (1880) explored stories about his fate.[15] Rumours of sightings of him continued from the 1860s and into the 1890s.

The Mutiny brought good as well as bad fortune to the Venables family. William Venables was given by Lord Canning[16] in perpetuity one of the estates forfeited by a disloyal Indian prince. Its value was £1,000 a year (£40,000 today) or £500 to £800 a year if William lived in England. William wanted very much to leave India because of his health and had applied on the grounds of the service given there by his brother Edward who had died suppressing the Mutiny.[17] True to its tradition, and even in the aftermath of the Mutiny, India could be for some fortunate ones a pot of gold, a boost in their struggle to get on. Edward Lockwood arrived in India just as the Mutiny started but he described his time there as 'the most joyous period of my life', an outlook founded partly on his large salary and on the fact that (in Monier-Wiliams's words) 'Every Englishman in India is regarded as a petty prince'.

No doubt William Venables felt entitled to the Indian prince's estate because of India's betrayal of the Raj. Nevertheless, his entitlement to that estate was considerably less, and much harder to justify, than that of Nana Sahib to the estate of the prince who had adopted him. However, at this time most Britons would have heartily approved of William Venables's good fortune and considered the bad fortune of Nana Sahib no more than he deserved. Post-Mutiny British attitudes towards Indians were extremely harsh. A poem in the 12 September 1857 issue of *Punch* was a strident call for revenge:

> Who pules about mercy? The agonised wail
> Of babies hewn piecemeal yet sickens the air ...
> Our swords come for slaughter: they come in the name
> of Justice ...

Another *Punch* poem (21 November 1857), entitled 'Mercy for Nana Sahib by a humanitarian', mocked pleas for mercy:

> First catch your NANA SAHIB; then, though you
>   may speak your mind to him,
> Oh! pray do not harsh language use, or be at all unkind to him.
> Point out how naughty 'twas of him with cruelty to slaughter
> The mother and her little boy, and helpless infant daughter:
>   But there stop.
> Don't doom your brother Nana Sahib to the drop.

The Rev. Venables was all for dooming Nana Sahib 'to the drop' and was angry that he might have escaped it by committing suicide. Kilvert was similarly deaf to calls for mercy: 'If [the soldiers with Gough] had caught the rebels then no mercy would have been shown to those who showed none'. He took satisfaction in Gough's description of '500 mutineers executed at once, the rank and file shot by musketry, the ringleaders blown from guns'. He described the latter form of execution: their arms tied to wheels of cannon, chests pressed against their muzzles; 'At the discharge the man was blown all to fragments but his arms remained tied to the wheels'.

This dreadful, barbarous punishment, sometimes known as 'cannonading', was not devised specifically to appease British indignation at the Mutiny, but was a threat which 'kept the sepoys in line throughout most of imperial history', as Gott noted. It had been used to deter sepoy mutinies on numerous occasions, the first at Manjee in 1764 when twenty-four ringleaders of a revolt suffered it. The British knew that both Hindus and Muslims had a particular horror of it. Gott quoted an explanation given by William Butler, a missionary at the time of the Mutiny: 'What the sepoys object to was the dishonour done to the body, its integrity being destroyed', so that a proper funeral ceremony could not take place. The punishment was 'the glue of terror that enabled the British to maintain their mercenary armies over such an extended period'.[18]

Such treatment of mutineers was part and parcel of the national demand for revenge in 1857: 'In response [to the Mutiny] the British inflicted terrible reprisals, acts of inhumanity born out of an outrage fuelled by feelings of racial and cultural superiority'.[19] Ferguson wrote 'In churches all over the country, the theme of the Sunday sermon switched from redemption to revenge', and he quoted the *Times*: 'every tree ... should have its burden in the shape of a mutineer's carcass'.[20] The hope was fulfilled: accounts by soldiers sent to suppress the Mutiny are filled with references to bodies, sometimes scores of them, hanging from trees. At Allahabad, British soldiers and civilians exacted revenge on the Indian population, 'killing them regardless of sex or age'. Troops boasted of sparing no-one, of 'peppering away at niggers', an activity they 'enjoyed amazingly'.[21] These troops were commanded by Colonel Neill and they later went on to Cawnpore.

> 'He was the Victorian militant Christian personified, who believed that God had chosen him to take part in suppressing the revolt... Six thousand Indian men, women and children are estimated to have been killed

in and around Allahabad in June, following Neill's arrival'.

They were brutally killed: burnt alive in their villages and mown down by artillery.[22] An *ILN* report for 26 September 1857 told its readers that at Cawnpore Neill made high-caste Brahmins wash and lick blood of victims from the floor while being whipped by British soldiers. 'The wretches, having been subject to this degradation, which includes the loss of caste, are then hanged... The punishment is said to be Colonel Neill's own invention, and its infliction has gained him great credit'.[23] Early accounts made much of British women being raped, which raised even higher the lust for revenge at home, but a British enquiry later disproved the rape charge.

It is easier to understand the lives of Album people against the background of the Mutiny because it impacted, sometimes in highly significant ways, on the lives of many of them. Dr. John's son, William, had gone to India in 1858 with his regiment to suppress it. He would have seen evidence of Indian atrocities and was likely to have participated in some British ones. A main cause of the Mutiny was Indians', and particularly sepoys', fear that the British were intent on supplanting their religions with Christianity, and their native ways with European ways. Some historians see missionaries as 'social disruptives, forcing alien values and spiritual teaching on a resistant population and the sepoy army units'.[24] Missionaries thought they were benefiting Indians by freeing them from superstitions and introducing them to modern civilisation. Dr. John's brother Edward who, as has been noted, suffered a rapid decline in health around the time of the Mutiny and retired soon afterwards, may have been one of these. Although nine years had elapsed since the Mutiny when Frederick Kilvert went to India, memories of it would have been relatively fresh and its psychological and emotional impact still potent. Sam Wyndowe had actually been involved in fighting mutineers and when Emily Kilvert first met him in early 1860, he was home to recuperate from his ordeal. One imagines that talk of the Mutiny took place between them then and on many subsequent occasions as man and wife in India.

It is interesting to note that the Album photos of Sam and Emily are followed by that of Colonel Montague Cholmeley. Does this indicate Anna Maria's awareness that Lieutenant-Colonel Wyndowe and his wife were particular friends of Colonel Cholmeley because of their close involvement with India? In Montague's background are to be found several of the social and professional elements typical of the Album group as a whole. Born on 21 December 1820, he was the third son of a clergyman, the Rev. Robert Cholmeley (1780-1852), Vicar of Wainfleet, Lincs. An older brother of Montague was a solicitor whose son became a tea planter in India. Another brother was a doctor in the EIC and married Joanna, daughter of William Cumin, a Bath doctor. Two other brothers were clergymen.[25]

Montague's military career began with an act of patronage when he was nominated for a commission. He began training in August 1835 (his army record indicates he did not attend Addiscombe College but 'passed public examination' on 12 June 1837 when he became an ensign). He arrived in Madras on 14 December 1837 and joined the 27th Native Infantry. Early in 1838 he was 'examined in the Hindustani language and reported creditable progress'. He became a lieutenant on 19 October 1839 and continued with regimental duties until August 1843. A sign of his potential was that he was appointed adjutant of his regiment in March 1842. (Adjutants served senior officers by communicating orders and handling correspondence.) A regimental report, dated 19 January 1843, stated of him: 'His general conduct and character good, and reported to be steady, intelligent and zealous'. In August 1842, he had attained the appointment which Lieutenant Yorke (in *The Dilemma*) craved: he became a staff officer (at Malacca). To be a staff officer meant that one was attached to the most senior commanding officers as an executive assistant. He was adjutant at Vellore between January and July 1857. During the Mutiny he was attached to the force under the command of Major MacDonnell, 'restoring and maintaining peace in the Chota Nagpore District in 1857, 58 and 59'. Montague was by then a captain (from early 1848). He was awarded a medal for his Mutiny services. He continued as staff officer with his regiment at Vellore from February 1860 until December 1861. He had become a major on 21 July 1861 and was commanding officer of the 27th Regiment from 1861 to 1865. He became lieutenant-colonel in July 1864 and full colonel in June 1868.

One wonders whether, for long-serving officers like Montague, action during the Mutiny, dangerous and disturbing though it was, came as a welcome change from months of repetitive regimental duties and social rounds in barracks. During his long service, he fell victim to 'the cursed East', as Kilvert's diary entry for 28 February 1870 confirms: 'Bad news expected of Montague in India'. *Allen's Indian Mail* had reported on 6 July 1865 that he had been granted eighteen months' leave 'on medical certificate'. His service record, however, notes leaves on medical certificate for five and a half years, only three of which 'were allowed to reckon as service'. His total period of service that could count towards his retirement pension was almost twenty-five years, out of a total of twenty-seven and a half years actually served.[26] He did not survive long back in England, dying aged only fifty-three in 1874.

Montague's connection to the Kilvert family resided in the fact that he had married a niece of Dr. John, as Emily Kilvert recorded. She stated that Adelaide 'married at the age of 22 Captain Montague Cholmeley ... and they went out to India very soon afterwards'. Adelaide (born 1830), called Adele by her father, uncle Francis, was the youngest of his three daughters so her early marriage might have been painful for her sisters. Emily Kilvert naturally tended to locate events involving people who had gone out to India in relation to the Mutiny and this was the case with Adelaide, who 'returned home just before the Mutiny bringing her two children, Adelaide Maria,[28] born 1854, and Montague... After this visit home she went out again when the Mutiny was over'. On her next homecoming (June 1865) she travelled, Emily was pleased to remember, in the same P. and O. steamer as Emily's future husband, Sam Wyndowe, 'who was then coming home on 3 months' privilege leave to be married'.[28] According to Emily, Montague died in Bournemouth.

William Macrone was another Album character who was in India prior to the Mutiny and continued his career there after it. His photo is separated from the other Album Anglo-Indians only by that of Kilvert himself, as though he was seen as a member of that group by Anna Maria Kilvert. He sports the moustache and ample side whiskers of Colonel Cholmeley, leans casually against a chair, legs crossed, one hand in pocket, the other holding a walking stick. William Bordwine Macrone (born 1837) had an EIC background. His maternal grandfather, John

Bordwine (1778-1835), was for twenty-five years Professor of Fortifications at Addiscombe Military College. William was living in 1841 in Croydon with his mother, Elizabeth Adeline (née Bordwine), who had married John Macrone there in 1835. William does not appear in censuses for 1861 and 1871 because he was in India. In 1856, aged 19, he was appointed as an 'Uncovenanted Civil Servant' (like Fred Kilvert) to the Bengal Public Works Department as an Assistant Superintendent, Aligarh Division, Ganges Canal (an irrigation scheme). The building of the Canal had offended Indians, as Ward noted: 'The diversion of the sacred course of Mother Ganges had appalled the Brahmins and displaced and discomfited the native merchants'.[30]

The fact that William's maternal grandfather held such an important position in the EIC would have helped him secure an opening in it, as would the loss of his father, who died the year William was born. The number of orphans entering the service of the EIC was, Bourne stated, 'astonishing'. In addition, 'Between 1810 and 1854, a quarter of the Company's military patronage was distributed to families in which the head of the household was dead'.[31] When the Mutiny broke out, civilians like William had to play their part in suppressing it by joining the District Volunteers, many of which became irregular cavalry units and scoured districts in pursuit of rebels. India Office Records list his Mutiny services: 'Served with the Aligarh District Volunteers throughout [the Mutiny] and was at several petty affairs. Was also at the surprisal [sic] of the outpost of Gulloutee and the occupation of Nauffer, and went out to the relief of the Volunteers at Burroute'. For these services, William was awarded the Indian Mutiny Medal.[32]

For people like William and his wife, India was a different place after the Mutiny. Blunt wrote: 'The "Mutiny" of 1857-8 posed an unprecedented threat to British rule in India and its consequences for imperial rule and the place of British women were far-reaching'.[33] One result was the replacement of the now disgraced EIC by British Crown rule. The *Punch* article of 15 August 1857, 'How to Make an Indian Pickle', listed the ingredients that had produced the Mutiny: allow the EIC to use 'as much corruption as they please', 'throw in ... incompetent judges, cruel tax-gatherers, and overbearing military officers',[34] 'mix the above with native superstitions', and allow 'to quietly ferment for several years without taking any notice of how things are going on'.[35] From 1858 India was ruled through the India Office.

Another result of the Mutiny was growing distance between British rulers and their Indian subjects, deriving largely from the fate of British women during the uprising and made worse by the increase in numbers of those women living in India after 1858. There was now 'a persistent ... tendency among the British to remain as far as possible, culturally, socially, and racially distinct from the Indians they ruled over'.[36] Racialism revived after the Mutiny and Indians were referred to more frequently as 'niggers'. Even though the EIC itself had gone, the old profit-motive remained plus the assumption that the British knew best with regard to Indians, whom they viewed as children. The post-Mutiny reconstruction programme was partial and one-sided. The British stopped short of real change. All that happened was that their power was established more firmly.[37] It is possible to see in Kilvert's very favourable reaction to Jemima, the Indian nurse of the children of his sister Emily, an element of surprise and even of relief. He had found that this 'short elderly woman with a nice good-tempered face' did not seem alien, and certainly not at all threatening, but was just like any English woman of his acquaintance, even though he registered (with some amusement) the startled response of locals to 'the ayah's brown face, nose ring, bangles and shawl'. In immediately warming to her, he was resisting racial feelings in himself. The Mutiny was another evil thing that had come from 'the cursed East' where she too originated, but he could see her simply as another human being.

The British liked to think that their policy of 'improving' India included providing practical things like railways, a telegraph system, and a better justice system. Middleton, the outspoken character in *Oakfield*, had asserted that the British mission should concentrate on building roads, railways, mines, and canals. William Macrone's duties with the Public Works Department, to which he returned after the Mutiny (he became Deputy Superintendent on 20 February 1860), were concerned with irrigation schemes. By 1866, he was Officiating Engineer on the Boolundshuhur branch of the Ganges canal. Such schemes were vital to Indian agriculture but had been neglected by the British. Muckerjee noted the findings in Bengal of the well-known British hydraulic engineer, Sir William Wilcocks, who studied Bengal's ancient irrigation system:

> ... innumerable small rivers ... were originally canals which under the English regime were allowed to escape from their channels and run wild. Formerly these canals distributed the flood waters of the Ganges and provided for proper drainage of the land... Some areas, cut off from the loam-bearing Ganges water, having gradually become sterile ...

The result was recurrent famine in Bengal, once a fertile and prosperous region. The neglect of irrigation schemes affected other areas too. Muckerjee stated that 'as late as 1851-52 less than one per cent of the gross revenue from the three Presidencies of Bengal, Madras and Bombay was spent on "roads, canals, bridges, and other works of public necessity".'[38]

In his branch of public works, William Macrone continued to make progress: he was promoted to Executive Engineer 2nd Grade in October 1866 and to 1st Grade in September 1868, when he transferred to Burma as Assistant Secretary to the Chief Commissioner for British Burma in Rangoon – at the age of thirty-one. There had been a long struggle between Burma and Britain. The latter was made nervous by the former's westward expansion towards Bengal and it declared war on the Burmese Empire in 1824. The British force that captured Rangoon was led by General Campbell, who had commanded troops in the war against Tipu Sultan in 1799. 'To General Campbell plunder was part of soldiering' and his soldiers stole the gold and silver images of the smaller Buddhist temples.[39] However, they paid a high price for their plunder because three thousand of them died from starvation, malaria and dysentery. Burmese soldiers fiercely resisted the British invasion of Burma in 1852, which was ordered by Lord Dalhousie, Governor-General of India. After British victories, the King of Burma was told that Britain was going to annex his province of Pegu adjoining the border with Bengal; Pegu then became a permanent part of the British Empire.

William Macrone's career exemplified how a young man could get on in the East that had been conquered by British power. He retired on a pension in late 1877 when only forty. His Album photo, which shows a man of about forty wearing clothes that belong to the 1870s, could have been taken when he retired from India. He was living as a boarder at a house in Glasgow in 1881. In 1893, he died at Barton, near Cheltenham. He and his wife, Fanny Anne, had two daughters, born at Mynpoorie, West Bengal: Fanny Adeline was born on 6 July 1860; Emily Josephine was born in 1862. Like Emily Kilvert, William was prepared to risk his family to the 'cursed East' and post-Mutiny India.

No doubt William visited Bath while on leave from India to see his mother Elizabeth Adeline, who rented a house there from 1854 living on investment income, presumably a friend of Dr. John Kilvert's family. She was living from that date at 7 Darlington Place, at the bottom of Bathwick Hill about 600 yards from Dr. John's home in Darlington Street. Bath censuses for 1861 and 1871 show her at 7 Darlington Place with two of her unmarried sisters, women who had failed to 'get off'. At that address in 1871 were Elizabeth's grand-daughters, Fanny Adeline (aged 10) and Emily Josephine (aged 9), the daughters of William Macrone. His sister, Josephine, first appears at Darlington Place in the census of 1881 and is listed in ratebooks as occupier (after her mother's death in 1883) until 1892. In the 1891 census she is listed as head of household, unmarried and aged 53, with her brother William and his wife. Her mother and brother dead, Josephine had moved by 1901 to Tyning House, Tyning Road, Widcombe, where she was living alone, apart from two servants. She died on 30 December 1906.

CHAPTER NINE
More Album characters, more photographers

A nother Album family with links to Bath were the Buées. Something of their importance to Dr. John Kilvert's family lies in the fact that no less than four of the former are pictured in the Album: William Urban Buée, Mrs. Buée, Urban Buée, and Katie Buée. Three of the four photos were taken by photographers in Eton and Windsor because the family lived in Slough from 1851. In 1841 William was working in London as a 'surgeon / apothecary', a fact that links him to Dr. John Kilvert and to other surgeons among Album families. He formed a link to Bath in May 1845 when he loaned money to a builder there who proposed to erect nos.12-16 Sydney Buildings, a street running parallel to Darlington Place, home in the early 1850s of William Macrone's mother, only a short distance from Dr. John's.[1]

To understand who and what the Buées were, we need to begin far from Bath on Dominica, one of the Windward Islands in the West Indies, where William's grandfather (also William Urban) was causing a considerable stir by growing cloves. Cloves were an important element in the spice trade, the main objective behind the setting up of the EIC, which was determined to break the almost exclusive spice monopoly maintained by the Dutch until the eighteenth century. The EIC tried to break the monopoly by sending their botanist, Christopher Smith, to the Molucca Islands, known as the Spice Islands (in modern Indonesia), to obtain plants of cloves and nutmeg and by 1802 there were over 6,000 clove plants flourishing in the EIC's spice garden at Penang.[2]

Vast profits were to be made from spices and the French too were bent on growing cloves for themselves and successfully transferred living plants to Cayenne on the South American coast (now French Guiana).

William Urban Buée took specimens from there to Dominica in 1789 and their fruit was as good as any from the East Indies. Dominica, lying between the French islands of Martinique and Guadeloupe, had been settled by the French in 1715 but when the Seven Years' War ended in 1763, it became a British possession. The Buées, originally from Normandy, had settled there sometime in the eighteenth century. In 1797, William wrote a pamphlet on clove cultivation, *A Narrative of the Successful Manner of Cultivation of the Clove in the Island of Dominica*, printed by order of the Privy Council. The year before he had presented a memoir on the subject to the Lords of the Committee of Council for the Affairs of Trade and Plantations. A copy was sent with specimens of William's cloves to the great botanist, Sir Joseph Banks. The former's achievement was noted in leading journals of the time and he became a celebrity. However, his potential trade was ruined by taxes imposed on West Indian spices by 'the jealousy of influential persons who were interested in the trade of the East', i.e. the EIC.[3]

The author of the pamphlet on the growing of cloves in Dominica is sometimes referred to as William Urban Buée and sometimes as Abbé Buée, which introduces another link between the Buée family and Bath. A certain Abbé Adrien – Quentin Buée (1748-1826) was a French priest among a group, mainly of aristocrats and clergymen, who fled from France to England from 1792 onwards to escape the Terror that followed the Revolution (just as Kilvert's aunt Sophia de Chièvre did). Some of these émigrés were intellectuals and were welcomed by their English counterparts. Abbé Buée established himself in Bath and began producing learned papers on mathematical subjects. His *Recherches Mathématiques* was published there by subscription.[4] That Abbé Buée and the William Urban Buée who presented his work on clove growing in 1796/97 were one and the same seems impossible, yet the fact that the former came to live in Bath, a city to which other Buées, descendants of the latter, had links later, is too much of a coincidence. A Mrs. Buée was living in 1833 at 2 Daniel Street, which is off Bathwick Street, only a few hundred yards from Dr. John's. She may have been related to the clove-grower or was the wife of the Rev. W.U. Buée referred to later in this chapter.

We know that William got married in Liverpool on 12 November

1778 to Margaret Penketh, a local woman, and a son, John Penketh, was born on 18 July 1780. He grew up there, went to Cambridge in 1797 where he took a law degree, and became curate of Halsall, near Ormskirk (Lancs.) around 1804. In April 1814 he became Vicar of Cawthorne, a village a few miles west of Barnsley. His eldest son, the William Urban Buée of the Album, was christened there on 14 January 1815. In spring 1845 he married Matilda Theophila May (born 1826), daughter of another surgeon, George Henry May, of Burnham, Bucks. The first child of this marriage was Catherine Matilda (born 1847), the Katie Buée of the Album. Her link to Dr. John Kilvert's family is shown by the fact that at the time of the 1871 census she was living as a visitor at 12 Darlington Street, inhabited then by his widow Marianne and her daughter Eliza, aged 34 and as yet unmarried.

The photographs of the Buée family appear in the Album between that of Lucy Stringer Falkner and Fred and Mrs. Koe; no reason for these juxtapositions suggests itself. Not much can be gathered of the photo of William Buée because it is a vignette: he is in profile, little can be seen of his clothes and the photographer is unknown. The photo of William's son Urban shows a young man in his early twenties, looking pale and frail. He died in fact on 24 July 1873, aged only twenty-three. His mother had been christened Theophila (i.e. lover of God), suggesting that hers was a family of some piety, and she chose to christen her first-born son Urban Theophilus. The photograph of Theopholus was taken in Windsor by Benjamin Charles Paice, originally a clothier. His wife and daughter also worked in his studio at 17 Thames Street. Theopholus's picture appears opposite that of his sister Katie, who is posed, half-face and looking serious, as she leans with both hands on the back of a chair and wearing a dress with a full skirt. She seems in her early twenties so the photo would have been taken around 1870. Even fuller than Katie's skirt is that of Mrs. Buée, who sits, one hand on her knee, the other on an open book on the table, with a curtain behind. A strip of dark-coloured braid demarcates her right sleeve from the white inner sleeve. She faces her husband. She looks about fifty and the photo dates therefore from the early 1870s.

Hills and Saunders of Eton and Oxford took that photo and the one of Katie, probably at the same time. Robert Hills and John Henry Saunders had established their business in 1852 and had studios at different times in various places. The firm still exists in Eton, advertising its longevity and its reputation as 'Photographers of the rich and famous including royalty'. On the back of the pictures of Mrs. Buée and Katie is the claim 'by appointment to Her Majesty'. The firm opened its studio in Eton in 1863; the Buées would naturally favour it with their custom even though it photographed many more famous people. It did CDVs of the geologist Sir Charles Lyell, George Campbell (8th Duke of Argyll), Prince Leopold, Lewis Carroll, Harriet Leveson-Gower (Duchess of Sutherland), the Emperor and Empress of Germany and their children, and Queen Victoria herself. The firm was in constant demand when the Court was in residence at Windsor. Hills and Saunders were appointed official photographers to the Prince of Wales while he was at Oxford (where they had a studio).

The Buée family lived for over fifty years in Slough, Bucks., or more precisely in the Upton-cum-Chalvey part between it and Windsor. Census records picture in brief their life there. In 1851, William, described as 'surgeon and apothecary', was thirty-six and his wife Matilda, who was from the village of Burnham only five miles from Upton, was twenty-nine. With them at Bath Road were the children of the Album – Catherine Matilda, aged four, and Theophilus Urban, aged one – plus Edith, aged two. They employed three servants. On one side of them lived a draper, on the other a military engineer. The address of the family is given in the 1861 census as 'The Cedars' 3 William Street. William's occupation is given in 1861 as 'Medical General Practitioner'. The children born earlier must have been at school or visiting elsewhere because the only children who are recorded at this point were Francis William, aged six, and John Walter, aged seven months. A 'medical assistant' lived in and there were three servants. Francis was away at school in 1871 and now the children at home were Edith, unmarried aged twenty-two, Theophilus Urban, unmarried aged twenty-one (a clerk in the Royal Exchange), John, Henry aged six, Charles Lewis aged five.[5] The Buées' niece Louise was a visitor. In addition there was a medical assistant and one servant. 1881 finds the family still at 'The Cedars' but reduced in numbers: Katie was there, unmarried aged thirty-four, and Kenneth aged eighteen. There was a 'surgeon's assistant', a cook and a housemaid.

William Urban was still practising in 1891 although aged seventy-six;[6] Katie was still at home. By 1901, there were only three Buées at 'The Cedars': Matilda, then seventy-nine and described as 'feeble-minded', Katie and Edith. Within the house was a 'separate household', in which lived a fifty-three-year-old widow 'of independent means', who probably paid rent to Mrs. Buée.

We must assume that Eliza Kilvert and Catherine (Katie) Buée knew each other because their parents knew each other. Dr. John and Marianne Kilvert could have known William Buée from visits he made to Bath in connection with his 1845 investment in 12 Sydney Buildings, built by John Pinch. William had a financial interest in another property near to Dr. John's home – Bathwick Tavern, the rent and profits of which became his when Pinch was forced to put it up for sale in 1851 when he defaulted on repayments of the loan made to him earlier by William. The Tavern was located at 10 Sydney Buildings and was frequented by bargemen on the Kennet and Avon Canal, which lies behind it. Another significant common denominator between Dr. John Kilvert and William Buée was that they both were members of the PMSA.

Katie Buée did not see her friend Eliza get married at the age of thirty-four in St. Mary's Church, Bathwick, just across the road from her home. Katie was ten years younger than Eliza and perhaps hoped to be married herself some day. However, it was not to be and we find that as the years went by she devoted herself to religion. When she was thirty-five, she began holding meetings of believers in a Slough cottage. Three years later in 1885, a Mission Church was built on the site, to be replaced in 1905 by a church, so that Katie had effectively established a new parish.[7] Katie's story is paralleled by that of the only sister of Kilvert's to remain unmarried, Frances Henrietta (1846-1929). At the age of forty-three she entered the Community of St. John the Baptist at Clewer, Windsor, coincidentally (or did they know each other?) only two miles from Katie Buée's home in Slough. The latter died in 1917 at Lea Rectory, Ross-on-Wye, the home of her youngest brother, the Rev. Charles Lewis Buée. Her sister Edith was employed as a (daily) governess in a school at the time of the 1891 census, the fate of many women who failed to get off in Victorian times, just as it was the fate of many others to enter religious communities as Katie had done.

We have already seen that the Buée family, like many Album families, was involved with the Empire through the enterprise of William Buée's clove-growing grandfather. Another Empire connection exists in the person of John Buée, who is referred to in the Cambridge University Alumni entry on William's father, John Penketh Buée: 'John Buée (eldest son of the Rev. W.U. Buée of Bath), Lieut. 15th Native Infantry, died 1838 at Vellore, East Indies'. This John Buée may have been William's brother or a cousin. One of William's own sons continued the family tradition of seeking fame and fortune in remote regions of the Empire: Kenneth Tooke Buée became a doctor like his father but not for him the quiet life of a GP in Slough.[8] Kilvert took a lively interest in colonial wars and on 6 February 1874 he recorded 'good news from Cape Coast Castle' that he had read in newspapers: 'Sir Garnet Wolseley was within a march of Coomassie. The King of Ashantee had ... agreed to pay the £200,000 demanded by Sir Garnet'. The Empire of Ashanti (in modern Ghana) was a powerful, warlike one which was the location of three wars with the British government. Kenneth Buée was involved in the final one, after which the Ashanti were annexed into the Empire while remaining semi-independent.

Kenneth was a doctor in the Gold Coast Medical Service and in December 1900 was with a force of a thousand men sent from Accra to relieve the British Governor besieged in Kumasi by the Ashanti. A report of the battle of Kumasi refers to Dr. Buée, his 'hospital train', and to his being 'busily engaged among wounded soldiers with bottles, lint and bandages endeavouring to extricate bullets'. In the view of the report's author, the battle was a 'duel between savage cunning and civilised organisation'.[9] A memorial tablet in the Holy Trinity (Anglican) Cathedral, Accra, Ghana, records the name of Kenneth Frederick Tooke Buée, Senior Medical Officer, West Africa Medical Service, died Accra, 7 January 1906 after ten years' service.[10] His death was reported in the *Slough, Eton and Windsor Observer* on 13 January 1906.

Aged only forty-three when he died, Kenneth was another, like William Kilvert and Lechmere Thomas, who never came back from the colonies. William Buée did not live to suffer the sadness of Kenneth's death because he had died in 1900, but Mrs. Buée did, dying on 25 July 1908. Kenneth's probate, handled by his brother Henry, shows that he left £904 (worth £50,000 today). There is a parallel between Dr. John Kilvert and William Buée in that they were both GPs and descendants of theirs became doctors. The Buée family is typical of Album families because in it are represented not only the profession of medicine but the other professions in which Album characters were regularly to be found: the Church, the law, and the army.

In compiling her album, Anna Maria must have taken pride in having CDVs of individuals who had achieved success in their professions or other occupations, who could be counted among her family's circle. She would have been able to say to herself: this is who I am, this is what my family is, because we mix with such eminent people. Her album held pictures of five army officers: her brother (Lieutenant William Kilvert), Colonels Wyndowe, Cholmeley, and Vander Meulen, and Captain Bampfylde. There was also a son and a daughter of an army captain (the Hewitts). There were no less than four clergymen. Individuals like her brother Fred and William Macrone had given years of service in the ICS (and Mrs. Middleton was the widow of another such). Other women in the Album were daughters or grand-daughters of army officers, clergymen, doctors, barristers, and bankers. There were businessmen like Henry Lancaster and Anna Maria's brother-in-law, Thomas Parsons. And of special importance, because it reminded her of her father, there were several doctors.

The fact that Anna Maria could include in her album the CDV of a judge must also have given her particular satisfaction. Arundel Rogers was born on 28 February 1825 in Helston, Cornwall. His CDV was taken by Owen Angel of 11 High Street, Exeter. Born in 1821 at Totnes, Devon, Angel had established himself in Exeter in the early 1840s as an engraver and printer. He had become a photographer by 1855, advertising 'daily photographic portraits' in the *Trewman's Exeter Flying Post*. He was at 5 High Street, Exeter, by August 1855 and was advertised then as 'photographer to the Exeter School of Art and the Cornwall Photographic Society'. He liked to maintain a connection with painting because on the back of his CDVs he styled himself 'Artist Photographer'. He also advertised a service whereby portraits could be 'Painted in Oil or Water Colours by Artists of great experience'. The 'Artists' may have been himself or his wife and daughter, who assisted in his studio (just as Miss Perkins helped her father Joseph in his Bath studio). Angel remained in business until 1903. In 1861, he opened his premises at 11 High Street, Exeter.[11]

Rogers looks mid-forties in his CDV so it dates from around 1870. He looks very dignified, Dundreary whiskers very prominent. His pose is designed to bring out his position as a judge: he wears his court wig, gown and cravat and his hands touch what are obviously meant to be law books, one held on his knee, the other held upright on a table. Law and the West Country were continuous elements in Rogers's life. After being articled to his solicitor father, he practised as a solicitor himself in Penzance from 1849 until becoming a student at London's Inner Temple in May 1859, while simultaneously studying at Trinity College, Cambridge. He was called to the Bar on 27 January 1862.

On 23 April 1870, he married Ellen Gwynne, daughter of a barrister, Lawrence Gwynne of Teignmouth, Devon. Arundel was living and working in Chelsea with Ellen in 1871. Their first son, Arundel Gwynne, was born on 2 May 1871 and their second, Arthur Strangeways, was born on 24 January 1873. Arundel senior became a judge on the Western Circuit of County Courts in 1879 and accordingly is to be found in the 1881 census at the Green Dragon Hotel, Hereford. Five barristers were staying with him in the hotel at the same time, plus a Government Inspector of Constabulary. After he retired in 1885, Arundel went to live in Cheltenham, at 21 Lansdown Place with his two sons, who had both become pupils at Cheltenham College in September 1882. We have seen that the College was also chosen for the education of Sam Wyndowe and the Rev. William Smith. Chapter five noted that it was founded on a modern conception of education which took account of science and commerce, as well as favouring merit instead of patronage as the means of getting on. Arundel's elder son went to Peterhouse College, Cambridge, in 1891. He became a lieutenant in the Gloucester Volunteers in 1889. Arundel senior is another Album character who wrote books. He published *The Law and Practice of the Supreme Court of Judicature* in 1875 and followed it in 1876 with a volume showing how much he was a son of Cornwall – *The Law Relating to Mines, Minerals, and Quarries.* Perhaps it was these volumes that he can be seen proudly holding in his CDV. He died in Torquay in 1889.

Another author among Album people, and one of the four clergymen represented, was the Rev. Leveson Russell Hamilton, who published his *Parochial Sermons* (1866), preached at St. Mary's, Bathwick where he was curate from the late 1850s, and *The Lineage of the Sovereigns of England from the Norman Conquest, Designed as a key to the Study of English History* (1868). Hamilton was an Irishman, born in Dublin in 1823, the first son of John Leveson Hamilton, clergyman. His background was obviously Anglican, not Catholic, which meant that he did not raise the problem that Frank Russell, M.D., raised for Dr. John's family, members of which must have listened to his sermons until his early death in 1869.

A clue to Hamilton's background is that in 1841, when he was eighteen, he went to Christ Church, the most aristocratic of Oxford's colleges. Kilvert's Clyro squire, Walter Baskerville, was a student there, as were many sons of the aristocracy and of the landed gentry. Its ethos was that of an exclusive club. Hamilton belonged to what became known as the Protestant Ascendancy, the social, political, and economic group of landowners, Protestant clergy, and members of professions, which dominated Ireland from the seventeenth to the twentieth century. It excluded not only all Catholics (and therefore most of Ireland's population), but members of other, usually lower-class, Protestant denominations. Hamilton's mother was a daughter of the Rev. Richard Woodward, D.D., Rector of Glanworth in County Cork. Hamilton's father's family too came from County Cork. In 1849, Hamilton married Marianne Meade, daughter of Richard John Meade and Frances Arnold,[12] who had married in Torquay in 1817. The Meades were a particularly powerful and prestigious family in the Protestant Ascendancy.[13] One branch of it were Earls of Clanwilliam, Cork; one member of the Ballymartle branch was Dean of Cork in 1736.

Hamilton's father-in-law, a Canon of Wells Cathedral, Somerset, was also vicar of nearby Castle Cary with Hamilton as his curate (from 1845). Prior to Christ Church, Hamilton had been tutored by a clergyman in Abbotsbury, Dorset. The 1841 census shows Hamilton there in company with two other pupils, one of whom was Sir Charles Montgomery. Hamilton was staying in an expensive hotel in Torquay in 1851 with Marianne, his wife, and Catherine, then four months old. Two years later, Marianne was dead, and Hamilton can be found in 1861 as Curate of Bathwick, living with Catherine, aged ten, Thomas Meade, his nephew, aged sixteen (probably his pupil), and Richard Woodward, aged twenty-one, of Hamilton's mother's family. There were three servants, one described as a 'nurse'.

No photographer's name appears on the back of Hamilton's photo but we can date it because it shows Catherine, born 1850, looking about twelve. It was made therefore in the early 1860s. She stands by her father, her hand on one of his, which is holding some small object. It is a domestic shot with a plain background. He sports very bushy side-whiskers. She is in profile, looking dutifully down on what he is holding; she wears a dark dress that complements his dark suit. Her wide skirt is trimmed with flounces and she has her hair in a bun. A powerful but absent presence in this study of father and daughter is a wife and a mother. However, by 1866, Catherine had a stepmother and Hamilton a new wife, Wilhelmina Wilkes, from Teignmouth, Devon, whom he married in that year. Stepmother and daughter were living together in 1881 at the same house, in the village of Charlcombe just outside Bath, that Hamilton and Catherine inhabited in 1861. Then it was recorded as 3 Alma Villas; in 1881, it was known as 'Glanworth', which was the parish in County Cork where Hamilton's mother was raised. The 1881 census return described Wilhelmina as 'Gentlewoman'. Catherine was unmarried and aged thirty. Five servants lived in: cook, groom, lady's maid, parlour maid, and housemaid.

Hamilton liked to have plenty of servants and had probably been used to them during his life. When he died on 14 October 1869, he was a very wealthy man. His probate return located the value of his estate as around the £25,000 mark, getting on for half a million pounds today. Probate was granted to the Rev. Harry Mengden Scarth, who was the Vicar of Bathwick. He hailed from County Durham, where he had won the favour of the first duke of Cleveland, whose patronage secured for him the rectory of Bathwick in 1841. Scarth (1814-1890) was a close friend of Kilvert's uncle Francis, whose obituary sermon he preached in 1863; they were both antiquaries, Scarth being particularly expert on Bath's Roman remains. Scarth was in fact Hamilton's brother-in-law because he had married Elizabeth Sally Hamilton in 1842.[14] Through this connection, Hamilton became Curate of Bathwick. Scarth moved in 1871 into Brompton House, built in 1775 as Rectory for St. Mary's. To the north of it is the church of St. John the Baptist, which was founded by Hamilton in 1862. It is evident that Hamilton was a man of piety and, though a humble curate, was both wealthy and socially eminent, as Anna Maria no doubt knew.

Hamilton's daughter Catherine is one of the few children whose CDVs appear in the Album. Apart from Maggie Lancaster, the only other children are those of Anna Maria's sister Lucy. She married Thomas Cox Parsons, who was, according to Emily Kilvert, Lucy's cousin.[15] The marriage, at St. Mary's, Bathwick took place on 27 December 1862 – a date which some might consider as strange and inconvenient as that chosen for the marriage of Lucy's sister Eliza (see chapter three). This was a wedding ceremony that Marianne *did* attend: she must be the 'Mrs. Kilvert' who was a witness (the 'Mrs' is not clear on the certificate). The other witnesses were Anna Maria and Frances Jane Parsons, Thomas's sister. Interestingly, whatever the degree or starting point of the coolness between Marianne's family and that of Kilvert, the latter's father had been invited to conduct the ceremony. The residence of Thomas, the bridegroom, is given on the certificate as Islington, his occupation as Silk Broker, and that of his father, also Thomas, as 'Merchant'. Census returns give Lisbon or Portugal as the birthplace of Thomas junior.

The 1871 census, which states Thomas's occupation as 'in Silk Broker's Office', shows him in Greenwich with his family of four: Fred (7), John (5), Harold (3), and Lucie (1). These are the children who appear in the Album photo captioned 'L.S.P. Fred and Johnnie' ('L.S.P.' stands for Lucy Susannah Parsons). It seems to have been taken around 1871 and in St. Leonards-on-Sea, where the family was perhaps on holiday. John has been supplied with a suitable holiday prop in the form of a fishing net and bucket. The children have been grouped together at varying heights. Fred looks relaxed as he stands with one arm on the back of the chair in which Harold sits, still wearing a dress, as was the custom with young boys in Victorian times. Lucy, out of focus and indistinct partly because she was in white, sits on the floor. The photographer was Henry Knight, who bought the studio at Regina House, 20 Grand Parade, from John Thorp, owner of a photographic business there from 1862 until 1869. Knight had originally had a studio on the Isle of Wight. He operated at Regina House for almost twenty years. On the back of some of his CDVs he claimed to be photographer to the Crown Prince and Crown Princess of Germany, while on others he stated 'Patronised by Her Majesty the Queen'. At the time when the Parsons were holidaying in St. Leonards, they were living in Greenwich. The 1871 census gives the birthplace of the four children – Frederick, John, Harold, and Lucie – as Blackheath in London. A cook was employed as well as a nurse and housemaid, the former from Melksham, the latter from Yeovil. One of the Parsons' Greenwich neighbours was a manager in a shipbuilding firm (he too was from Somerset) and another was a paper manufacturer.

The photo of Harold Bertram Parsons (the caption reads 'H.B. Parsons') has his age – four years and six months – on the back, so it was taken in 1872/3 by Mrs. Williams of Bath (who also photographed Captain Bampfylde, William Macrone, and Fanny Lawrence). Harold sits on an upholstered bench and had been given to hold what appears to be a whip for whipping a top. The photo of his sister, Lucie Gwendoline (the caption reads 'L.G. Parsons'), was probably taken at the same time since it was by Mrs. Williams and the age of Lucie written on the back – two years nine months – means it was taken in 1872/3. Seated in a padded chair, Lucie has what might be a work basket with frilled top by her side. The ovals in which the images of Harold and Lucie sit have been raised from the page to emphasise them.

Some Album photos of Parsons children were taken while they were on holiday, as is the case with families everywhere. We may assume that pictures of Harold and Lucie were taken when the family were visiting Marianne in Darlington Street. Thus, the photos as a whole commemorated occasions when the children were in specially important, memorable locations. Lucy's children are the only grandchildren of Marianne in the Album. Marianne had other grandchildren: John, son of Fred Kilvert, and Oswald, son of Eliza Kilvert. Inevitably, their absence from the Album takes us back to the strange weddings, with their underlying tensions, of Fred and Eliza, which were examined in chapter three.

The photo of Lucy Parsons herself, one of the earliest in the Album, follows those of Eliza and her husband Frank Russell. An empty space comes next, which probably contained a photo of Thomas Parsons, thus completing the pattern of Eliza and her husband and, following Lucy

('Mrs. T.C. Parsons') and the empty space, Fred and his wife, 'Mrs. Fredk. Kilvert'. In her photo, Lucy stands, her back to a vaguely classical backdrop, leaning with one hand on the back of a chair. Resting there too is the elbow of her other arm, its hand up to her chin in a pose suggesting a pensive mood. Her dress, with full skirt and a bustle, has flounces on it. The photographer was Frederick C. Bird of 38 Milsom Street, Bath, who seems to have been favoured by Dr. John's family because he also took the photos of Eliza and Frank Russell. Bird had a business at 38 Milsom Street from 1864 until late in the century. On the back of one of the Album photos taken by him, he described himself as a 'Photographer and Portrait Painter' as other photographers did. In addition, he featured the crest of the Prince of Wales with its motto 'Ich Dien' ('I Serve'), and 'By Appointment' above, a claim which was genuine. His son, Owen Graystone Bird, continued the business, winning several photography prizes, until well into the 20th century.

There is a second uncaptioned photo of the Parsons children, again taken at a holiday location – Eastbourne – the work of William Hicks. Originally running a studio on the Isle of Wight from 1856 to 1860, Hicks established a studio in Eastbourne in 1864. He called his establishment 'A First-Class Photographic Studio' and charged 10s.6d. for a dozen CDV portraits. The children seem about three years older so it dates from around 1875/6. In 1881, when the Parsons family was living in Blackheath, only three of the children were at home. John was probably away at school. Fred is still listed as a 'scholar' though he was seventeen. Lucy Parsons continued to favour servants from home (it is a pattern evident with other Album characters): her housemaid and nursemaid were both from Somerset. A visitor in the house was Annie Leigh Gwatkin, the thirty-two-year-old unmarried daughter of Theophilus Gwatkin, Anna Maria's husband. Thomas Parsons's occupation is given as 'Merchant (silk broker)'. One of his neighbours was a retired bank manager, another a retired brewer. His address at this time was 39 Burnt Ash Hill, which is only half a mile away from the home of another Album character – Fred Koe. Fred's address from 1876 to 1886 was Clarence House, 19 Belmont Park, Blackheath and from 1886 to 1889 he was at 15 Bennett Park, Blackheath; both addresses are very close to the Parsons' home. Thomas Parsons had retired by 1891 but had changed his address by that time, though it was still in Blackheath. Only Lucie remained at home then, twenty-one and unmarried. Their neighbours were a newspaper proprietor, a retired secretary, and an architect. Lucy died in 1902, her husband in 1907.

Much has been said in this chapter (and chapter four) about Album and other photographers. Photographers too were eager to get on from the moment it became apparent that the new medium of photography was going to revolutionise society and social interchange. In the mini-biographies that have been given of photographers, they can be seen making the transition from being artists who painted portraits to photographic artists who created CDV portraits. We have documented how they set up studios, sometimes carrying on a photographic business of an earlier practitioner, sometimes moving to better premises or premises in better locations, sometimes moving from unfashionable towns to more fashionable ones such as coastal resorts (John Thorp migrated from Hull to St. Leonards) or to spa towns like Bath and Cheltenham where better business opportunities beckoned. For a photographer to be able to claim aristocratic clients which many did, as we have seen, was one way of stealing a march on one's rivals, as was the assertion that one possessed artistic talent and experience. The degree of competition in the new industry is apparent in the sheer numbers of studios springing up everywhere. Bath's fashionable Milsom Street had four studios which took photos of Album people in the 1860-1880 period. However, another dozen operated in Milsom Street in that same period. Furthermore, Turton Smith listed no less than 167 photographers in Bath between the 1850s and 1910. Energy and enterprise characterised the city's photographic business, especially between 1860 and 1880 when Album people were flocking to its studios in the grip of cartomania.

CHAPTER TEN
A man of mind marries a Catholic:
Fred Koe and Mr Koe

The family of Frederick Pemberton Koe displays many of the features that made Dr. John's family distinctive. Members of both were involved in the navy, trade, medicine, the law, the army, the Church, India and various periods of foreign travel. Members of both kept diaries and had books published. The histories of both families illustrate the struggle to get on in the nineteenth century, the importance of patronage in that struggle, and the insecurity of middle-class family fortunes. Both experienced huge setbacks resulting from business failures and bankruptcy.

Fred's story is one of the 'inside stories that frame the pictures [in an album], animating the most stilted of studio portraits with family secrets and subversive tales', in Langford's words. Fred's studio pose replicates that of other male subjects in Album photos:[1] he leans on the back of a chair, full face to the camera, carved plinth and drapes lending dignity to his serious, almost solemn expression, one leg crossed over the other, wearing light-coloured trousers. He looks about fifty so the picture was taken around 1879, by a photographer based in Southampton.[2] The face is more than usually serious and sensitive, with a hint of vulnerability. Langford favoured regarding an album as 'an act of communication', which means 'reactivating a suspended conversation that fills in those gaps by reawakening the actors'.[3] (The 'gaps' she had in mind were those normally filled by the real-life 'presenter' of an album.) The idea of a 'suspended conversation' with reawakened actors seems particularly appropriate to the story that can be told of Fred Koe and Mrs. Koe. The Album picture of the latter is only a vignette so little can be gathered of her clothes. Since she looks about forty and was born in 1839, it was probably taken at the same time as that of her husband. We don't know who took it or where. She wears a severe expression.

Fred's unusual surname was originally Norwegian. His grandfather, born John Kaae in Oslo in 1739, was a merchant who settled in London, became a naturalised Briton in 1767, married an English woman, and changed his name from Kaae to Koe (Kaae is pronounced Koe in Norwegian and means jackdaw). He became bankrupt in 1778 and died in 1785. His younger son, Fred's father, John Herbert Koe, was born in 1783 in Brompton. He and his brother, John Heide Koe (born 1777), were left fatherless and in poverty, as were the Kilvert sons a generation later. Patronage then appeared in the brothers' story, although it is not known how or why. By 1795, John Heide (Heide hereafter) was living at Queen's Square Place, Westminster, acting as secretary to Jeremy Bentham (1748-1832), astute political commentator, advocate of Utilitarianism, and radical reformer, 'the great questioner of all things established'.[4] Heide gave up this position two years later and went to sea on board H.M.S. *Dart*, a sloop designed by Bentham's brother Samuel. Dr. John Kilvert had adopted a similar course when he was young and seeking a career.

Heide was replaced as Bentham's secretary around 1800 by his brother John Herbert (Herbert hereafter). The radical philosopher was so impressed by Herbert's intelligence that he asked Samuel Bentham to give him tickets for lectures at the Royal Institution. 'Jeremy evidently became very attached to the young man and very dependent on him'.[5] Herbert began to study law at Lincoln's Inn in 1804 and became a barrister in 1810. During these years, he continued to live at Bentham's London home. In 1814, the latter became tenant of the magnificent Ford Abbey in Dorset, from which the former was married in August 1815 to Anne Jump, daughter of a naval captain from Devon. A year later, Herbert's first son was born and christened Bentham. Herbert and Anne lived at Queen's Square Place between 1816 and 1818, while Bentham lived at Ford Abbey.

In this period the philosopher was hard at work on his book *Church-of-Englandism and its Catechism Examined*, an attack on the Church's education system, in particular on the schools of the National Society for the Education of the Poor in the Principles of the National Church.

The National Society had been founded in 1811 to promote the teaching of the Church's doctrines, including the Catechism. All teachers in Church schools taught the Catechism to their pupils in the nineteenth century. Thus, Kilvert recorded in his diary in January 1878: 'Gave the upper standards of the school questions on paper on the Catechism'. The words children were asked to repeat and memorise were designed *inter alia* to inculcate subordination at a time when the French Revolution was still fresh in the mind of England's ruling classes. One part of the Catechism required each child to swear 'to submit myself to all my governors, teachers, spiritual pastors and masters; to order myself lowly and reverently to all my betters'. Bentham's book 'contained a scathing clause by clause attack on the Church's Catechism'. In his view, by 'making children learn [it] by heart and thus encouraging false declarations of belief, the Church was purposely instilling habits of insincerity and mendacity'.[6]

Herbert Koe was closely involved in the development of *Church-of-Englandism*, copying out sections of it and supplying Bentham with books and papers needed in its composition. It was read by Bentham's friend Sir Samuel Romilly, law reformer and former Solicitor-General. Bentham wrote to Herbert on 29 September 1817 about Romilly's reaction to it: 'first – it was a sad thing such a book could never be published: then it was most admirable: and last that he never had been so much captivated with any thing he had ever read in his life'.[7] However, Romilly found that there were so many 'dangerous passages' in it that he advised against publication because it would result in Bentham's prosecution and conviction. He regretted this as the work proved that 'Church-of-Englandism was wholly different from true Christianity'. Herbert helped to seek out a publisher for the book and it appeared in 1818.

While working on it, Bentham had invested heavily in a Devon marble quarry and a cement business, in which Heide was a partner. When these businesses failed, Heide became bankrupt and Bentham lost £8,000. In spite of his loss, Bentham was prepared to make Herbert an allowance of £100 per year for life when the latter moved from Queen's Square Place in September 1818 to set up his own home. However, the allowance was stopped a year later because Bentham believed that Herbert had been neglecting his (Bentham's) affairs and could now be independent.

During the years that Herbert and Anne lived at various fashionable addresses in central London, seventeen children were born to them, although two died in infancy. Their eldest son, Bentham, a barrister like his father, died in 1842 aged twenty-six at the start of a promising career. India had already claimed in 1840 the life of their second son, a surgeon in the Indian army, in the Khyber Pass. Another of Fred's brothers Stephen went out to India in 1857, arriving just as the Mutiny began in Bengal. He worked on the Madras railway system. He paid a visit in 1859 to his youngest sister Julia, who had married and settled in Bombay. Also in 1859, he went to Bangalore to meet Fred, who by then was on a world tour (more will be said about this later). Stephen later became a manager of Bowling Iron Works in Bradford. Another of Fred's brothers, Robert Louis, became a clergyman in 1844.[8]

Fred, born on 15 January 1829, twelfth child of Herbert and Anne, was raised in an educated, sophisticated and energetic family, which displayed various talents and whose sons pursued various professions. Wendy Koe, the historian of the family, noted that 'The younger children were sent to France in batches to learn French'.[9] Anne, Fred's mother, was

> ... pretty with enormous blue eyes and was extremely clever and witty. She wrote large numbers of books for children, but unfortunately only one of these appears to have survived titled *Lives of Learned and Eminent Men taken from authentic sources adapted for the Use of Children of Four Years Old and Upwards in two volumes*.[10]

This work seems to be characteristic of the Koe family, whose sons were raised – *from the age of four* – to emulate 'Learned and Eminent Men'.

Fred's own career is an illustration of his family ethos. He was sent away to boarding school around the age of eight, first in company with his twin brother Ralph Pemberton Koe to a school in Putney, then to the College School, Gloucester[11] (again with Ralph), where their brother Stephen was already a pupil. When Fred left this school at the age of twelve in 1841, he had already won a scholarship to Pembroke College, Oxford. He received private education before beginning his maths degree at the College in 1845 aged sixteen; he graduated in 1849 while still only twenty. He was obviously extremely clever.

For some time afterwards he tutored the sons of Mr. J.T. Macaulay of Bayswater and of Lord Carrington. In 1852 he was ordained and obtained a curacy at St. Martin-in-the-Fields. Teaching was, however, the career that interested him most. His career was interrupted in 1858 when his brother Frank came home on sick leave from Gibraltar, ill with yellow fever contracted in Antigua. He and Fred toured the Mediterranean in the hope that the former's health might be restored. On a steamer bound for Naples, Fred met Jane Bethell, the Mrs. Koe of the album. Frank had become weaker, died off Messina, and was buried in Naples.

> No doubt Jane was a comfort to [Fred] in his sorrow. He fell deeply in love with her, but on his return his family and friends were horrified at the very idea of a Church of England clergyman even considering the idea of marrying a Roman Catholic ... a tutorship was found for him to take a young man named Charles Simpson on a two-year world tour[12] – thus hopefully to remove him from the charms of Jane ...[13]

The extreme hostility to Catholics referred to in connection with the marriage of Eliza Kilvert and Dr. Frank Russell, where it was a submerged element, was very much on the surface in the case of Fred and Jane. Fred returned via America, arriving in Liverpool on 7 January 1862. While he had been away, his father had died and his mother was ill and living in Kingston-on-Thames with two of his sisters.

We are very fortunate to have insight into the character and mind of Fred Koe, as he journeyed round the world at this time of crisis in his life, from Dr. Robert M. Cutler's *A Rediscovered Source on Bakunin in 1861: the Diary of F.P. Koe*. In his introduction, Cutler explained that on 17 September 1861 Mikhail Bakunin (1814-1876), the Russian revolutionary, 'having escaped from Siberian exile, left the port of Yokohama on the American ship *Carrington* for San Francisco'. A fellow passenger was Fred Koe, who was 'chaperoning a young boy Charles Simpson on a round-the-world tour'. To Cutler, Fred's diary was of value in relation to Bakunin's 'person and activity in three particular respects'. First, the diary gives Fred's impressions of the revolutionary. Second, it provides Bakunin's views of the relations between Fred and Jane Bethell. Third, we learn from Fred of Bakunin's current political views and plans. The value of the diary for this study of the Kilvert Album is that we learn about

Fred's feelings for Jane Bethell and the dilemma she presented him with, as well as his own political views at the time. We learn too what kind of issues occupied Fred's mind when he was thirty-two years old in 1861, the year when Anna Maria Kilvert began to compile her album.

The Bakunin that Fred met on the *Carrington* was forty-seven and large in girth, voice, beard and personality. The 18 September 1861 entry in Fred's diary, a lengthy one summarising the history of Bakunin's political activities in Europe, begins: 'The greatest passenger we have on board is a Man named Bakunin'. The account tells that in 1849 Bakunin was a member of the Provisional Government in Dresden, then spent eight and a half years 'in a dungeon' and the last four in Irkutsk (Siberia) in exile.[15] 'He has just made his escape and is now on his way to London to meet his wife who is gone home through Russia'. Fred noted that Bakunin was the eldest son of a noble family, had spent time in the army 'but left it having ... led a most dissipated life'.

Fred enjoyed Bakunin's company because 'We have much talk on various subjects', and his next comment about the revolutionary is very revealing about Fred himself: 'He is a man of mind and interests me much'.[16] It is also revealing that the greater part of their conversation was in French so it seems that Fred had benefited, along with his siblings, from being sent to France when they were young 'in batches' to learn the language. One of the things that interested the two men was what Fred called 'the subject of that second or inner self-world or life. It is in this sphere only that friendships are made'. Fred found to his delight that Bakunin had developed ideas on this subject which corresponded 'to what I had so often thought. I used to want always to get at that inner self of everyone I met'. One wonders whether Fred found others in the extended family of the Album who shared his ideas, as the Russian revolutionary did, about this inner self which could give rise to true friendships. Fred, however, was conscious that 'many people doubt if they have it, or if others have it' – a hint perhaps that he had been disappointed in the past when he had risked opening up his inner self to others.

Little details about conditions on board the *Carrington* suggest the intimacy, physical as well as emotional / spiritual, into which Fred and Bakunin had entered. On 1 October, Fred noted in his diary: 'I remained on deck about 2 hours and then could get no sleep. Bakunin and I however had our bath. Nothing but potatoes and bacon and ham could be cooked'. On 10 October, Bakunin sang some Russian songs. 'Some of them were melancholy or rather plaintive', Fred noted, and they reminded him of Neapolitan airs.

The intimacy which the two travellers shared embraced issues of love and marriage. For some reason Fred 'had to take care of Miss Hepburn', a fellow passenger. It was, he said, 'a duty I liked much. It is to me a great pleasure to look after women. It takes me back home and I fancy I am with the girl [Jane Bethell] again'. 'During the long trip,' wrote Cutler, 'Koe retained an affection for her but had become somewhat ambivalent about marriage'. Even though Miss Hepburn had reminded him of Jane at home, 'he nevertheless mentions his own opposition to marrying her'. Cutler continued: 'Responding to this, Bakunin, with whom Koe has "much talk" about Jane, contends that such opposition "proceeds from pride".' One of Fred's diary entries recorded that Bakunin had stated, on the question of Protestants marrying Catholics, that his own wife 'is a Catholic but under gentle treatment she begins to think that she is becoming Protestant'. The meaning or purpose of this remark, according to Cutler, is that 'Bakunin was trying to encourage Koe not to give up the hope of happiness with Jane Bethell'.

Bakunin was famous for his passion for liberty and equality. Nineteenth-century societies were made up, he believed, of two classes – an oppressing class and an oppressed class. He rejected all privilege in society, declaring it is 'the peculiarity of privilege to kill the intellect and the heart of man'. Inevitably, one of the political questions he discussed with Fred was the emancipation of the serfs in Russia. Fred wrote a diary entry for 8 December 1861 on this subject, by which time he was meeting with Bakunin in New York, and the U.S.A. was in ferment over the issue of slavery and the threat of civil war:

> We had a long chat about all kinds of things. He tells me that one suggestion has been made with reference to the extinction of slavery and that is to raise the position of slaves to that of serfs... This would of course be only a step but it would be a great one.[17]

Further evidence confirming Fred's interest in and knowledge of 'all kinds of things' exists in his diary entry for 7 December: 'Bakunin came here in the morning and gave us letters for Boston which I hope I shall be able to use, Agassiz, Longfellow and one or two others'. The letters in question were letters of introduction to Louis Agassiz, famous at this time as naturalist and geologist (an expert on glaciers), and to Henry Wadsworth Longfellow, the American poet and intellectual.

Bakunin had been able to journey as far as New York through the generosity of Fred Koe. In his diary on 10 October, the latter wrote: 'I find I shall have to lend him the money to reach New York, some $250'. In San Francisco, he actually handed over $300 or £60, which is £2,500 in today's values, to his departing ship-board friend. It was 14 October 1861 when Fred wrote in his diary: 'Poor old Bakunin, I was sorry to part with him. He has been more like a friend than any one I have met for a long time'. Fred had rejoiced to have access to the mind of a leading European revolutionary on board the *Carrington,* just as his father had enjoyed having access as a young man to another leading revolutionary mind in the person of Jeremy Bentham. Being confined together in the ship's small space had helped to induce a closeness between two men of different backgrounds and experience: one an upper-middle-class English clergyman, whose social position brought with it status, privilege and comfort; the other, equally high-born but who had cast away all trappings of rank and endured humiliation and suffering for his beliefs. For one, the *Carrington* was the means of pleasure and education, while for the other it was the means of escape from a Siberian work camp and of rejoining his wife. Fred's easy acceptance of Bakunin is all the more remarkable because he represented the 'red republicanism' of Europe feared and hated by the British public.

What had brought them together was a shared perspective on the burning questions of the day – European revolutions, the emancipation of the serfs, slavery and the imminent American Civil War, geology and evolution, the growing power of Catholicism. This fact is some guide to what figured certainly in Fred Koe's conversation and perhaps in that of some other Album characters. The thing that brought Fred and Bakunin closest was the possibility of deep friendship between individuals, which their journey from Yokohama to San Francisco had made a reality. It was a question which mattered also to Kilvert the diarist. There are many *Diary* passages concerned with the possibility of establishing close rapport with strangers. Kilvert explored the idea in some depth in his poem *The Pilgrimage* in which he wrote: 'We cross the path of many travellers and stand a moment face to face'. Some meetings were significant, he believed, and came about not by chance but by God's agency. One such was his meeting on a train on 19 June 1872 with a girl he christened Irish Mary who, although a saucy street hawker, attracted him profoundly. The fact that she was Irish (and probably a Catholic) was immaterial.

Kilvert recounted how close he came to running away with Irish Mary: 'Shall I leave all and follow her?' He knew all social convention opposed such an action. Fred Koe too was aware that severe social disapproval would be the result if he married Jane Bethell. Many months at sea had not banished from his mind the image of Jane nor his desire to marry her and he made an agreement with her father that any children of the marriage would be brought up as Roman Catholics.[20] The marriage took place on 29 July 1862 in the Roman Catholic Chapel in Richmond, Surrey. The witnesses were Ralph Koe, Fred's twin brother, and Jane's solicitor father John Bethell, who had married Louisa Abraham in February 1833. Louisa was then a minor and permission for her to marry was given by her father Robert (1775-1850). He was born in the parish of St. Pancras, where Jane's baptism was recorded on 30 September 1839. Her address was given on the baptismal certificate as Bedford Place, a fashionable street off Russell Square. Robert, son of a London builder, became an architect and developed an extensive practice, doing work for several leading Roman Catholic families, among whom were the Duke of Norfolk and the Earl of Shrewsbury.[21] Abraham's wife, Jane's maternal grandmother, was Eliza Brown, a gifted painter of flowers.[222] The Abrahams lived at Keppel Street, a stone's throw from Bedford Place.

Talented and entrepreneurial people were also to be found on the paternal side of Jane's family. The use of creosote on a commercial basis began in 1838 when John Bethell took out a patent for his 'Bethell process' whereby timber was placed in a chamber and subjected to a vacuum which removed all moisture from it. The timber was then impregnated with creosote. One of creosote's main uses was the treatment of railway sleepers to prevent them from deteriorating through dampness. John Bethell, born in Bristol in 1805, was a son of Dr. Richard Bethell of Bradford-on-Avon. John's brother Richard was a child of precocious intelligence, enrolling as a student at Oxford when he was only four-teen. Later he became a Liberal M.P. and eventually Lord Chancellor (as Lord Westbury).

After John Bethell died in 1867, Fred managed the business success-fully but a trade depression sent it into bankruptcy. Wendy Koe noted that Fred suffered greater financial loss than the Bethells, and 'but for the help of his friends and relations would have been destitute. As it was, Fred and Janie now lived in extreme poverty'.[23] It seems that Fred could not escape from bankruptcy; it had overtaken both his grandfather and his uncle. Wendy Koe believed that Fred's father 'brought out the second edition of *Montague and Ayrton's Law and Practice in Bankruptcy*' because he was haunted by what had happened to his father and brother.[24] In the period 1876-1886, Fred lived at Clarence House, Belmont Park, Black-heath, and died in 1889 at 15 Bennett Park, Blackheath. Just before his early death, and perhaps contributing to it, he suffered the pain and humiliation of the bankruptcy of his business.[25] Jane herself was only sixty-one when she died there in 1900.

After her beginnings among the fine houses around Russell Square, Jane continued to live in style. By 1841, her family were living at St. John's Hill in Battersea with no less than seven servants. Servants out-numbered children (eight as opposed to seven) at the time of the 1851 census when the Bennetts lived at 22 Craven Hill in Paddington, a quar-ter of a mile from Hyde Park. Two of the servants then were from Wilt-shire. Jane, aged twenty-one and unmarried, was at home with her six siblings – and seven servants – when her family surfaced in Bath in 1861 at Winifred House, 22 Sion Hill. Living with them was Jane's eldest brother Henry, a civil engineer, and his wife Sarah, who had been born in India. Neighbours of the Bennetts at this time were Captain and Mrs. Bampfylde, who lived at 11 Sion Hill.

The Bennetts' house was named after St. Winifred's Well, a spring providing water for the new houses in this part of Lansdown.[26] It is a matter of speculation as to how important it was for the Bethells, newly converted to Catholicism, to settle in a house associated with St. Wini-fred, whose veneration was originally limited to her well at Holywell, Flintshire. Her relics were later (1138) enshrined at Shrewsbury. An ar-ticle on the various St. Winifred's Wells noted that pilgrimage to Holywell Church, Flintshire, was reviving in 1838 after Catholic Emancipation.[27] The fact that the Bethells had settled in Bath in the early 1850s means not only that they had opportunity to mix from that time with Dr. John's family, but also to learn about Winifred House. From 1851 to 1855 the Bethells lived at 12 Primrose Hill, which is very near Sion Hill where Winifred House is situated. And, after a period at another address (29 Royal Crescent – from 1856), they seized the opportunity to take Winifred House when it became vacant around 1860.

After being widowed in 1867, Louisa Bethell, Jane's mother, first spent some time in Holdenhuish, a district of Bournemouth, where the 1871 census finds her. However, she then returned to Bath to live with her son at 16 Royal Crescent,[28] the most beautiful (and prestigious) crescent in a city of beautiful crescents. A neighbour of her son Henry in the mid / late 1870s were the Album characters Mrs. Middleton, who lived at no.25, and Emily Ellis, who lived at no.2.

Fred and Jane Koe are intrinsically interesting as a couple. The former has been characterised in this chapter's title as 'a man of mind', which was the way he had characterised Bakunin. He warmed to the Russian revolutionary, however, largely because he recognised a kindred spirit. The emotional warmth, spontaneity and generosity in Fred also responded to the same qualities in Bakunin. Both were men of feeling as well as of intellect; both were well read as well as well travelled.[29] Given what is known of the intellectual and enterprising individuals in Jane's background, and the fact that she appealed to Fred, it is likely that she was 'a woman of mind'. Though not as well-travelled as he, when she met him in 1858 she was travelling round the Mediterranean, no doubt chaperoned, but still only nineteen. Knowing that Mr. and Mrs. Koe were part of the extended family of the Kilvert Album helps us to take its measure more accurately in terms of its values, achievements and horizons.

Postscript

Much of the pleasure involved in telling the story of the lost Kilvert Album derives from laying bare its mystery – the reasons for its existence, the purposes behind its compilation, the factors that brought its subjects together, and the kind of lives they lived. We have seen that members of Dr. John's own family come first in the Album, followed by some of the daughters and one son (Kilvert the diarist) of Dr. John's brother Robert. The great majority of the Album people have been identified with certainty so it is a pity that some who come near its end have remained stubbornly mysterious. (It should be added that another Album person, Fanny Lawrence, not one of the final five, remains unidentified.) It has been shown earlier that Album people are linked to a degree by the photographers who took their CDVs. Similarly, something of a pattern can be discerned among the last five Album characters and their photographers, and this proves to be of some help in identifying them. Nevertheless, very little, sometimes nothing, has been discovered about them, their background, and the links they had both to each other and to the remainder of the Album's occupants. Together, the mysterious five constitute a kind of postscript to the Album as well as to the effort, represented by this book, to reconstruct a bit of history, an endeavour which rarely achieves total success.

When we examine the photographers of the mysterious five, certain common factors are apparent. Firstly, they were not based in Bath; in fact, they were located a long way from it. Other Album photographers were located far from Bath but reasons have been found to explain why they were engaged. Secondly, three of the mysterious people were photographed by Thomas Edge: the unknown gentleman, whose photo is no.41 (no photographer's name is to be found on its back but 'T. Edge' appears on the bottom of its front), and Hannah and Sarah Mitchell.

On the back of the Mitchells' pictures is Edge's name plus the addresses of his two studios: 28 Avenham Street, Preston, and Gloddaeth Street, Llandudno. The photographer of another of the mysterious five – Mrs. Whitworth – was Silas Eastham of 217 Lord Street, Southport. The last of the five (the last in the Album) was photographed by James Elliott, 12 Orme Square, Bayswater Road, London. Since this photo has no caption, the identity of its subject is unknown.[1]

Silas Eastham, who took Mrs. Whitworth's CDV, also had a studio in Manchester at 7 Market Street, the city's principal shopping street, just as Lord Street was Southport's. One of his advertisements boasted of 'several improvements' introduced into his establishments: 'Portraits in ivory, porcelain, carbon, ceramic, and colours'. He also claimed: 'Young children and babies are made a speciality and most wonderful results are obtained'. Photography was only one of Eastham's business interests. In 1869 he was an investor, holding 40 shares of £5 each, in the Southport Turkish Baths Company, as well as being one of its directors. He was also a shareholder in the Southport and West Lancashire Banking Company, an enterprise which suffered a collapse in 1881.

Partly because of these business links, many of Eastham's clients were local worthies. It may be relevant to the identity of Mrs. Whitworth that two of his fellow shareholders in the Southport Bank were Edward Whitworth and William Westfield Whitworth, cotton manufacturers, based in the village of Facit near Rochdale. There were Whitworths too in Southport itself, where Eastham took Mrs. Whitworth's CDV. In 1873, Richard Whitworth, a saddler, lived there. A chemist's business belonging to James Whitworth was in the town in 1876. A Mrs. Elizabeth Gee Whitworth resided at Thornton House, Talbot Street in 1878.

Hannah and Sarah Mitchell are the only individuals among the mysterious five who can with any certainty be identified. The 1851 census shows two sisters, Sarah aged thirteen, and Hannah aged ten, living in Harris Court, Bath. Only their heads are visible in their CDVs. The close physical resemblance between them seems to confirm that they were sisters. Their pictures follow that of Mrs. Whitworth, which may imply some connection. Following them is the unknown gentleman, whose CDV is the last in the Album. One fact undermines, however, the likelihood that the Bath Mitchell sisters are the Album ones: they were the daughters of James, a general labourer, and his wife Mary. Two older daughters were employed as dressmaker and servant. The 1861 census gives details of a Hannah working as a bootbinder in Bath; she was aged twenty-one and could therefore be the 1851 Hannah. The 1861 woman had a one-year-old son James (named after her father?), although she was unmarried. The background of these two sisters seems at odds with the ethos – middle-upper-middle class, professional, 'respectable' – of other Album characters. Furthermore, no link has been found between the former and the latter.[2] However, the fact remains that two sisters named Hannah and Sarah Mitchell were living in Bath at the same time as, and of the same generation as, the daughters of Dr. John. If the sisters were linked to Mrs. Whitworth, their CDVs were likely to have been taken in Southport as hers was, but they were taken in Preston by Thomas Edge.

In their photos, the sisters appear to be aged late thirties or early forties and, since they were born in 1838 and 1841, the date of the photos would be the early 1870s. Since Edge closed his Preston studio in March 1875 and moved to Llandudno, Preston seems to be the more likely location for the sisters' portraits. Edge's move to Llandudno stemmed from his contact with the Preston artist Thomas Ogle. Edge, born there in 1821, probably worked as a cotton weaver in his early life and may have attended Preston's Institution for the Diffusion of Useful Knowledge where Ogle taught landscape and figure drawing. Ogle became interested in photography and in 1855 was advertising himself as a 'portrait painter and photographic artist', based in a studio at 28 Great Avenham Street, Preston, in a middle-class, residential area, where he was in partnership with Edge. The partnership was dissolved in January 1860. The two men had begun to specialise in scenic views, particularly of the Lake District and their stereoviews sold well all over the country. Ogle went to live in the Lake District in 1861.

Some of Edge's clients were distinguished people, which partly explains why seven of his portraits are in the National Portrait Gallery Collection. Two of them feature the Liddell sisters as children: Ina, Edith and Alice. The last named was of course the inspiration for Alice in Wonderland by Lewis Carroll, who was himself very interested in photography. Some of his many pictures of the Liddell daughters showed them nude and have become controversial. Their father was Henry George Liddell,[3] Dean of Christ Church, Oxford, where Carroll was a lecturer in maths. Denis de Vitré is the subject of one of the seven portraits by Edge in the National Portrait Gallery. De Vitré (1806-1878) was born in Carlisle, took his M.D. at Edinburgh University, and moved to Lancaster in 1832 where he became Physician to its County Lunatic Asylum. The seventh of Edge's portraits is of Sir Monier Monier-Williams, the expert on India whose picture of the world of the District Collector was quoted in chapter three. After Oxford, he had attended (1840-1) the EIC College at Haileybury, becoming a lecturer in Asian languages there from 1844 to 1858. In 1860, he became Oxford's Professor of Sanskrit.[4]

The reputation of Thomas Edge as a photographer meant that he could command commissions from famous people, even though based (up to 1875) in Preston. The fact that four of the five mysterious characters, whose CDVs come at the end of the Album, had those CDVs taken by photographers who lived only twenty miles apart (i.e. the distance between Preston and Southport) raises the possibility that they themselves were located in Lancashire or had links to it. Because they are mysterious to us, it is tempting to believe that linking them together was some story whose nature determined not only that they were allocated the last places in the Album, but also that two of their photos were not provided with captions. Chapter one suggested that Anna Maria added all the captions to the photographs at the same time in order to ensure that their subjects would be known to future viewers of the Album. Why then did she fail to identify two of the last five? It seems a considerable oversight on the part of one who otherwise had shown herself to be a diligent album keeper. Langford warned, as was noted earlier, that absent photos in albums are neither 'mistakes nor secrets' but just 'silences'. Must we make the same assumption about absent captions?

The explanation for the absence of the photo of Marianne, Anna Maria's mother, may simply be that it was lost; the caption 'Mamma' tells us that it was once there, so it cannot be a mystery nor a secret. However, something of a mystery is attached to her as we have seen. It is concerned with the antipathy of the diarist's family to her family, or more specifically, Mrs. Kilvert's antipathy to Marianne. The mystery is also concerned with the 'secret' weddings of two of Marianne's children: Fred and Eliza. The secret behind the wedding of Eliza seems to have been that her husband was both a Catholic and an Irishman. The secret behind Fred's wedding is still a mystery.

Chapter ten characterised Fred Koe's as an 'inside story' involving 'family secrets and subversive tales', largely because he too married a Catholic. How far this fact was made known to other people, including Album people, is a matter of speculation. The same is true also of Mrs. Middleton's secret: that her mother was an Indian woman, who lived the life of an exotic dancer before becoming an Englishman's concubine and siding with so-called 'rebels' against the British during the Mutiny. We may speculate too about the extent to which Fred Koe revealed to others his quest 'to get at that inner self of everyone I met'.

It has not been possible to penetrate far into the inner selves of Album people in this book. Nevertheless, it is hoped that at least some of the inner world of the Album – its triumphs and tragedies, pride and prejudice, mysteries and secrets – has been revealed. The Album story is a fascinating one for its own sake, whether its readers are familiar with Kilvert's Diary or not. It is hoped that those who are not will now be encouraged to read it. For those who are, the Album story can be the means of approaching the Diary with a fresh perspective, providing insights into many aspects of it which have remained undeveloped or even puzzling and mysterious. One example is the effort Kilvert can be seen making to establish a friendship with his cousin Anna Maria, the Album's compiler. We can now recognise that he was seeking a reconciliation with her, the explanation for which is the antipathy his mother felt towards hers. To understand this antipathy, we have to learn what kind of people the members of Anna Maria's family were. In so doing, we also learn more about Kilvert's family.

The Album's story takes us not only into the arena of close family relations but also into the society of Bath and Chippenham, in which those relations were embedded. Most of the Album subjects had connections with Bath and researching their lives has enabled me to fill out the picture of the Bath that Kilvert and his family knew. The families of Album characters are families very much like Kilvert's own: they had similar origins, education, careers, interests, fears, aspirations. This fact alone means that our understanding of Kilvert's family is enhanced by the Album story. The story also provides an expansion and a deepening of some of the Diary's main concerns – one may call them themes: the challenges of gaining an education and building a career, religious and racial prejudice, fear of financial ruin, leisure pursuits, the importance, especially for women, of getting married. Not least of these concerns is photography itself, the new phenomenon that brought the Album into existence. The Album story is therefore one which helps us to understand what it meant to be a mid-Victorian, middle-class person.

Notes

INTRODUCTION

1 'Rambling Recollections', in *More Chapters from the Kilvert Saga*, Leamington Spa, Kilvert Society, no date, p.111.
2 Although there are 45 photos in total in the Album, two people are unnamed, two cannot be identified, and six are of children.
3 The word, from the Hindi 'bangla' meaning 'of Bengal', has become part of the English language.
4 Statements by Robert Kilvert in this paragraph are from his 'Memoirs of the Rev. Robert Kilvert' in *More Chapters from the Kilvert Saga*, pp.36-7, 45.
5 The quotations from J.M. Bourne's *Patronage and Society in Nineteenth-Century England* (London, Edward Arnold, 1986) are from pp.89-90, 64, 31.
6 Martha Langford, *Suspended Conversations. The Afterlife of Memory in Photographic Albums*, Montreal, McGill-Queen's University Press, 2008, p.21. The Langford quotations in the preceding paragraph are from pp.20-1, 5.
7 Robin and Carol Wichard, *Victorian Cartes-de-Visite*, Princes Risborough, Shire Publications, 1999, p.80.

A NOTE ON COSTUME

1 E.J. Hobsbawm, *The Age of Capital 1848-1875*, London, Cardinal, 1991, pp.270-1.
2 Oliver Garnett and Penelope Byrde, 'From Crinoline to Bustle: 1850s-1870s', in *Museum of Costume. Assembly Rooms, Bath, Authorised Guide*, 1994, p.36.
3 A new development in fashion was the department store, appearing first in London. Jolly's of Bath opened in 1830. The store is still there today.
4 Garnett and Byrde, *op. cit.*, p.36.
5 Heather Toomer, *Antique Lace: Identifying Types and Techniques*, Atglen, Pennsylvania, Schiffer Publishing, 2001, p.192.
6 Santina M. Levey, *Lace. A History*, London, Victoria and Albert Museum, 1990, p.102.
7 Asa Briggs, *Victorian Things*, London, Batsford, 1988, pp.269-271.

Acknowledgments

1 www.cartedevisite.co.uk/about-2/ron-cosens/. Accessed on 2 August 2012.
2 www.cartes.freeuk.com. Accessed on 1 August 2012.

Biographical note on Francis Kilvert

1 *Francis Kilvert Priest and Diarist 1840-1879*, Leamington Spa, Kilvert Society, 2000, p.51.

Chapter One

1 On the 'Victorian and Edwardian Photographs – Roger Vaughan Personal Collection' website, the 'W.G. Maddy Victorian Photograph Album – Carte-de-Visite' is presented. It is an album dating from 1864 with the name 'W.G. Maddy' inside the front cover. Vaughan wrote of this album: 'It is highly unusual to find so many named and dated photographs – unique in my collection' (www.rogerco.pwp. blueyonder.co.uk/list123/ list123html). Accessed on 2 August 2012.
2 'Images and Impressions: Painting, Reproduction and Photography' in *Victorian Vision. Inventing New Britain*, edited by John M. Mackenzie, Victoria and Albert Publications, 2001, p.228.
3 Robin and Carol Wichard, *op. cit.*, p.21.
4 Ryan, *op. cit.*, p.226. By the end of the 1860s, there were almost 300 photographers in London.
5 Wichards, *op. cit.*, p.33.
6 *Ibid.*, p.75.
7 Helen Verity Vafeas, *Uneasy Allies. An Englishman in Australia: Henry Vigors Hewitt 1839-1931*, unpublished M.A. thesis, Melbourne University, 1985, p.13.
8 John Tagg, *The Burden of Representation*, Basingstoke, 1988, p.37, quoted by Patrizia Di Bello, *Women's Albums and Photography in Victorian England. Ladies, Mothers and Flirts*, Aldershot, Ashgate, 2007, p.18.
9 Quotations in this paragraph to this point are from Wichards, *op. cit.*, pp.21-7.
10 Elizabeth Siegel, *Playing with Pictures. The Art of Victorian Collage*, with additional essays by Patrizia Di Bello and Marta Weiss, New Haven, The Art Institute of Chicago in association with Yale University Press, 2010, p.18.
11 Alice Dew, daughter of the Rev. Henry Dew of Whitney-on-Wye, was then eleven. The date was 25 July 1871 and the entry appears in *Unpublished Extracts from Kilvert's Diary relating to the Bevan and Dew families*, Hereford, Kilvert Society, no date.
12 Wichards, *op. cit.*, pp.75, 79.
13 George Simpson, 'Photography', *British Quarterly Review* 44 (1866), 346-90, quoted in Di Bello, *op. cit.*, p.107.

14 Siegel, *op. cit.*, p.16.

15 He referred to seeing the 'Great Girls' article in the journal 'for last week'. Mrs. Linton wrote many of the articles in this series: 'Beauty and Brains', 'The Fashionable Woman', 'Feminine Amenities', 'Spoilt Women', 'Grim Females', 'Feminine Affectations'. Born in 1822, daughter of a clergyman, she originally wrote for the *Morning Chronicle*, then for the *Saturday Review*. She also had articles published in Dickens's *Household Words*.

16 'The Perfect Victorian Lady' by Martha Vicinus, in *Suffer and Be Still: Women in the Victorian Age*, edited by M. Vicinus, Indiana University Press, 1972, pp.ix, xii.

17 Deborah Gorham, *The Victorian Girl and the Feminine Ideal*, London, Croom Helm, 1982, p.27.

18 Joan Perkin, *Victorian Women*, New York, New York University Press, 1996, p.153.

19 Before her marriage, Kilvert's sister Dora acted as his housekeeper when he became Vicar of Bredwardine.

20 Jose Harris, *Private Lives, Public Spirit: Britain 1870-1914*, London, Penguin Books, 1994, p.66.

21 Gorham, *op. cit.*, pp.5, 11.

22 The 1861 census confirms she was at 12 Darlington Street, Bathwick.

23 Di Bello, *op. cit.*, pp.31-3.

24 *Ibid.*, pp.2-3.

25 Sontag, On Photography, New York, 1978, quoted in Langford, op. cit., p.27.

26 Ryan (*op. cit.*, p.223) noted: 'Authors of contemporary photograph manuals placed the "art / science" of photography on a par with the steamship and the telegraph as one of the wonders of the age'.

27 Di Bello, *op. cit.*, pp.88, 146.

28 Quoted in Di Bello, *op. cit.*, p.88. The letter was to Mary Mitford. The Daguerrotype, was named after its inventor, Louis Daguerre. It was superseded by the 'talbotype' of Henry Fox Talbot, from which a negative could be made, facilitating further copies. Emily Kilvert remembered this development as a milestone: 'Mr. Talbot invented the talbo-type which ... succeeded the daguerrotype, in the early days of sun-pictures' (*op. cit.*, p.115).

29 The quotes in this paragraph are from pp.95, 105 of Langford (*op. cit.*).

30 *Op. cit.*, p.18.

31 The Langford quotes in this paragraph are from pp.35, 102, 199.

Chapter Two

1 R.S. Neale, Bath *1680-1850. A Social History,* London, Routledge, Kegan & Paul, 1981, p.292.

2 *Op. cit.*, p.36. The earlier quotation in this paragraph from the 'Memoirs' is to be found on p.44.

3 Llewellyn Lloyd of Llowes, a village near Clyro, once underlined to Kilvert the

problem of being a son in a large family: '[he] spoke touchingly about his deep regret that he had not been able to go to the University to take his degree. "But," he said quietly, "my father has eleven children".'

4 Colborne's three daughters were the most regular members of Mrs. Kilvert's missionary working parties.

5 Geoffrey Best, *Mid-Victorian Britain 1851-75*, London, Fontana Press, 1985, p.185.

6 She also mentioned that Dr. John's grandson, son of the one who went out to India for his health, 'was brought up to the Medical profession' (her capital 'M').

7 Mary Abbott, *Family Ties. English families 1540-1920*, London, Routledge, 1993, p.97. She also noted that naval surgeons were not commissioned officers until 1843.

8 Information about the medical profession in this paragraph from Peter Gay is to be found in his *The Cultivation of Hatred. The Bourgeois Experience, Victoria to Freud*, vol.III, pp.487-8. The Society of Apothecaries used to license surgeons to act as apothecaries.

9 M. Abbott, *op. cit.*, p.97.

10 For the information about Dr. John Kilvert's professional training, I am greatly indebted to Philippa Mole, Assistant Archivist and Records Manager of the Royal College of Surgeons.

11 P. Gay, *op. cit.*, p.486.

12 The plaque, commemorating his death, states that he was 'resident in this parish thirty-seven years'.

13 It was created partly out of materials from the original twelfth-century parish church.

14 One of his sermon collections is called *Sermons preached at St. Mary's Church, Bathwick* (1837). The DNB entry on him states that he was an evening lecturer there. A plaque dedicated to him is on the wall of the Church.

15 *Op. cit.*, p.120.

16 The school was at East Tytherton near Langley Burrell, Wiltshire.

17 Letter to William Money, 8 May 1824, Wiltshire Record Office L14/329. Emma was the grandmother of the Harriet Money Kyrle who married the Rev. Andrew Pope, one of Kilvert's closest friends, on 9 September 1874. Kilvert was best man at the wedding.

18 The Dillwyn quotations come from *The Dillwyn Collection. The Journal of Lewis Weston Dillwyn*, transcribed by Richard Morris (www.swansea.ac.uk/lis/historical-collections).

19 Dillwyn's father was a Quaker and, like Francis, married a Quaker.

20 From 'Trevellyk or How Little Turns the Scale', an autobiographical fragment, in *More Chapters from the Kilvert Saga*, p.74.

21 The family of Theophilus Gwatkin was eminent: it included army generals and the artist Sir Joshua Reynolds.

22 In the *Diary* entry recording his visit to the Gwatkins in Liverpool in June 1872, Kilvert referred to Anna Maria as 'Maria' and 'Mrs. Gwatkin'.

23 Hugh Barbour, *The Quakers in Puritan England*, New Haven, Yale University Press, 1964, p.173.

24 Isabel Grubb, *Quakerism and Industry before 1800*, London, Williams and Norgate, 1929, pp.145-6.

25 In census returns and her marriage certificate she appears as Mary Anne.

26 Andrew appears in the 1830 *Bath Directory* and in Poll Books for 1835 and 1837, when he was at 22 Bladud Buildings on the opposite side of the Avon from Bathwick.

27 He could not have been the officiating minister because he was not ordained until 1827.

28 Present at this meeting was Dr. Charles Bailey of Chippenham, who had so impressed Emily Kilvert when he showed her a frog's leg under a magnifying glass.

29 Asa Briggs, *The Age of Improvement 1783-1867*, London, Longmans, p.103.

30 Information from *Bath Poll Books*, Bristol City Library, Bath Collection (13 EL 1410).

31 John could have attended BLPA lectures as a visitor. Visitor records have not survived.

32 *Talbot Correspondence Project*, document numbers 7983, 7985 (foxtalbot.dmu.ac.uk/ letters/letters.html). Accessed 4 September 2012. John's sister Mary was the wife of John Matthews, Vicar of Lacock (died 1853). Matthews wrote himself to Talbot in late November / early December 1850 on the threat of Tractarianism. That John believed in the technological future is evident in the fact that in 1837 he bought £20 worth (£1,000 today) of shares in the Bath and Weymouth Great Western Union Railway.

33 Quoted in Best, *op. cit.*, pp.256-8.

Chapter Three

1 He complained of the 'poisonous East wind' on 15 and 17 February 1870. On 20 February 1870 he noted 'a blessed change in the weather. Wind westerly and no longer deadly poison'. 'A keen and cruel wind [was] whistling and wheeling from the East' on 21 March 1872.

2 'The concept of Original Sin ... was the linchpin of the Evangelical creed' (Elisabeth Jay, *The Religion of the Heart. Anglican Evangelicalism in the Nineteenth-Century Novel*, Oxford, Clarendon Press, 1969, p.54). That Kilvert was interested in the origins of Man is clear from his excitement over Edward Hine's *The English Nation identified with the lost house of Israel*, which he heard about on 29 November 1872.

3 Helen James, 'The Assassination of Lord Mayo: the "First" Jihad?', *International Journal of Asia Pacific Studies*, vol.5, no.2 (July 2009).

4 Asa Briggs, *Victorian Things*, p.266.

5 This has implications for the date / period of the Album's compilation. Anna Maria could of course have inserted his photo when his death was confirmed.

6 Information from *Hart's Army List*.

7 In 1881 it merged with the 75th Regiment to become the Gordon Highlanders.

8 The 1861 census shows him at home with his family at 12 Darlington Street, Bath-wick.

9 This journal gave full details of the workings and activities of the British adminis-tration in India, including departures and arrivals of army / civilian personnel and their families. Its full title was *Allen's Indian Mail and Official Gazette for British and Foreign India*. 'Foreign India' presumably referred to those parts not ruled by the British.

10 *Op. cit.*, p.120.

11 *Op. cit.*, p.12.

12 In 1793, they were banned from trading and their salaries increased.

13 Philip Lawson, *The East India Company: a History*, London, Longman, 1993, pp.72-3.

14 *The British Empire. Resistance, Repression and Revolt*, London, Verso, 2012, pp.1-6.

15 *Ibid.*, pp.396-400.

16 Rob Graves, 'The Ladies of Llanthomas', *Kilvert Society Journal*, no.35, September 2012, p.183.

17 This caused the Bengal famine of 1770 in which 3 million people died.

18 Nicholas B. Dirks, *The Scandal of Empire. India and the Creation of Imperial Britain*, Cambridge (Mass.), Belknap Press of Harvard University, 2006, pp.30, 10.

19 Nirad C. Chaudhuri, *Clive of India. A Political and Psychological Essay*, London, Bar-rie and Jenkins, 1975, p.278.

20 Lockwood underlined the way patronage and nepotism worked in his own family. His uncle was an EIC Director and not only secured Lockwood's appointment but 'gave cavalry appointments to my four brothers' ('A Glimpse of Old Haileybury' in *The Early Days of Marlborough College*, London, Simpson, Marshall, Hamilton, Kent, 1893, p.145).

21 Bourne, *op. cit.*, p.105.

22 Edward actually spent his career in the Inland Revenue of the English Civil Serv-ice.

23 Bourne, *op. cit.*, p.106. The quoted words are from R. Sencourt, *India in English Literature*, London, 1923.

24 Sir Monier Monier-Williams, 'Camp Life in India, 1850', in *Indian History Sourcebook*, Fordham University, New York, Paul Halsall, November 1998 (www.fordham.edu/halsall/india/1850monier.html). Accessed on 28 August 2012. The Monier-Williams passage appears in Eva March Tappan (editor), *The World's Story: a History of the World in Story, Song and Art*, Boston, Houghton-Mifflin, 1914, vol.II, pp.224-233.

25 The reasons for this were complex and are covered in correspondence between senior officials (and including one letter by Fred himself) in the period 1876-1880 (IOR/L/PJ/6/8, File 393, British Library). Envy and/or favouritism seem to have played a part in the omission of Fred's name from the list because one official de-clared 'it was not unintentional'.

26 'Patna during the Mutiny' in Lockwood, *op. cit.*, pp.197, 157. Niall Ferguson

observed that it was not Oxbridge's intellectuals who opted for the ICS but 'rather those whose prospects at home were modest: bright young sons of provincial professionals' (*Empire. How Britain Made the Modern World*, London, Penguin, 2004, p.187).

27 Lockwood had studied Hindustani at Haileybury as well as Indian administration.

28 In 1825, the Anglo-Indian community in Calcutta offered a prize to any steamer that completed the voyage from Britain in 70 days or less. P. and O. took over the London-Bombay service in 1855, taking four weeks for the journey. By 1870, the time has been reduced to 26 days (Mark Ravinder Frost, 'Asia's Maritime Networks and the Colonial Public Sphere, 1840-1920, *New Zealand Journal of Asian Studies* 6, 2, December 2004, pp.68-9).

29 His health would have been likely to suffer during the period 1871-74 because Terai, the district in which he was stationed (between the plains and the Himalayan foothills) was notorious for its fever-ridden swamps.

30 It was quite natural for Kilvert to sleep overnight at Marianne's, as he did on 8 October 1873 when attending the Bath Church Congress.

31 On 15 February 1875, Kilvert called on his relatives the Miss Mascalls, who were 'justly indignant that Mrs. Prodgers and her children should have been introduced into the new painted east window in Kington St. Michael's Church'. It was a situation in which photography had played a key role, for Mrs. Prodgers and her children 'actually sat for their likenesses'. Their appearance, 'in the most prominent position' in the window was 'the laughing stock of the village'.

32 Caer Badon was the ancient name for the village of Bathampton near Bath. Bathampton Down is surrounded by an earthwork called Caer Badon. Caerbadon House was split into two flats in 1955 and is now known as Brandon House. (I am indebted for this information to Colin Johnston of Bath Record Office.)

33 In these last words, Kilvert was paying Eliza the highest compliment because he attached great value to naturalness and lack of affectation in women.

34 P.120.

35 D.G. Paz, *Popular Anti-Catholicism in Mid-Victorian England*, Stanford, Stanford University Press, 1992, p.299.

36 *The Irish in Nineteenth Century Britain: Integrated or Assimilated*, Salford, University of Salford, 1994, pp.5-6.

37 The photo was taken by Frederick C. Bird of Milsom Street, Bath, who also took those of Eliza and of her sister Lucy.

38 The family was then living in Hastings.

39 He had died in 1863. Lizzie was the Elizabeth Frances to whom Emily Kilvert referred when reviewing the fortunes in the marriage stakes of her uncle's daughters (see Introduction).

40 Cf. Best, *op. cit.*, pp.271-2: 'Barristers carried much more social weight than solicitors'.

Chapter Four

1 *White Mughals. Love and Betrayal in Eighteenth-Century India*, London, Harper Press, 2012, p.265.
2 He was elder brother to Arthur Wellesley, who became the Duke of Wellington.
3 Quoted in Dalrymple, *op. cit.*, p.273.
4 *Ibid.*, p.49.
5 Gott, *op. cit.*, pp.138-140.
6 The name Ochterlony is Scottish, originating in Forfarshire.
7 His career record is from *Bengal Civil Servants 1790-1842* (British Library).
8 Asian journals give glimpses of the Middletons' movements: *The Quarter Oriental Magazine Review* for March 1825 reported Mrs. S. Ochterlony, Charlotte Ochterlony, and Mary Ann Middleton travelling on the *Cornwall* to India from England; *Allen's Indian Mail* records Mrs. Middleton's return from England to Calcutta in 1846 and both Middletons embarked from India to Ceylon in 1848.
9 It is possible that he was related to the Captain Child who had known for years that William Kilvert had died in Calcutta.
10 Directory of London and Westminster and Borough of Southwark 1794.
11 The National Archives refers to the interest this firm had in a merchant ship, the *Sophia Elizabeth*, in 1783-4.
12 This regiment was originally raised as the Second Battalion of the 42nd Royal Highlanders in 1780.
13 The information and quotations in this paragraph are from Gott, *op. cit.*, chapters 23 and 54.
14 *The Gorilla Hunters*, London, Collins, no date, pp.10-11.
15 For an account of Kilvert's attitudes towards colonialism and missionary work, see J. Toman, *Kilvert's World of Wonders: growing up in mid-Victorian England* (Lutterworth Press, 2013), chapter eleven.
16 Ringlets of the kind she was wearing were popular in the 1840s and 1850s but were out of fashion by the 1860s.
17 35 Milsom Street was the location until 1862 of the photographer J.G. Newport. During 1866 Mrs. Williams worked in partnership with another female photographer, Mrs. J. Roper. In 1888, the former moved her business to London.
18 It is hard to believe that Dr. John could have found this sort of money to purchase a commission for his son William. Perhaps patronage played a part.
19 The 1851 census states that she was born in Punjab.
20 It was part of his interest in and respect for soldiers. His brother Edward used to attend national reviews of Volunteer detachments.
21 Bath Directories for the 1860s record that he was Adjutant of the 1st Battalion Somerset Rifle Volunteers.
22 Vafeas, *op. cit.*, p.14.
23 It seems that Captain Bampfylde gave evidence in September 1856 at a Portsmouth Court Martial relating to events in India in 1854. The *Times* (22 September

1856) mentioned that he and others were occupying a house in the Murree Hills in July 1854. On 6 May 1857 he and his wife attended a soirée of the West Cowes Choral Society (*Hampshire Advertiser*, 9 May 1857). The fact that the CDV of Fred Koe was taken by a Ryde (I.O.W.) photographer is probably a coincidence.

24 Younghusband Collection: Album of CDV portraits, shelf mark MSS Eur F197/675. Dame Eileen was a pioneer in the field of social work. She taught at the London School of Economics, 1944-58.

25 MSS Eur F197/57(1). Perkins also made a CDV of Col. A.P. Chesshyre of Bath, another Anglo-Indian, dating from the 1860s, which is among the India Office Select Materials, shelfmark Photo 459/(86).

26 The village has long been associated with the Younghusband family, some of whom were living there in the 1850s and 1860s. The family were therefore local clients for Joseph Perkins.

27 For more on the Hewitt family, see chapter seven.

28 Lambert was proud to announce in one of his advertisements that he was 'Late operator at Mr. Beard's, King William Street, London'. Richard Beard had opened England's first daguerreotype studio around 1840 on the roof of the Polytechnic in Regent Street. When the daguerreotype process was superseded by others, his business declined and he handed it over to his son in 1857. Lambert opened his studio at 10 Fountain Buildings, Bath in 1860 where he photographed Anna Maria's 'Grandmamma'. He also advertised that he took photos of 'Family Mansions'.

29 That the photos of Mrs. W.R. Smith and Col. Cholmeley came from the same studio is confirmed by the appearance in each of the same curtain and the same table (with the same vase on it).

30 The College was known as Bath Proprietary College in this period.

31 The *Worcester* was the Thames Marine Officer Training School.

32 He was James Brooke (1803-68), an adventurer who showed what getting on in the Far East could mean. Born in India, he received some private tutoring in Bath before becoming an ensign in the Bengal Army of the EIC. He won the trust of the Sultan of Brunei by helping to suppress a rebellion. He was rewarded by being appointed First White Rajah of Sarawak.

33 The Rev. Sabine Baring Gould was a Devon clergyman / antiquarian, remembered for writing *Onward Christian Soldiers*.

CHAPTER FIVE

1 *Oakfield; or Fellowship in the East* (1853), edited by Kenneth Allott, Leicester, Leicester University Press, 1973, vol.I, pp.161, 69.

2 Trollope's *The Way We Live Now* (vol.I, p.51) refers to Sir Patrick Carbury who 'had come home from India as an invalid'.

3 *Calcutta Review*, 'The English in India', vol.I, 1844. This journal was founded in May 1844 by Sir John Kaye, who was attached to the Bengal Artillery. His aim was to

produce 'useful information and propagate sound opinions' (his preface to vol.I). His target audience was the English-educated middle class of Bengal.

4 The College 'History' stated that 450 pupils went to Addiscombe in the first 50 years of its existence.

5 'A History of the College', in *Cheltenham College Register 1841-1889*, edited by Andrew Hunter, London, George Bell, 1890.

6 See J. Toman, 'The other brother: Edward Kilvert at Marlborough College', *Kilvert Society Journal*, No.35, September 2012.

7 See J. Toman, *Kilvert's World of Wonders: growing up in mid-Victorian England*, Cambridge, Lutterworth Press, 2013.

8 This was true also of Marlborough College. Bourne characterised Marlborough as one of the public schools offering middle-class parents 'a safe route into government service, the armed forces and the professions' (*op. cit.*, p.105).

9 The highly Evangelical Rev. Francis Close, Perpetual Curate of Cheltenham, was on the College's original Board of Directors.

10 His name is not to be found in the list of its cadets at the end of Colonel H.M. Vibart's *Addiscombe. Its Heroes and Men of Note*, Westminster, Archibald Constable, 1894. Several heroes of Indian wars, such as Robert Napier and Sir Henry Lawrence, passed through it. In 1858, the government took it over and it became the Royal India Military College.

11 'Surgeons in India – Past and Present', p.244, vol.23, July-December 1854.

12 *Crawford's Roll of the Indian Medical Service.*

13 *Op. cit.*, p.108.

14 It may have appeared in the original diary and been omitted by Plomer.

15 Dalrymple, *op. cit.*, pp.xxxviii-ix.

16 The next six months of the *Diary* are missing so this event is not covered.

17 All the information about Sam's career in the India Medical Service is from *Medical News*, 5 April 1919.

18 Edward became a member of St. Alban Hall on 2 April 1840. I am indebted for some of the information about the Hall to Julian Reid, Archivist at Merton College, Oxford, with which it later merged.

19 *The Church in Madras: being the history of the ecclesiastical and missionary action of the East India Company in the presidency of Madras*, London, Smith and Elder, 1904, vol.I, p.341. Edward wrote *Eight Papers on Ritualism*. Ritualism (roundly condemned by Kilvert) played no part in the earlier years of the Oxford (Tractarian) Movement though it later caused controversy in the Church of England. Edward Cardwell, Principal of St. Alban Hall when Edward was a student, was very hostile to Tractarianism.

20 Eric Stokes, *The English Utilitarians and India*, Oxford, Clarendon Press, 1959, p.xi.

21 Robert Johnson, *British Imperialism*, London, Palgrave Macmillan, 2003, p.29.

22 Bathwick has a Vellore Lane, off Sydney Street, three hundred yards from Dr. John's home. Further reminders of India's importance to Bath are graves of Bengal Army soldiers in Bathwick cemetery where Dr. John is buried.

23 Lawson, *op. cit.*, p.151.

24 *Op. cit.*, p.113. In 1873, Kilvert heard Sir Bartle Frere, educated at Bath Grammar School and the EIC College at Haileybury, at the Bath Church Congress. He spoke 'admirably well', Kilvert noted, in a lecture (8 October) entitled *Remarks on the Organisation of Missions to Uncivilised Populations*. In a 1872 lecture, *Christianity Suited to all Forms of Civilisation*, to the Christian Evidence Society, he had spoken of Christianity as 'a civilising and humanising influence' on India, justifying Britain's rule there.

25 Quoted in Ramkrishnan Muckerjee, *The Rise and Fall of the East India Company*, Berlin, Veb. Deutscher Verlag der Wissenschaften, 1995, p.186.

26 *Ibid.*, p.195.

27 Madras in 1782-3, North-Western Provinces 1837-8, Agra and Punjab 1860-1, Bihar 1873-4, Madras and Bombay 1876-8 (5.5m people died), Orissa and North Bihar 1888-9, Madras, Bombay, Bengal, United and Central Provinces 1896-7.

28 Gott, *op. cit.*, p.46.

29 Earlier that year (17 May) he recorded that he 'preached for the Bengal Famine Mansion House Fund' at Langley Burrell Church.

30 The quotations in this paragraph are from *Oakfield*, vol.I, pp.175-179, vol.II, pp.222-225.

31 Andrew Ward, *Our Bones are Scattered. The Cawnpore Massacres and the Indian Mutiny of 1857*, New York, Henry Holt and Company, 1996, p.90.

32 Frank Perry, *op. cit.*, vol.III, p.341. One wonders whether his fragile mental state on his return to England was a factor leading to the incarceration of his wife Emma in Brislington Asylum, Bristol. Kilvert visited her there on 2 October 1874.

33 E.J. Hobsbawm, *op. cit.*, p.152.

34 *Op. cit.*, p.150.

35 During his time as an educational administrator in Punjab he secured the passing of a law which meant that Hindus in public schools were no longer required to study the Bible.

Chapter Six

1 Editha, born 1841, died 1941.

2 *Op. cit.*, p.120.

3 *Op. cit.*, p.186.

4 This was the title of a lengthy poem by Kilvert, which he had printed on cards for distribution among his parishioners.

5 NLW edition, April-June 1870.

6 The Trollope quotations are from *The Way We Live Now* (Oxford, Oxford University Press, 1991), vol.I, p.199; vol.II, pp.261, 424; vol.I, p.193; vol.II, p.427.

7 On 7 April 1874, Kilvert visited the Christian Malford (Wilts.) Rectory of Rev. Robert Law. Mrs. George Law was there and told Kilvert that she and her husband Colonel George Law were going to a station on the west coast of India in July.

Behind the entry is the unspoken fear of dangers.

8 Chesney (1830-1895) attended the EIC's military college at Addiscombe before joining the Bengal Engineers in 1848. He was severely wounded during the siege of Delhi during the Mutiny. He worked in various administrative departments in India and wrote the widely read *Indian Polity* (1868). He was best known for his short story *The Battle of Dorking* (1871) about a supposed invasion of England by the Germans.

9 The words were actually A.C. Brown's and Bourne quoted them from B. Parry, Delusions and Discoveries. *Studies on India in the British Imagination, 1880-1930*, London, Allen Lane, 1972, p.31.

10 'India 1857-9', in *The Victorians*, London, Hutchinson, 2007, p.101.

11 The quotations in this paragraph are from *Extracts from the Letters and Journals of William Cory*, selected by Francis Warre Cornish, Oxford, 1897. (Johnson changed his name to Cory.) He was the author of the famous *Eton Boating Song*. On 25 January 1870, Kilvert recorded hearing a sermon by 'Mr. Furse, Vicar of Staines'. The Rev. C.W. Furse was Johnson's brother (Furse was their mother's maiden name).

12 *The Dilemma* quotations in this paragraph are from pp.9, 21, of volume I. The edition used is the *Nabu Public Domain Reprints* one of the original William Blackwood, London, 1876 publication.

13 Dalrymple, *op. cit.*, p.10.

14 *The Way We Live Now* is not only full of references to India, but has a chapter entitled 'The India Office'.

15 Warlow was a clergyman as Kilvert was. In 1863 he was joint chaplain of St. George's Cathedral, Madras. Later, he became Archdeacon of Madras, dying there in 1884.

16 The account of the Emily / Edward reunion is in the entry for 21 May 1870 in the NLW edition, April-June 1870, of the *Diary*. Edward (born 1849) would have changed from the sixteen-year-old who saw Emily leave for India in 1865 and the twenty-one-year-old welcoming her return in 1870.

17 *Op. cit.*, p.71.

18 Kilvert's parents looked after Katie and Annie from February 1872 to April 1875.

19 Nearly two months later (28 June 1875) Kilvert was reassured that tiny Mayndie was 'much improved in looks ... and much heavier'.

20 Cf. Dalrymple, *op. cit.*, p.75: '... many British children of the period alarmed their parents by speaking the Hindustani of their ayahs as their first language'.

21 *Op. cit.*, p.99.

22 Dedication of girls continues in modern India, though the system of devadasis has been abolished.

23 Dr. Kusum Pant Joshi, *From Temples to Brothels: India's Devadasis* (www.confluence.org.uk/2012/08/18). Accessed on 12 November 2012.

24 Pran Nevile, *Stories from the Raj: Sahibs, Memsahibs and Others*, Indialog Publications, excerpt in The Sunday Tribune, 25 July 2004, p.3 (www.tribuneindia.com). Accessed on 12 November 2012.

25 Sukla Chatterjee, *Contested Virtue: Imperial Women's Crisis with Colonized Woman-*

hood, Kolkata, Institute of Development Studies, 2010, p.3.

26 Quoted in Joshi, *op. cit.*, p.2.

27 Nevile, *op. cit.*, p.3.

28 Joshi, *op. cit.*, p.1.

29 Chatterjee, *op. cit.*, p.4.

30 Quoted in Chatterjee, p.5.

31 Joshi, *op. cit.*, p.2.

32 Chatterjee, *op. cit.*, p.3.

33 *Op. cit.*, p.10.

34 *Op. cit.*, p.41.

35 This, and the earlier quotation in this paragraph, come from Harshawardhan Nim-khedkar, *Sir David Ochterlony's thirteenth wife*, India-British-Raj Archives (archiver.rootsweb.ancestry.com/th/read/india-british-raj/2009-11/1258276445). Accessed on 24 November 2012.

36 *Op. cit.*, p.526, note 1.

37 *Ibid.*, p.382.

38 Her will, proved in Bristol 19 July 1878, had two clergymen as executors. In it, she referred to her god-daughter, Mary Anne Charters, who was the Bengal-born lady living with her in Bath at the time of the 1871 census. Her will also referred to 'my models of buildings', which may have been Indian ones.

39 Rakashi Chand, 'Meet the Ochterlonys', Online Object of the Month, *The Massachusetts Historical Society* (www.masshist.org/objects/). Accessed on 24 November 2012.

40 The Commissioner in *The Dilemma* suffers from cirrhosis of the liver. The *Calcutta Review* for 1844 was recording that liver disease was a common complaint among Anglo-Indians. In Trollope's *The Way We Live Now*, it is suggested that an already dissolute character be sent out to the Colonies. His mother rejoins: 'Yes; - be sent away that he might kill himself with drink in the bush' (vol.II, p.210).

41 Ward, *op. cit.*, p.139. 'Tatties' were grass mats which were kept wet to cool the air. 'Punkahs' were cloth mats which fanned the air when their cords were worked by Indian servants.

42 The Chesney quotations in the last three paragraphs are from vol.I, pp.36, 20, 186, 541, 90, 20, 157, 196.

43 Letter of 23 February 1820 to the Rev. George Cornish, *The Life and Correspondence of Thomas Arnold*, edited by Arthur Penrhyn Stanley, London, Ward Lock, 1890, p.36.

44 The quotations in the last two paragraphs from *Oakfield; or Fellowship in the East* (Surrey, Unwin Brothers, second edition [1854], 1974), are vol.I, 10, 119, 16, 118, 45, 39, 118, 74-5. The book was published first in 1853 under the pseudonym Punjabee, because Arnold feared a backlash; the second edition bore his real name and in its preface he stated that things in India were improving.

CHAPTER SEVEN

1 Vafeas (*op. cit.*, p.9) quoted this story as one which Henry told to one of his children in 1913. The date of the episode is given by him as 1834 but it must have been later because Caroline was only four at the time of the 1841 census.

2 *Ibid.*, p.9.

3 Jane also looked after her 78-year-old father, Caleb Barrett. Between 1850 and 1865, boarding and day schools for young ladies came and went in Clifton with extraordinary rapidity because they were run by unmarried women. By 1861, 20 Richmond Terrace housed a young ladies' school run by the Misses Hawson. In 1863-4, it had become a prep school for young gentlemen.

4 In his 1913 letter describing the fire on the *Earl of Eldon* (Vafeas, *op. cit.*, p.9).

5 Edkins and his wife were both aged 62. Like Dr. John Kilvert, Edkins had joined the Provincial Medical and Surgical Association in its early days; he was a member in 1834. In 1873, he was serving on a committee for local affairs.

6 Valentine's wife lived there too, his cousin, and several other visitors, plus Arthur Goodwin, 'medical assistant'.

7 *Sir Rowland Hill. The story of a Great Reform. Told by his daughter*, London, Fisher Unwin, 1907, p.16.

8 Colin G. Hey, *Rowland Hill. Victorian genius and benefactor*, London, Quillan Press, 1989, p.103.

9 *Darwin Correspondence Project*, Letter 1352, 4 September 1850. (www.darwinproject. ac.uk/darwins-letters). Accessed 23 June 2012.

10 Brian Turton Smith, *Photographers in Bath 1841-1910* (Royal Photographical Society, RPS Historical Group Newsletter, Supplement 47, May 1980, Bath, p.5).

11 This Vafeas quotation and the earlier one in the paragraph are from pp.8, 19.

12 Quoted in Peter Bailey, *Leisure and Class in Victorian England, Rational recreation and the contest for control, 1830–1885*, London, Methuen, 1987, p.73.

13 Located on one of the downs overlooking Bath, Hampton Rocks rise spectacularly out of the ground, revealing rock strata tipped on end.

14 Vafeas, *op. cit.*, p.17. He attended St. Bartholomew's Hospital where he 'saw a girl's leg cut off'.

15 At Stone's Rooms there would have been drinks, food, entertainment, girls. Cyder Cellars was a popular supper-house. 'Olympic' probably means the Olympic Theatre on Drury Lane where equestrian and rope-dancing shows were performed, plus farces, melodramas, comedies.

16 Vafeas, *op. cit.*, p.22.

17 In 1851, Eversley was living in Widcombe at the same time as Henry's father. Eversley died in Bath on 12 November 1879.

18 He never qualified as a solicitor.

19 Dickens, a friend of the Hills, also used to visit Bruce Castle School, and he too favoured Australia as a place of new beginnings. He tried unsuccessfully to persuade 'fallen women' to emigrate there to seek husbands. He toyed frequently with the

idea of emigrating himself; two of his sons did emigrate there and never came back. Characters from *David Copperfield* find new lives there. He gave his backing to Australia emigration societies.

20 *Op. cit.*, p.28. The earlier quotation in this paragraph is from p.26.

21 Vafeas suggested (p.36) that J.J. Falkner, the Bath lawyer who tutored Henry, may have been her brother but none can be seen in the Falkner family tree.

22 He often wrote long funny poems. He believed literature should be amusing and enjoyed social satire.

23 Vafeas, *op. cit.*, p.92.

24 *Ibid.*, p.125.

25 *Ibid.*, p.173.

26 *Ibid.*, p.390.

27 Vafeas gave 1884 as the year in which Henry's father died but it seems he died in 1878.

28 Vafeas, *op. cit.*, p.406.

29 Among the India Office Select Materials is the Hogg Collection: Carte-de-visite album of Major-General George Hogg, a relative of Col. Hogg.

CHAPTER EIGHT

1 *Eighteen Fifty-Seven*, Government of India, Publications Division, 1987, pp.29-30.

2 *The Rebellion in India, by a Resident in the North-Western Provinces of India*, quoted in Sen, *op. cit.*, p.23.

3 Captain Medley, *A Year's Campaigning in India from March 1857 to March 1858*, quoted in Sen, *ibid.*, p.27.

4 *The Shannon's Brigade* in India, quoted in Sen, *ibid.*, p.29.

5 *The Mutinies in Rajpootana*, quoted in Sen, *ibid.*, p.31.

6 Joseph Sramek, *Gender, Morality, and Race in Company India, 1765-1858*, New York, Palgrave Macmillan, 2001, pp.129-137.

7 'Embodying war: British women and domestic defilement in the Indian "Mutiny", 1857-8', *Journal of Historical Geography*, 26, 3 (2000), p.403.

8 *Op. cit.*, p.114. On 29 November 1870, Kilvert's brother referred to its presence in the Kilvert home, as the *Diary* entry for that date confirms. The 29 November 1871 *Diary* shows Kilvert's friend Daisy Thomas bringing him a copy of it, as though she knew he liked it.

9 *ILN*, 19 September 1857, quoted in Blunt, *op. cit.*, p.413.

10 The quotations in this paragraph are from Ward, *op. cit.*, pp.438, 552.

11 *Llysdinam Collection* of Venables letters, National Library of Wales, letter B1111.

12 *Ibid.*, letter B1311.

13 *Op. cit.*, p.412.

14 Ward, *op. cit.*, p.512.

15 The novel had such alternative titles as *The Stream House* and *The*

Demon of Cawnpore.

16 Lord Canning was Governor-General of India at the time.

17 *Llysdinam Collection,* letter B1325 dated 22 January 1860.

18 Material in this paragraph is from Gott's book, pp.6, 44.

19 Lawson, *op. cit.,* p.161.

20 *Op. cit.,* p.152.

21 Quoted in Gott, *op. cit.,* p.457.

22 Rosie Llewellyn-Jones, *The Great Uprising in India, 1857-58. Untold Stories, Indian and British,* Woodbridge, Boydell Press, 2007, pp.155-6. One of the Andaman Islands (see chapter three) was named Neill Island in his honour.

23 Quoted in Blunt, *op. cit.,* p.415.

24 Referred to in Lawson, *op. cit.,* p.151.

25 One of these was the Rev. Robert Cholmeley, D.D., Vicar of Findon, Sussex, where Kilvert attended the wedding on 10 August 1874 of Addie Cholmeley, daughter of Montague; she was only twenty at the time. One of her brothers was a solicitor; another was in the ICS. She had three children in quick succession before dying of scarlet fever aged twenty-four.

26 The account of Colonel Cholmeley's military career is based on three Madras Army service entries L/MIL/11/41f.497, L/MIL/11/77f.161, and L/MIL/11/83f.89 (British Library).

27 The marriage took place on 27 October 1853, when Adelaide was in fact twenty-three. Emily's memory was at fault or perhaps she was over-keen to emphasise how young Adelaide was when she married.

28 She was the 'Addie' whose wedding Kilvert attended on 11 August 1874. Dr. Cholmeley, her uncle, performed the ceremony and 'touchingly alluded to the happy spiritual presence among us of his dear brother Montague, the bride's father', Kilvert wrote.

29 *Op. cit.,* p.111.

30 Ward, *op. cit.,* p.78.

31 Bourne, *op. cit.,* p.94.

32 *List of Officers of the Public Works Department under the Government of India,* V/13/195-200. *Medal Roll for Civilians entitled to the Indian Mutiny Medal,* L/MIL/5/86. Aligarh is seventy miles south of Delhi and two hundred miles north of Cawnpore.

33 *Op. cit.,* p.422.

34 The *Punch* writer may have had General William Hewitt in mind.

35 A *Punch* article in the 17 April 1858 issue referred to 'John Company' (the familiar nickname of the EIC) as a 'convict' who was 'under sentence [but] showed no signs of penitence for his innumerable crimes'.

36 Sramek, *op. cit.,* p.43.

37 Kiernan, *op. cit.,* pp.47, 52.

38 Muckerjee, *op. cit.,* pp.186-7. The quoted words are from the report of Dr. Buchanan-Hamilton, a British expert.

39 Gott, *op. cit.,* p.246.

Chapter Nine

1 Chris Morrissey, 'No.12 Sydney Buildings', Sydney Buildings History Group, 2009.

2 Henry Nicholas Ridley, *Spices*, Macmillan, 1912, p.160.

3 'Chinese White Wax', Bulletin of Miscellaneous Information, Royal Gardens, Kew, vol.1893, no.76/77, p.84.

4 *Catalogue of the Library of the University of London*, London, Taylor and Francis, 1876.

5 Only Katie and Urban of the Buée children appear in the Album perhaps because they had sustained contact with Anna Maria's extended family.

6 *The Slough, Eton and Windsor Observer* (2 January 1897 p.5) contained an item on 'the retirement of Dr. Buée'. He was then eighty-five.

7 'Sense of Place South-East, St. Paul's Mission Church, Stoke Road, Slough, 1900', Slough Library.

8 He went to London University in January 1884.

9 Captain Harold C.J. Bliss, *The Relief of Kumasi*, London, Methuen, 2nd edition, 1901, pp.107-109.

10 *Historical Notes and Memorial Inscriptions from Ghana*, by M.E.J. Crew, Ofinso Training College, Ofinso, Ashanti, Ghana, 1988-90.

11 For information on Angel, I am indebted to Brett Payne's *Victorian and Edwardian Portrait Photo Collection: Photographers' Profiles* (www.freepages.genealogy.rootsweb. ancestry.com/~/brett/photo2) Accessed 14 September 2012.

12 Frances died in March 1855 at Wolverton, Bath.

13 Richard John Meade appears in *Burke's Peerage*.

14 The *DNB* entry on Scarth notes that 'He was much esteemed in Bath, and a window was erected to his memory by public subscription in St. Mary's Church, Bathwick'.

15 He might have belonged to the Shropshire Parsons family from which the 'Grand-mamma' of the Album came, but he has not been located in it.

Chapter Ten

1 E.g. those of Colonel Cholmeley, W.B. Macrone, Colonel Meulen, Henry Hewitt.

2 He never lived there as far as we know but, as a world traveller, he must have used the port.

3 *Op. cit.*, p.19. The Langford quote at the start of the paragraph is from p.5.

4 The words of John Stuart Mill, quoted in Asa Briggs, *The Age of Improvement*, p.178.

5 *The Bentham Newsletter*, edited by Professor Burns and Dr. J.R. Dinwiddy, the Bentham Committee, University of London, March 1979, No.2, p.31. One of Herbert's sons stated that his father was adopted by Bentham and brought up by him.

6 Editorial introduction to *The Correspondence of Jeremy Bentham*, vol.ix, Oxford, Clarendon Press, edited by Stephen Conway, 1989, pp.xi-xii.

7 *Ibid.*, p.xix.

8 Another of Fred's brothers was christened Heber after the Bishop of Calcutta, who died young and was a hero to many Evangelicals.

9 *The Jackdaws: A History of the Koe Family*, privately printed by R.G. Taylor, husband of Wendy Stuart Koe, 1981, p.48.

10 *Ibid.*, p.48.

11 Founded in 1541, it catered for Gloucester Cathedral choristers, who became fully integrated into what later became the King's School in the 18th century. It was popular in the first half of the 19th century, then began to decline.

12 Cf. Trollope's 1875 novel *The Way We Live Now* (vol.2, p.457) in which Lord Carbury told friends that 'he intended to devote the next few months to foreign travel, and that it was his purpose to take with him a Protestant divine – as was much the habit with young men of rank and fortune some years since'.

13 Wendy Koe, *op. cit.*, p.67.

14 Originally published in *Canadian Slavonic Papers* 35, nos.1-2 (March-June 1993): 121-130. (www.robertcutler.org/bakunin/ar93csp.htm). Accessed 12 July 2012.

15 He was involved in a series of revolutionary movements in Europe. Speaking out while in Paris in 1844 (where he met Karl Marx) against Russian oppression of the Poles led to his deportation from France. He supported the revolutionary movements of 1848. His arrest in Dresden resulted from the backing he gave to the May uprising there in 1849.

16 Charles Simpson, who was in Fred's charge on his two-year world tour, was apparently 'an unpleasant companion' (Wendy Koe, *op. cit.*, p.67).

17 Cutler explained the meaning of such a move in a note: 'The supposed progress in this is whereas slaves can be sold and thus alienated from their family, serfs being attached to the land are less likely to be separated from their kin'.

18 Agassiz was brought up in Switzerland. His work was well known in Britain (and probably to Fred Koe, who was clearly keen to meet him). In 1836 the Geological Society of London awarded him its Wollaston Medal for his work on fossils of fish. He collaborated with the influential British geologist William Buckland in 1840 in investigations of mountain ranges in England, Wales and Scotland. In 1847, he had been appointed Professor of Zoology and Geology at Harvard University in Boston.

19 Longfellow had spent several years in Europe early in his career and was particularly fluent in French. Kilvert was reading his play *The Spanish Student* (1843) on 24 May 1870. Bakunin had already been in Boston meeting Longfellow and Agassiz, who were close friends.

20 Four sons and five daughters were born of the marriage.

21 The Bethells must have had some contact with and perhaps had been influenced by the Catholic families who were Robert Abraham's clients. We don't know exactly when John Bethell became Catholic, but his name appears in *Converts to Rome: a list of about 4,000 Protestants who have recently become Roman Catholics*, London, 1855.

22 One of her works was displayed at the Royal Academy in 1814. Jane's paternal grandfather, Richard Bethell, was a doctor in Bristol.

23 Wendy Koe, *op. cit.*, p.67.

24 *Ibid.*, p.48. The second edition of this law book was published in 1844.

25 An order in the High Court of Bankruptcy stated that 'Frederick Koe and Charles Bethell, trading as John Bethell and Co. of Goodacre, Weybridge, Surrey, Tar distillers and Creosoters of Timber, became bankrupt on 3 June 1886'. Fred's address was given as Montpelier House, Blackheath, Kent.

26 Up to 1966, there was a St. Winifred's Chapel on Sion Hill from pre-Reformation times (*Historical and Archaeological Report on Somerset Place, Sion Hill, Bath*, October 2006: (kaye@thehousehistorians.co.uk). Accessed on 17 October 2012.

27 Roy Fry and Tristan Gray Hulse, *The Other St. Winifred's Wells* (http://people.bath. ac.uk/liskmj/livingspring/ sourcearchive/ns1/ns/tgh). Accessed on 17 October 2012. Next door to Winifred House at 23 Sion Hill was Winifred Well Cottage. The legend of Winifred held that she was beheaded by her suitor, angry at her decision to become a nun. A spring appeared where her head stopped after it had rolled down a hill. Gerard Manley Hopkins, poet and Catholic priest, wrote a verse drama, *St. Winifred's Well*, in the 1880s.

28 Designed and built (1767-75) by John Wood, the younger.

29 'During his two-year world tour, Fred spent one year in Australia, travelling often on foot' (Wendy Koe, *op. cit.*, p.67).

Postscript

1 Nothing has been discovered about the photographer, James Elliott.

2 One possible link is that the Mitchell sisters were the servants of one of the Album people. Langford referred to the 'hierarchical logic' of one family album that began with the Royal Family and proceeded down the social scale to include servants. No Mitchell women have been found working as servants for Album people.

3 Edge's photo of him is one of the seven in the National Portrait Gallery Collection. Two others show the Liddell sisters together, another is of Ina alone. Carroll's photos of the three sisters are on display at the National Media Museum in Bradford.

4 Edge probably obtained his commission to photograph Monier-Williams through contact with Henry Liddell – or vice-versa.

W M Sechrest

1861